# HORNCHURCH OFFENSIVE

# HORNCHURCH OFFENSIVE

## THE DEFINITIVE ACCOUNT OF THE RAF FIGHTER AIRFIELD, ITS PILOTS, GROUNDCREW AND STAFF

### VOLUME TWO
### 1941 TO THE AIRFIELD'S FINAL CLOSURE

### RICHARD C SMITH

GRUB STREET · LONDON

Published by
Grub Street
4 Rainham Close
London SW11 6SS

First published in hardback 2001
Copyright this edition © 2008 Grub Street, London
Text copyright © Richard C. Smith

**British Library Cataloguing in Publication Data**
Smith, Richard C.
Hornchurch offensive: the definitive account of the RAF fighter airfield, its pilots
groundcrew and staff
Vol. 2: 1941-1962
1. Great Britain. Flying Corps – History
2. RAF Hornchurch – History  3. RAF Hornchurch
I. Title
358.4'009422'09041

**ISBN 978-1-906502-15-7**

Typeset by Pearl Graphics, Hemel Hempstead

Printed and bound in Great Britain by
MPG Books Ltd, Bodmin, Cornwall

Grub Street only uses FSC (Forest Stewardship Council) paper for its books

# CONTENTS

# ACKNOWLEDGEMENTS

Without the help of the men and women listed below, with their own personal memories of their time at RAF Hornchurch, this second volume of Hornchurch's history would not have been possible. Once again, they helped with facts, figures, photographs and most of all, the all-important testimonies of their own lives, whether in the war years, when they held the torch of freedom along with many others, or during the post-war period, when they still continued the tradition of service to Monarch and country. They all played their part in what is the history of this famous airfield. Sadly, as with the first volume, since being interviewed some have since passed on. I salute them all.

Flight Lieutenant William 'Tex' Ash, MBE
Squadron Leader Robert Beardsley, DFC, RAF Retd
Squadron Leader Gordon Braidwood, DFC, RAF Retd
The late Air Chief Marshal Sir Harry Broadhurst, GCB, KBE, DSO, DFC, DSO
Squadron Leader Peter Brown, AFC, RAF Retd
Lieutenant General Baron Michael Donnet, CVO, DFC, FR, AE Retd
Wing Commander Frank Dowling, OBE, RAF Retd
Flight Lieutenant Trevor Gray RAF Retd
The late Wing Commander Joe Kayll, DSO, DFC
The late Wing Commander John Kilmartin, DFC
Squadron Leader Arthur Leigh, DFC, DFM, RAF Retd
The late Air Vice-Marshal David Scott-Malden, DSO, DFC
Air Commodore George Mason, DFC, DFC (US), FBIM, RAF Retd
The late Group Captain Wilfred Duncan-Smith, DSO, DFC
The late Squadron Leader Jack Stokoe, DFC
Mervyn Young
Mr Alfred Allsopp
Mr Robert Ballard
Mr Bernard Batchelor
Mr Harold Bennett
Mr William Bird
Lady Jane Broadhurst
Mr Max Bygraves OBE
Mrs Joy Caldwell
Mrs Patricia Churchill
Mr John Cox
Mrs Pamela Duncan-Smith
Mr Ken Finding
Mrs Ada Hewitt
Mr Robert Kingaby
Mr Howard LaRoche
Mr Roy Little
Mr Don McNaught

Mr Stan Reynolds
Mr G.F 'Ricky' Richardson

Special thanks to Lieutenant General Michael Donnet; it is an honour to have him contribute the Foreward to this book. Thanks are in order once again to Squadron Leader Peter Brown AFC for his Introduction, help and advice. To Peter 'Onion' Oliver for all his time and help at the Public Record Office, which made all the difference. Thanks to my publisher John Davies, and Anne, Louise and Dominic at Grub Street for another excellent production. To aviation artist Barry Weekley for another amazing painting to grace the front cover. Thanks to all those who support the work of 'The Hornchurch Wing'.

Thanks also go to friends and fellow historians for their continued support and help:

Jack and Pamela Broad, Squadron Leader Peter Brown, AFC, RAF Retd, Steve and Val Butler, Alison and Dave Campbell, Mrs May Clark, Mr Reg Clark, John Coleman, John and Anne Cox, Joe and Drene Crawshaw, Dave Davies, Wing Commander Frank Dowling, OBE, RAF Retd, Ted Exall, John Gill, Squadron Leader 'Dave' Glaser, DFC, RAF Retd, Alan and Sue Gosling, Flight Lieutenant Les Harvey, John Jones, Gary Lilley, Frank and Philippa Mileham, Geoff and Lesley Nutkins, Emma Palmer, David Ross, Ricky and Joyce Richardson, Ken Slaney, Air Marshal Sir 'Freddy' Sowrey, KCB, CBE, AFC, RAF Retd, Squadron Leader Gerald 'Stapme' Stapleton, DFC, RAF Retd, Wing Commander John Young, AFC, RAF Retd, Historian of the Battle of Britain Fighter Association.

Thanks also to the Public Record Office, Kew, The Imperial War Museum, Lambeth, The Battle of Britain Fighter Association, RAF Historical Branch, RAF Innsworth Personnel Management Agency, No.452 Air Training Corps, Hornchurch, The Purfleet Heritage and Military Centre, *The Romford Recorder*, The Sanders Draper Senior School, Alan Cooper & Joan Bedford of The London Borough of Havering Council and Christine Hipperson of the Elm Park Library.

Finally, a special big thank you to my family for all their patience, help and understanding in my days and nights of research in getting the whole project together.

# FOREWORD

## by
## Lieutenant General Aviateur Baron Michael Donnet,
### CVO, DFC, FR, AE

It is a great honour for me to write these few words for the book, which narrates the history of the Royal Air Force Station, Hornchurch, during the years following the Battle of Britain. In doing so I am particularly touched, to follow Air Marshal Sir Frederick Sowrey KCB, CBE, AFC, whose father flew as a pilot from Sutton's Farm airfield during World War One and shot down a German Zeppelin in 1916. This had always fascinated me, and to my surprise I discovered a piece of structure from an enemy airship which had been framed, when I entered the Hornchurch Officers' Mess, on my arrival as a pilot of No.64 Squadron in October 1941. We were to remain 18 months in the sector.

I was impressed by the layout of the station and its smooth running, and also the efficiency of the staff and of the personnel of all trades. A great devotion to duty was most noticeable. The scars left from the bombing during the Battle of Britain were hardly visible and the station had recovered its vigour.

The summer of 1941 had seen the Royal Air Force on the offensive. The battle on the airfront had been moved over to the German-occupied countries in Europe. The Luftwaffe had to be kept under pressure and its fighters engaged in air battle; Hornchurch squadrons were to pay heavily in these operations.

In the winter of 1941/42 it was relatively calm, except for the excitement created by the sailing through the Channel of the German battle-cruisers; the spring however, brought in a period of intensive offensive air operations. The Hornchurch Wing consisted of three squadrons sometimes carrying out two sorties a day. Many different squadrons made up the Wing, coming from British, Commonwealth and Allied countries; including pilots whose countries had been overrun by the Germans.

The pilots all displayed the same keenness and fighting spirit. There were successes, but also casualties; the air battle during the Dieppe landings was an illustration of this.

Hornchurch remained in the front line until the time of the invasion of Normandy, when the scene of the air battle moved south.

Through all these years, Hornchurch lived up to its reputation mainly due to the qualities and efficiency of its leaders, the Station Commanders first, men such as Harry Broadhurst and George Lott, and the fighting spirit of the Wing Leaders, Eric Stapleton, Peter Powell, 'Paddy' Finucane and Peter Hugo and many other great fighter pilots.

One has to mention the station personnel, men and women of all ranks and all trades. They all displayed the same high spirit and the same devotion to duty. They lived up to the reputation established by those who had preceded them during World War 1, and by their action, they did contribute greatly to the final victory in World War 2.

# INTRODUCTION

by

**Squadron Leader Peter Brown** AFC, RAF Retd
**Flying Officer No. 41 Squadron, Hornchurch 1941**

The first volume of the Hornchurch history covered the years 1915 to 1940. During this period the young pilots of the squadrons based at Hornchurch and its satellite airfields defended London and southeast England against terror and pre-invasion attacks by German aircraft in two wars. In the Battle of Britain in 1940 the first and third highest scoring squadrons in Fighter Command were No. 603 and No. 41 based at Hornchurch. The top-scoring pilot in the Battle was Pilot Officer Eric Lock of 41 Squadron. Sadly 41 Squadron recorded the second highest number of casualties. The great contribution of Hornchurch Fighter Station to the Victory is self-evident.

September 15th 1940, the day when the Luftwaffe squadrons attacked London twice in one day and were harassed and mauled as never before, tolled the bell for the ending of any German plans for the invasion of England in 1940. After October 1940, German bomber formations never again flew operations over England during the day. However, night terror attacks by German bombers as single aircraft continued until May 1941.

When the author opens *Hornchurch Offensive* at the beginning of 1941, major changes in Fighter Command had taken place. Air Marshal Sir Hugh Dowding, although the Architect of Victory, had been removed without honour from office and replaced as Commander-in-Chief by Air Marshal Sholto Douglas. Air Vice-Marshal Keith Park, who had commanded No. 11 Group with great professionalism, had been down-graded to command a Training Group. He had been replaced by Air Vice-Marshal Trafford Leigh-Mallory who had been the exponent of the use of five squadron wings as the best fighter defence for Britain. This myth was soon dispelled in 1941 and such large wings were never again considered in a defensive role. There was still a possibility that there would be a second and more powerful attempt at invasion in 1941. It was only when Hitler invaded Russia in June 1941 that an invasion of Britain could be dismissed from strategic and operational planning. Within a few days of the start of the new year, Fighter Command philosophy and operations changed from defence to offensive. On the 10th January, a Hornchurch Wing of three squadrons of Spitfires took part in the first sweep over France, escorting six Blenheim bombers to attack the Forêt de Guines airfield in northwest France. There were six squadrons of fighters – seventy-two aircraft – to protect the six bombers with another three squadrons in support. This was clearly a 'coat trailing' exercise and this type of operation was given the name of 'Circus'.

In March 1941, Leigh-Mallory appointed official Wing Leaders at each Fighter Station in 11 Group. Offensive operations over France were normally based on three squadron wing formations, except for the low-level intrusion by pairs or fours – not a popular exercise with most pilots. Until

June, Circus sweeps were spasmodic and there were a number of Channel patrols to establish a presence. Although Fighter Command was nominally on the offensive, it is difficult to understand the strategy, if indeed there was one, other than 'we are going on the offensive'. Leigh-Mallory, who was basically an 'office' commander lacked the depth of fighter experience to command such an offensive operational group.

It was not until June, when Hitler attacked Russia, that there was a high level instruction for Fighter Command to 'lean on' the Germans to make them keep a large fighter defence in Western Europe in order to ease pressure on the Russian Front. Sholto Douglas then 'leaned forward' with almost continuous sweeps. The sweeps over France in 1941 and 1942 with aircraft of limited range was costly in men and machines and achieved little. As the Luftwaffe was based in occupied France, most of the damage caused by six tons of bombs from six Blenheims or one four engine Stirling bomber would not have seriously concerned the Germans, except by direct hits on a Luftwaffe airfield or installation. The 'coat trailing' technique is only effective if high profile military targets or major capital cities are in range. This was not the case.

The Luftwaffe could choose to attack only when conditions were in their favour and then dive out of the action. Fighter Command had to operate in large multi-wing formations to protect the few bombers, though the enemy had freedom of mobility with small formations. Combat reports show that the ME109s and FW190s usually attacked in small numbers of four, eight or sixteen, similar to our defensive attacks in the Battle of Britain. Their technique was to bounce the squadrons and dive away. Our pilots over-claimed by several times the actual number of aircraft shot down. The common error was the belief that black smoke from an ME109 or FW190 meant an engine out of action, whereas in fact, it frequently meant maximum boost for escape. The imperative need not to follow an aircraft down through cloud or to see it crash also led to an error in claims. As a result of those errors, the claims of aircraft shot down far exceeded our own losses. These exaggerated figures, readily accepted by Leigh-Mallory, justified to him his continued philosophy of 'coat trailing', but led to the sacrifice of pilots and the loss of valuable aircraft, time and petrol.

A Fighter Command pilot shot down, was generally either killed or captured. A Luftwaffe pilot shot down might bale out and fly again the next day. It is difficult to substantiate precise figures of claims, losses, and enemy losses, but the following figures give a fair comparison. In 1941 Fighter Command claimed significantly higher victories against their own losses of over 600. The actual losses of Luftwaffe aircraft were around 150. In 1942 Fighter Command again claimed much greater victories than their own losses of over 500. The actual Luftwaffe losses for that year were nearly 200. The tragedy was that we had lost so many of our Squadron and Flight Commanders, and experienced Section Leaders, all battle trained in 1940. Aircraft losses of four a week could be acceptable to the Germans. For a pilot to defend his homeland was a natural, inspiring and total action, but flying over water and hostile territory to attack an electric power station serving a foreign country demands a different attitude and an aggressive philosophy to fight the enemy where ever they are. The high morale required of the pilots was reinforced by their belief in the high number of victories claimed and accepted by Fighter Command. These results gave meaning to their losses.

In early 1941 squadrons were equipped with Spitfire Is, IIs and Hurricanes against Messerschmitt 109s. In June the Mark VA and VB were brought into service. The Mark Vs gave some improvement in performance, and the introduction of cannons was especially welcome and made the aircraft a more effective fighting weapon. By the end of 1941 the Mark Vs had become standard in the Hornchurch Wing.

The German Focke-Wulf 190 came into service in August 1941, although when first reported by the pilots, the intelligence section refused to accept the sightings. The FW190 with a radial engine was an exceptional aircraft, which outclassed the Spitfire Vs, and it dominated the skies over France for the next ten months. It was less effective over 22,000 feet but the new improved ME109s were able to take over at heights above this. Hornchurch claimed the first FW190 victory. However courageous the pilot, an aircraft with an exceptionally high performance will always have the advantage – unless the opponent has the other advantages of height and position.

On 10th September 1941, RAF Fairlop, built a few miles to the northeast of Hornchurch came into operation. It had the benefit of concrete runways, especially valuable in bad weather conditions. With RAF Southend, RAF Hornchurch now had two satellite airfields. In 1942 the Luftwaffe carried out an offensive campaign with raids against coastal targets. These were flown by Me109s and FW190s, fitted with bombs, which were later given fighter support. They came in low and fast and were difficult to stop. Their activities caused Fighter Command to return to defensive tactics and were a hindrance to the policy of 'leaning forward'.

In July 1942, to the great relief of Fighter Command, the Spitfire Mark IX was brought into service. With the two-stage supercharger it was very fast and could operate up to 35,000 feet. With long range tanks it could penetrate into France for escort duties with American day bomber raids; the FW190 had met its match. No. 64 Squadron in the Hornchurch Wing was the first squadron to be equipped with the Spitfire IX and also claimed the first FW190 victim. In 1942 the 'coat trailing' activities continued with escorts for small bombing raids by aircraft such as Blenheims, American Douglas-Bostons and Mitchell bombers, now at squadron strength.

On 12th February 1942 Britain was stunned by a German achievement – the Channel Dash, which was a total victory for the Germans. Two of their battle cruisers and a cruiser made a successful dash up the Channel, by night and day, from their base at Brest in Western France to the Kiel Canal in Germany. Later that year, on 19th August a Canadian Division with British services in support made a 'reconnaissance in force' against Dieppe. Fifty-six fighter squadrons of Fighter Command including the Hornchurch Wing took part, making many sorties with a seventy-mile sea crossing to get into action. Leigh-Mallory claimed Dieppe as a great victory for Fighter Command on the basis of British over-claims. The RAF gave great support to the ground and naval forces, but lost 90 of their fighters against the 42 lost by the smaller number of German fighters. Fighter Command pilot losses over Dieppe for this one day, were similar to the total pilot losses of Fighter Command providing a protective screen for the 10 days during the evacuation over Dunkirk in 1940.

'Rhubarb' low level attacks continued in low-cloud conditions. The Air Ministry never understood the inherent dangers of attacking defended ground targets and many of our experienced pilots were lost or captured on these operations. Such pilot and aircraft losses could never be justified by these ineffective sorties. The loss of more than 1,000 pilots over France and the Channel in two years led to early promotion in Fighter Command.

One of the features of the 1942/3 period was the increasing number of allied squadrons that came into service with Fighter Command. At Hornchurch there was a continuous movement of Belgian, Canadian, Australian, French, Czech and New Zealand squadrons, serving side by side with RAF squadrons and sometimes with their own wings. They all fought valiantly and were easily and effectively integrated into operational service. To French and Belgian pilots, flying as free men over their homeland must always have been a moving experience.

As the war moved on into 1943, the Hornchurch squadrons equipped with Spitfire IXs escorted American B17 Flying Fortresses to inland targets – their work had changed significantly from the 'coat trailing' exercises of 1941. They also met and protected American squadrons returning from targets in northwest Germany. In 1943, No. 83 Group was formed to become part of the Tactical Air Force, ready to operate on the Continent after the invasion. These squadrons were based near the south coast. Hornchurch squadrons were not involved in this move and continued their support work in Fighter Command.

On 8th September 1943, a secret operation code named 'Starkey' was put into effect. The plan was to mislead the Germans into believing that the allies would land their invasion troops in the Calais area. For some time a major part of the Hornchurch Wing activities were concentrated on bomber protection and fighter sweeps over northern France and Belgium.

In 1940 and until mid 1941 London was subjected to continuous night bombing. This was followed by a break in 1942 and spasmodic raids in 1943. In 1944 and 1945 it was attacked day and night by V1 and V2 terror weapons. Hornchurch was situated 2 miles from the London Balloon Barrage. Frequently the shortfalls and near misses would fall on the town of Hornchurch and nearby communities and on the RAF Station itself. Although the squadrons took off daily to fight the war over France, as in 1940, the station personnel were still in the front line. In June 1944, the Germans brought into service their new V1 Vengeance weapons. The pilotless flying bombs had a 2000lb warhead. When the fuel was used up the engine cut out and the bomb dived to the ground and exploded. They flew very fast and were difficult and dangerous for fighters to shoot down. The Germans had also been researching and developing rockets fitted with a one-ton warhead. In their descent on London and the surroundings, the speed of the V2 rockets was much faster than the speed of sound and the explosion took place without warning. There was no defence.

The year 1944 was to see significant changes in the work of the squadrons and in the functions of the Station itself. The squadrons still continued their escort duties for day bombing raids and for covering the return of American bombers. Mobile radio units were being organised and trained ready for operation in France after the 'D' Day landings, and at Hornchurch a Mobile Control Centre was formed. This was an early indication of the gradual transition of the station from an active operational flying unit into a depot for vehicles and personnel. On 18th February 1944, the final order for the closure of the Hornchurch Sector Control Room was received. Squadrons still flew from Hornchurch and the satellites at Fairlop and Southend, but were controlled from North Weald. The controlling of wings escorting bombers was very different from the heady days of 1940, with squadrons always at readiness waiting to be scrambled at any moment to meet incoming raids of any size at any height. On one day, the Hornchurch Wing gave high cover to 72 B26 Marauders and later in the day provided withdrawal support to a large force of Liberators and Fortresses returning from a raid deep into Germany. The fighting sorties now undertaken by the squadrons had real purpose in the preparations for the 'D' Day Invasion. Hornchurch squadrons were still on the attack.

Over four years there had been many changes in the leaders and pilots of the squadrons, now of many nationalities. Although their tactical tasks were different the courage and tenacity needed for the fight with the Luftwaffe had not altered. The enemy – although now on the defensive – was just the same and just as dangerous.

As 'D' Day approached the Hornchurch Spitfire squadrons moved south to be closer to the scene of the action. There was no great ceremony to record the end of the fighting history of Hornchurch and its satellites. The squadrons slipped away one by one in March and April. On 6th June – 'D' Day – the Invasion had begun.

By August 1944, RAF Hornchurch had been designated as a Holding Establishment and as a Forward Station. No 55 Repair Unit was located there to carry out work on buildings damaged by flying bombs and later by rockets. In November the 55 RU left and Hornchurch became a base for a marshalling area to hold 400 vehicles.

The year ended with the station operating as a transit service for personnel travelling to and from Europe. The Battle for France and Germany continued but Hornchurch had no operational function and was now a depot. The Hornchurch Eagles would soar no more. On 7th May the Germans surrendered unconditionally.

The story of Hornchurch would not be complete without a tribute to the ordinary, or extraordinary, citizens who withstood the terror attacks by the Germans with their bombs, V1s and V2 rockets. In those times, courage and patriotism was the norm.

Hornchurch, its satellites, squadrons and personnel had served the country well between 1941–1945. They had fought against heavy odds over the Continent and had played a major part in the victory in the air. They had also faced the German bombing assaults over the years. It was a long and relentless war, and victory was celebrated by all including the European countries, who had been freed from the German yoke. There was still a heavy price to be paid for the victory for many years ahead – no matter – we were still a free people.

There is no national memorial to the pilots who continued the fight for freedom over France and Germany. The Military Cemetery at St. Andrew's Church at Hornchurch holds the graves of some of the pilots. Others are remembered on the walls of the RAF Memorial at Runnymede. Some of them rest in the war cemeteries in many countries in Europe where their graves are tended with care.

The young pilots who fought in the battles over Europe from 1941 to 1945 had the great qualities of courage, dedication, and love of their countries held by those who had fought over England in earlier years. Their great sense of humour and companionship helped them through the difficult days. Their honoured memory is in the Freedom they fought for, and which is still the treasured possession of the British people today. Let it always be so.

RAF Hornchurch continued its service to the nation during the 1950s, when it was selected as the main Aircrew Selection Centre for the Royal Air Force, for those young men who wished to enter into the service and wear the famous blue uniform.

But with the arrival of the jet aircraft, Hornchurch was no longer deemed suitable or required by the Air Ministry. This distinguished Royal Air Force Station with its remarkable record finally closed in 1962.

Peter Brown
March 2001

# CHAPTER 1

# ON THE OFFENSIVE
## January – June 1941

The year of 1941 arrived and with it the Royal Air Force was given new orders by Fighter and Bomber Commands to take the fight back to the enemy across the Channel into northern France. Fighter Command had a new officer in command after Air Chief Marshal Sir Hugh Dowding was replaced as Air Officer Commander in Chief. Air Vice-Marshal Keith Park, who had done so much as No.11 Group's commander during the Battle of Britain, was also unceremoniously replaced. Dowding's position was taken by Air Marshal William Sholto Douglas, while No.11 Group would now come under the command of Keith Park's main dissenter during the battle in 1940, Air Vice-Marshal Sir Trafford Leigh-Mallory.

The new fighter operations were to be called Sweeps, in the form of Circus, Ramrod, Rhubarb and Rodeo missions. The RAF fighters would escort a light bomber force over France in order to cause damage to the German installations on the ground, and also to draw up the Luftwaffe to be attacked. The various sweep operations were:

**Circus**, which consisted of a bomber force or fighter-bombers, which would be escorted by fighter aircraft to entice enemy fighters up into combat.

**Rodeo** was a fighter sweep without bombers.

**Rhubarb** saw the use of small sections of fighters, mainly in pairs attacking targets of opportunity such as trains, troop transport, airfields etc, which might be seen during the flight.

**Ramrod** was a bomber force escorted by fighters and had a definite target to attack.

The 1st January 1941 was fine with good visibility, but with a fair amount of low cloud. The Operations Room at No.11 Group showed that enemy activity was only slight and was mainly restricted to the French side of the Channel.

No.41 and 611 'West Lancashire' Auxiliary Squadrons who were based at Hornchurch, were sent up during the afternoon to carry out a standing patrol over Maidstone, and several other sections were also airborne during the remainder of the day, but no interceptions resulted.

It was noted in the New Year's Honours list that Group Captain Cecil Bouchier, former officer commanding RAF Hornchurch, had been awarded the CBE, as well as Mentioned in Despatches, for his outstanding work during the previous year's operations at the airfield. The new Station

1

Commander at Hornchurch, Wing Commander Harry Broadhurst, had now arrived to take over from Group Captain Bouchier, and remembers:

> I was posted to command RAF Hornchurch at the end of 1940, but my relief at Wittering hadn't arrived, so although I went down and reported and met everybody, I didn't take over Hornchurch until the first week in January 1941. We were then just about to send the first offensive Wings over to France from No.11 and 12 Groups.
>
> I came back in time to lead the first operational Wing to France, escorting bombers to Abbeville. I also brought my Hawker Hurricane aircraft with me from Wittering when I moved to Hornchurch, although I hardly ever flew it, but used it at night to save hours on Spits. One day soon after, somebody came down from Fighter Command and noticed the Hurricane amongst a hangar full of Spitfires and said, 'What the hell have you got a Hurricane here for?' I replied that it was mine, but they ordered it away – you couldn't own anything in those days.

Hurricane P2823 had been used by Harry Broadhurst during the Battle of France, and he now had the aircraft painted black with his initials HB painted in dark red on the fuselage. Wing Commander Frank Dowling OBE remembers the arrival of Harry Broadhurst:

> He was a very different type from 'Boy' Bouchier. Broadhurst was a real operational type with plenty of experience. He had that personality and persona about him, he would not suffer fools easily, a no-nonsense officer, but he would give praise to a pilot if he deserved it. George Carr had been the station adjutant, he'd been posted to command RAF Southend. My office was next to the station commander's and this is when I heard 'Broady' on the telephone to No.11 Group Headquarters asking, 'Where's my new adjutant.' Somebody must have said, 'You've already got him.' He came in and told me I had George Carr's old job; it was the start of a very long working relationship. I was then promoted from pilot officer to flight lieutenant immediately.

On 9th January 1941, Hornchurch's satellite airfield at Rochford was made independent and given the title of RAF Southend, although many of Hornchurch's squadrons would continue to operate from here as a forward base, and still refer to it as Rochford.

The first Circus Operation took place on Friday, 10th January 1941, at just after 12.00 pm. The mission consisted of six Bristol Blenheims of No.114 Squadron who were to be escorted by three Hurricane squadrons from North Weald and the three Spitfire squadrons from Hornchurch, No.41, 64 and 611. They were also to be supported by another three squadrons who would patrol the Channel area; these were No. 66, 74 and 92 Squadrons.

Flight Lieutenant Trevor Gray was a pilot officer at this time with No.64 Squadron; he had been with the squadron during the Battle of Britain and moved to Hornchurch in November 1940. He recalls:

> The very first sweep I remember we had wind of was around the 8th/9th January, there was to be a very big operation and we were sworn to silence. We was then given a big briefing in one of the lecture halls, and told that the sweep would be laid on for the following day, escorting Blenheims. It had been schedueled for the morning, but was cancelled until about mid-morning due to the weather over the Channel.

The target for the operation was the Forêt de Guines airfield in north-west France. The Hornchurch squadrons would act as top cover to the bombers at 16,000 feet. The Blenheims atacked their target from 7,000 feet and destroyed dispersal pens and huts on the airfield; although the enemy put up accurate anti-aircraft fire, none of the bombers were hit. The Hornchurch squadrons landed back at Hornchurch at 1.29 pm.

No.41 Squadron, who had been acting as rear guard during the return leg of the trip, flying at 19,000 feet, reported that two of its sergeants, Bob Beardsley and Henry Baker, engaged five Me109s, who were seen at 17,000 feet climbing to engage the squadron. During the combat that followed Sergeant Baker claimed a probably-destroyed after seeing one of the 109s diving vertically from 15,000 feet into the haze just above sea-level.

On 20th February, No.41 Squadron lost two pilots in action while on patrol, Flying Officer Peter Brown takes up the story:

> On 20th February 1941, I was leading a patrol of six Spitfires at 25,000 feet over the Dungeness area. The Controller reported that there were 'bandits' in the vicinity at 6,000 feet – some 19,000 feet below us. We were concentrating on sighting them below to take advantage of height for our attack. Our top cover Spitfire reported that he had engine trouble and left to return to base.
>
> After two or three minutes I checked the sky above and saw a group of Me109s diving down on us from 3 o'clock. I shouted a warning and led the flight into a steep climbing turn to meet them head on. As I pulled hard into the climb there was a loud banging noise in the rear fuselage and I thought that I had been hit by cannon fire. In fact my aircraft had gone into an uncontrolled high speed stall and I blacked out. When I came to I was in a steep spin. I recovered control and then climbed up to join the action again.
>
> As I climbed I saw a pilot on a parachute above me. I circled close to him and recognised that it was Sergeant John McAdam. He was not conscious and white smoke was coming from a hole in the middle front of his Sidcot flying suit. There were no Me109s in sight. I stayed with him until he landed in

the sea off Dover. While I continued to circle to guide the rescue boat, I was again attacked and fired at by four 109s, which then flew off back to France.

Sergeant McAdam must have been killed immediately by an incendiary shell which entered into the back of his body. He could not have been hit in the back when in the cockpit, as he would have been protected by armour plating and the fuselage, nor in the act of baling out. He must have been fired on after he had baled out and had pulled the ripcord. Who was responsible for this?

Major Werner Mölders, the famous German ace, was credited with the shooting down of Sergeant McAdam. Our squadron's Spitfires were not fitted with cannons at this time.

It has been proposed by post-war writers that Sergeant McAdam was killed accidentally by enemy fire that was meant for me; when I was circling him.

The suggestion that Mölders or one of his flight shot a pilot hanging on his parachute by mistake, when he was aiming at a circling Spitfire is beyond belief. McAdam had been shot before I climbed up to him and there were no Me109s in sight. When circling, my aircraft was always at right angles to the parachute and never in a direct line of sight. Sergeant Robert Angus had also been shot down, again credited to Mölders. Angus baled out landing in the sea, but was not found and was reported missing. A bad day for the Squadron.

The very next day No.41 Squadron lost another pilot in mysterious circumstances; his name was John Stanley Gilders. Sergeant Gilders was on a patrol with 'A' Flight led by the New Zealander Flight Lieutenant John Noble Mackenzie. The rest of the flight consisted of Pilot Officer Michael Briggs, Pilot Officer Roy Ford, Sergeant Bob Beardsley and Sergeant Hopkinson. They were sent off from Hornchurch at 12.10 pm to patrol over Canterbury, Ramsgate and Dungeness.

It was while he was flying off the coast at Folkestone at 32,000 feet, that John Gilders' Spitfire P7816 was seen by some of his fellow pilots to drop out of formation for no apparent reason. They tried to raise contact with him over the radio, but no reply came as his aircraft disappeared into the hazy cloud at 25,000 feet. The remaining Spitfires returned and landed back at Hornchurch at 2.05 pm, but what had happened to Sergeant Gilders who was reported as missing?

The patrol's incident was recorded in the Squadron's Operations Book, and read:

> Six aircraft were ordered to patrol Ramsgate, Canterbury and Dungeness.
> P/O Ford leading top pair did not see Sgt Gilders who should have kept with him.
> Sgt Hopkinson reports that he saw a Spitfire doing a steep

climbing turn below and then shoot away. He turned and saw the aircraft disappear through the haze at 20/25 feet. This occurred off Folkestone, the aircraft, presumably Sgt Gilders, being in a gentle dive. Two bandits were reported and searched for, but appear to have been on the French coast. The patrol landed Hornchurch 14.05 hours.

Squadron Leader Robert Beardsley DFC who had joined No.41 Squadron in September 1940 as a sergeant pilot, recalls the incident that day:

I remember 'Gilly' Gilders' tragic death when his aircraft just suddenly broke formation.

We tried to call him up on the R/T as he headed down; we followed him down, but we could not keep up without damaging our own aircraft due to overstressing and we had to pull up. When we arrived back at base, we were told that his aircraft had gone in vertically and was buried very deep. The conclusion was that he had suffered from anoxia as a result of his oxygen supply malfunctioning, and of the very high altitude. Gilders had passed out and had not recovered.

A number of pilots had died from not checking their oxygen supply before taking off.

The oxygen control was a simple nut which was not the safest of designs, I once completely unwound my own at extreme altitude, which came off in my hand, but I was lucky.

Sergeant Gilders' aircraft had dived into the ground and buried itself at Chilham Beeches, east of the River Stour, Kent. No.49 Maintenance Unit was sent to the crash-site where it recovered a small amount of wreckage, but no human remains.

John Gilders' family were notified of his death, but were told that no remains had been found and that he had possibly baled out into the sea and drowned. For the next 53 years, he remained buried with his aircraft.

In 1993, aviation archaeologist Mark Kirby started the proceedings to recover John Gilders' remains and finally give him a final resting place. He contacted John's younger brother Geoff and told him of his intentions.

Unfortunately, the Ministry of Defence, who grant or deny permission for the recovery of wartime aircraft, refused to allow Mark Kirby to go ahead with the excavation. Mark Kirby decided to ignore the Ministry of Defence and went to the family whose final wishes he would accept. So it was on 20th April 1994 that Spitfire P7816 and the remains of John Gilders were recovered. After an inquest, Sergeant Gilders was finally laid to rest at the RAF plot of Brookwood Cemetery, Surrey on 11th May 1995.

No.54 Squadron returned to Hornchurch from Catterick on 23rd February to relieve No.41 Squadron. No. 54 Squadron's new commander was Squadron Leader Robert Finlay Boyd. No.41 Squadron, who had fought with great distinction throughout its time based at Hornchurch, flew out for the last time, never to operate from here again.

On the first day of March there was very little air activity during the day.

No.611 Squadron sent up two flights on a combat patrol during the day, while two aircraft of No.54 Squadron carried out a dusk patrol, but no interceptions resulted.

On 2nd March, the Windmill Theatre girls again entertained at the airfield. They were later afterwards taken to the officers' mess for dancing and drinks. Once the party had ended, the girls spent the night at the Sutton's Institute.

Squadron Leader A.C. 'Joe' Leigh, then a sergeant pilot with No.611, remembers the girls' visit:

> I remember that during their visit to the airfield, we put two of the girls on the tail of an aircraft and ran the engine up; their skirts went up over their heads, but they took it all in good fun. Barrie Heath, one of our pilots, had arranged it all because his wife was a showgirl.

It was during this period that one of Britain's top post-war entertainers was stationed at the aerodrome and started his trip on the road to stardom; his name is Max Bygraves. Max recalls:

> I had been kitted out at Cardington, my RAF number was 1212094. You had to remember your last three numbers when you went up to collect your pay. I did some training at Bridgenorth, from there I went on a Riggers' Course, and on completion of that I was sent to No.611 Squadron. I was a rigger to start with, then moved up a bit, but most of the time I was trying my hand at entertaining. They had a very good station band down at Hornchurch, very, very good indeed. Whenever the chance arose to sing with them I jumped at it, it was what I wanted to do. So in between working on aeroplanes, I used to practise. In fact that's how I met my wife Blossom, who was in the WAAF.
>
> One night I was doing a concert, the popular song of the day was 'If I had my way, you would never grow old' and she just loved that song. She happened to bump into me the following day, and asked if I would write down the words to the song.
>
> I couldn't write them out fast enough for her. I loved the look of this girl, she was a 'cracker'. After that we started courting and 15 months later we were married; two years after we had our first baby.
>
> I can remember some of the pilots in the squadron. There was Flight Lieutenant Hayter, and we also had two Australians, one called McFarland the other Eade. We were allotted one pilot and sometimes they didn't come back from a sortie. Others who had had too much were sent away for rest, some of them would get the twitch, the flying was getting too much for them. But I admired the pilots. Once you were up in your Spitfire, you were on your own, a bit like being on stage, no one can help you, you're on your own merits.

All the WAAFs' quarters were situated over on the Elm Park side of the airfield. Blossom used to cycle past our dispersal hut and this would be about 5.30 am every morning. She'd go by, we used to give it some, 'Come on, Girl' and all that. She took it all in good part. A lot of couples used to do their courting in the air-raid shelters when they were empty or otherwise in the shop doorways over in Romford. I always did mine outside the Co-Op, so I could always be sure of my divi! There were also several pubs around the area where they would let you go up and do a turn. The Elm Park Hotel was one and the Beacon at Beacontree Heath, that was another. I loved going up, singing or telling a joke. I used to do an impersonation of Max Miller and the other boys in the squadron christened me; that's how my name became Max. If I had a date, I would have to bribe the sergeant. I was getting a couple of quid a turn and he would take half of it. When we eventually had a rest period, we were sent up to Drem in Scotland. It was a terrible, terrible place; I was there for a month one night!

At 2.35 pm on the 3rd, B Flight of No.54 Squadron was scrambled and vectored to 15,000 feet over Maidstone to meet an incoming raid that was coming in from south-east towards Folkestone. It sighted 14 Me109s, not below it as expected, from the information given, but directly above at 30,000 feet. The 109s peeled off and attacked. The flight managed to fight its way out, but one pilot, Sergeant Joseph Lockwood, failed to return. His Spitfire P7300 was later found to have crashed between Lympne and Hythe in Kent; Lockwood had been killed.

During the action an Me109 was shot down by Pilot Officer Alan Campbell, the aircraft crashing at Brenzett. Campbell also fired 200 rounds at another 109 before it escaped into cloud.

Harry Broadhurst was again leading the Hornchurch Wing on a sweep over northern France on 5th March 1941; in his report he recalls:

As leader of No.611 Squadron in a wing sweep over northern France, I led the front section of four aircraft into combat against five Me109s who were approaching us from the east, 10 miles off Le Touquet at a height of around 31,000 feet; this was at 2.00 pm approximately. They were slightly above and in a turn, which would have brought them into a position astern of us. As we closed in a tight turn to attack, two members of the section who were in line astern spun down about 2,000 feet and took no further part in the combat.

I attacked the nearest Me109 which was one of three flying in close line astern. The remaining two 109s were flying as a pair and about 1,000 feet behind.

After a burst of about five seconds fire, this Me109 began to smoke, rolled over on its back and dived out of the combat. I therefore opened fire on the next 109 which emitted slight traces of white smoke and dived away. The third Me109 had broken away also and was not seen again. The first 109 was seen to go down by one of the members of the flight who had spun down earlier, who gave his opinion that it was out of control.

I now climbed up into the sun and searched for further enemy aircraft, and thinking I could see one some distance below me, I dived on to it only to find that it was a Spitfire. I then returned to base. On landing I found that four guns in the port wing had failed to fire owing to freezing of the lubricant.

Harry Broadhurst claimed one Me109 probable and the other damaged.

The 13th March dawned with a clear sky and unlimited visibility. This resulted in a very busy day for the squadrons. In the morning No.54 and No.611 Squadrons patrolled over the Maidstone line; this passed without incident. At noon, Wing Commander Broadhurst led the three squadrons and carried out a 'mopping up' sweep over France after six Blenheims had bombed Calais-Marck airfield. With No.54 Squadron leading, No.611 was at 6,000 feet above. It sighted 12 Me109 fighters, but did not attack, as its position was unfavourable. The third squadron, No.64 which was acting as top cover to the wing, was attacked by nine Me109s from 36,000 feet. The enemy's tactics were excellent and during the combat Squadron Leader Donald MacDonell was shot down; later it was confirmed that he had baled out and had become a prisoner of war. He had been brought down by the German 'ace' Werner Mölders. The only other casualty was a Spitfire of 64 Squadron which was written off during a forced-landing near Faversham, due to shortage of petrol. The pilot was uninjured. Squadron Leader MacDonell's position was filled by Flight Lieutenant Barrie Heath who was posted to No. 64 Squadron at Southend from 611 Squadron.

On 15th March, Wing Commander Andrew Douglas Farquhar became the first Wing Commander Flying Hornchurch Wing. Wing Commander Farquhar was later posted away on 2nd June to command a training wing at 53 OTU Heston.

Squadron Leader Stanley Meares, the senior controller, took up his new job as flight commander in 611 Squadron. He had been connected with the Operations Room for over two years and he was to take over Flight Lieutenant Barrie Heath's flight. Squadron Leader Lea took over charge of the Operations Room. Other officers working in his operations team were Squadron Leaders Adam, Holmes, Milward and Tollemache, three flight lieutenants, Kemp, Elsbury and Green and Pilot Officers Adcock, Jones, Parker and Tullberg.

In charge of the Signals Section, which included all communication such as teleprinters and telephone systems, was Flight Lieutenant Pyke. The Operations Room, situated in the old Masonic Hall in Western Road, Romford, had over 100 telephone and teleprinter lines delegated to Fighter Command Headquarters, Observer Corps sites, Army posts and other airfields. It also had 10 General Post Office exchange lines with 15 internal extensions. Hornchurch itself had over 89 extension lines on the station.

This was all to be kept running efficiently by station engineers and electricians as well as civilian staff.

During the afternoon of 3rd April, there occurred an unfortunate accident at RAF Southend (Rochford), when the second of a pair of aircraft from No.54 Squadron crashed into a hangar while taking off on a shipping patrol. Sergeant Thompson was taking off towards a hangar, when personnel heard a terrific crashing sound. It was discovered that he had managed to hit the top of the hangar and had gone clean through both sides. It seemed impossible that there could be anything left at all of the aircraft or if anyone could survive the crash. Sergeant Thompson was seriously injured, as were two airmen working in the hangar at the time, one of whom died of his injuries later in the evening. The aircraft (P7610) was scattered throughout the hangar with pieces of wing, tail and guns strewn all over the place. It was a great compliment to the manufacturers of the Spitfire, that the frame stood up so well to the crash, and had it not been for the protection of the engine in front of Sergeant Thompson, he would have been certainly killed.

The following day, just after lunch, a sweep operation of three pairs of aircraft was ordered. 'Broady' Broadhurst led with pilots from 611 Squadron. Over Calais, Broadhurst decided to 'beat up' Calais-Marck aerodrome and dived to 3,000 feet. Unfortunately after firing a third of his ammunition at dispersal pens, his aircraft's perspex canopy was splintered by a burst of ground flak and he was forced to break away and return to base.

G.F. 'Ricky' Richardson was serving with No.54 Squadron as an engine fitter during this period, and remembers how Station Commander Harry Broadhurst dealt with a situation that arose one day:

> I had to change the oil filter on a Spitfire one day, now that was one of the filthiest jobs one could imagine. You had to get down on your knees, undo the nut, then five or six gallons of oil would go 'whoosh', and you would end up covered.
>
> Occasionally they would have a clothing parade where you could go to the stores and get a new overall or uniform. I went down to the stores straight away afterwards and while I was in the store an SP (Military Policeman) came in. I can visualise him now – he was only a little chap – and he said to me, 'You are filthy'. I said 'Yes, so what?' Anyhow, he then put me on a charge for being filthy. I then had to go in front of Harry Broadhurst.
>
> Harry said, 'Why were you filthy?' I said, 'I was changing the oil filter'; it might have even been his machine. He said to the SP, 'I'll tell you what we'll do. We can't give him "jankers" because he's working seven days a week as it is now. I'll put you working with him.' So I had this chap working with me. With the SP, we could go in and out of the camp at any time we liked. That's how Harry came to my rescue.

At 3 p.m., on 6th April, 14 aircraft of the Hornchurch Wing led by Group Captain Broadhurst took off on a 'propaganda' patrol over that morning's convoy in the Thames estuary and coastal towns as far as Harwich. During the patrol, Broadhurst's Hurricane's engine 'cut' with a broken conrod and he was forced to make an emergency landing at Martlesham Heath.

An early morning sweep by 611 Squadron on the 15th, was led by Squadron Leader Eric Bitmead, with the target again the airfield of Calais-Marck. During the sweep the squadron was attacked by 109s over St Omer. Sergeants Limpenny and Thomas were both badly shot up and were very lucky to get home.

On the 17th, No.54 Squadron was again active in the morning while on a 'flag flying' patrol over shipping in the estuary. It was diverted to intercept a hostile raid which proved to be four Messerschmitt Me110s. These aircraft were attacked by one flight of 54 Squadron and two enemy aircraft were destroyed, enabling the squadron to claim its 100th enemy casualty. This fine result had been achieved with the loss of only 12 pilots.

B Flight of No.54 Squadron was on patrol just off the Essex coast, near Clacton, on 20th April, when it was set on by a mixture of Messerschmitt 110s and 109s at 25,000 feet. During the ensuing combat, Pilot Officer Jack Stokoe shot down an Me110, which was later confirmed. The following account of what happened next is told by Jack Stokoe:

> One moment I was flying and fighting and firing my guns, the next second I found myself floating in mid-air, still attached to the bucket-seat of my aircraft. My Spitfire had completely disintegrated and I had been blown clear of the aircraft as a result of enemy cannon-shells hitting the armour plating behind. It was a strange sensation to be floating in one's seat at 20,000 feet. I looked down and could see my parachute had come loose from its pack: would it work or not? I decided to first free myself from the seat, which meant I had to turn and release the sutton harness which held me.
>
> In my anxious state, I nearly made the fatal mistake of also releasing my parachute as well. Once free of the seat, I now decided to pull the D ring on my parachute and prayed it would work. The parachute opened with a terrific jerk and I floated down into a cold grey green choppy sea.
>
> Once in the water, my first concern was to free myself of the parachute which was getting heavier. I did not want to be dragged down or get entangled in the shroud lines. But my hands did not function properly, perhaps due to shock or to the cold.
>
> I then remembered the small inflatable dinghy, which we all carried now. I managed to turn the air release valve on the small cylinder bottle which would inflate the dinghy, but due to my haste I over inflated it and the dinghy burst.
>
> Things were beginning to look bleak and I remember thinking to myself, 'What a way to die.' I managed to hang on to part of the dinghy which still had a small envelope of air captured inside it. Just as I had given up on being rescued, I saw a ship heading in my direction. It was a Royal Navy

minesweeper that had arrived in the nick of time. Suddenly rope lines were thrown out and after a couple attempts, I grabbed hold and was hauled in like a fish.

I was taken below and wrapped in blankets and plied with hot drinks. I was then put in a bunk and was soon asleep. I was later to learn from the captain of the minesweeper that an RAF Air Sea Rescue launch had been sent out from Harwich to pick me up. They had asked the captain to transfer me over to the launch, but he told them I was sleeping and that he would bring me in. I found out later, that if I had been put aboard the launch, I would probably have drowned, as the launch overturned in rough sea on its return trip to Harwich.

I spent seven days in hospital and then went on a week's leave. When I look back at the event, I must have had a guardian angel looking after me on that occasion. I later received a most unusual memento, a photograph of my rescue from the sea, taken by one of the sailors aboard.

Jack had been flying Spitfire P7666. This aircraft had been paid for by contributions from members of the Royal Observer Corps and had been presented to No.41 Squadron at Hornchurch in November 1940. It was transferred to No.54 Squadron in February 1941 and re-coded KL-Z. Also on this day, Flight Lieutenant Ashton of No.64 Squadron was given the task of collecting the station commander's Hurricane, which had been undergoing repairs. He was flown down to Martlesham in the squadron's Miles Magister.

The first day of May arrived and brought rain during the early part of the morning; the rest of the day was fine although a fair amount of cloud persisted. The squadrons carried out 11 shipping patrols on Barrow Deep, but all passed without incident.

The station was visited on this day by Air Commandant Her Royal Highness, The Duchess of Gloucester. When Her Royal Highness arrived at midday, she was taken to the WAAFs' Officers' Mess. She was accompanied by her lady-in-waiting, Flying Officer Sandford. Group Captain Broadhurst introduced himself, and then presented the Station WAAF Administrative Officers and Flight Officer Lady Sefton from the Air Ministry; also Flight Officer Salmon from No.11 Group and the Squadron Leader Admin. Her Royal Highness first inspected an NCOs' and airwomen's sleeping quarter. She was pleased by the cleanliness and homeliness of the houses, and chatted to the airwomen.

In one room she spoke to a new radio telegraph operator who had just done her first night duty. She asked her if she was missing her sleep owing to the inspection, and received the answer that the airwoman felt so proud to have had the opportunity of talking to Her Royal Highness that she did not feel tired.

She also inspected the WAAFs' garden, which bore evidence of many hours spent planting vegetables and seeds, which was favourably commented upon. At the WAAFs' Sick Quarters three patients were presented; here she became concerned about the smoky fire, but was told the fault was prevalent in all the houses of this type, and that it had been reported to Command. Her Royal Highness was then driven to the main camp and watched a game of netball and tennis, and inspected the airwomen's mess.

Here, she remarked on the comfort and cleanliness, and also expressed her pleasure that the NAAFI recreation rooms etc, were all under the same roof.

She was driven around the perimeter track to Sutton's cook house and saw the airwomen cooking and serving the airmen's lunch. She talked to one woman who had been cooking for soldiers in the last war.

The last place to be visited was the Operations Room at Romford. WAAFs were manning the majority of positions and the radio telegraph operators were busy typing in their cubicles. In the Signals Section she saw telephonists and teleprinters at work.

On her return, she was taken to the Officers' Mess for lunch; and in the card room of the Mess the squadron and flight commanders and a French pilot were all introduced to her. On her departure she shook hands with everyone and said how much she had enjoyed herself. Her charm and friendliness made everyone feel that the official visit had been transformed into an informal and happy day, and that their pride in Hornchurch was not without justification.

Pilot Officer Jack Stokoe returned to flying operations with 54 Squadron on 6th May and while on a patrol claimed an Me109 damaged.

A strange request befell No.54 Squadron on 7th May, when it was called upon to patrol over Westminster, while the Budget proposals were being made in Parliament. Opinions differed as to the wisdom of the patrol, but no enemy aircraft appeared over London, and the conscience of the pilots was not strained. During the afternoon of 8th May, Prince Bernhardt of the Netherlands paid an informal visit to the station, visiting the squadrons, and in particular the two Netherland pilots of 611 Squadron. After tea in the Mess, he left leaving everyone impressed with his charm, informality and amazing command of the English language.

Hornchurch's satellite airfield at Rochford near Southend was visited by the Luftwaffe on the 11th. At 9.30 am, 17 high flying Me109s approached Southend from the River Crouch estuary, circled north of the aerodrome and then dived in line astern formation to bomb and machine gun the aerodrome at 100 feet. In all 17 bombs were dropped, but only four fell on the aerodrome alongside a hangar. One of these hit a building containing the control room, in which five men were working. Four escaped with slight injuries, but the fifth was killed.

The only other damage was to an ambulance, its garage and a fire tender. Two of the enemy failed to return to tell their tale. One of these was shot down by one of the airfield's Hispano cannons, the crew of which were most praiseworthy in staying at their post in face of the intense gunfire. The second enemy machine was destroyed by Pilot Officer Sewell of 54 Squadron, who was returning with Pilot Officer Stokoe from a patrol, when they ran into four 109s, returning over Shoeburyness. They swung around and chased the enemy over Kent, finally shooting one down into the Channel.

Hornchurch itself suffered occasionally from the night bombing, when the Germans dropped their bomb loads short of London. Harry Broadhurst remembers just one occasion:

> The Station Commander and the Wing Commander Admin both had a separate building with their own back garden. I remember one night, I heard the screech of a bomb coming down, but I paid no particular attention to it. But it landed quite nearby as I was walking up the path. Two batmen, who had hidden under the stairs of the building to shelter, came running out to see if I was alright; it was the nearest I'd been to being blown up. I couldn't hear or see anything; here I was standing in a bit of a daze with two scared batmen.

Engine fitter G.F. 'Ricky' Richardson also remembers the night blitz that was occurring over London and one particular early morning, while he was working:

> I'd been working, I remember, on one of the squadron's aircraft till about 2 am in the morning. I went over to Sutton's Institute where Blossom (Max Bygraves' wife) was working, dishing out the food for some of the chaps. I had a meal, then had to go back an hour before dawn and run up the aircraft. There would be about six of them, I had to check the boost and check the magnitos.
>
> Once you started one up, the exhaust pipes on the aircraft would give off a blue light.
>
> Suddenly everybody was running around like mad, I thought what the hell's going on over there? I found out later that 'Jerry' had seen these two blue streaks, knew what they were and had started firing down with machine gun fire on the aerodrome.

On the 16th, No.64 Squadron changed places with No.603 Squadron at Turnhouse up in Scotland. The return of old friends No.603 was welcomed by the station, although there were many changes in the personnel who had flown from Hornchurch during 1940. At between 8.30 and 9.30 am, while on convoy patrol on 18th May, Sergeant Thomas of 611 Squadron crashed at Dengie Flats. His aircraft caught fire and he was killed. No. 603 Squadron was given the job of patrolling over Chatham on the 21st, when it provided air cover protection for Her Majesty, Queen Elizabeth on her visit to the area.

On the 26th, the station was visited by Major General Liardet, the Inspector General of Aerodrome Defences, who was given a full tour of the ground defence regiments and their anti-aircraft guns. The aerodrome was still very well defended during this period of the war, although the major threat of any German invasion was not expected. The 70th Essex Regiment, commanded by Captain Langley had six platoons of 'E' Company, which consisted of eight officers and 250 men; they were given the task of securing the east and south perimeters of the station. The South End Road section, which ran past the main entrance of the station, was made the responsibility of local volunteers of the Home Guard, one officer and 30 men. Hornchurch's anti-aircraft defence consisted of two officers and 80 men of the Royal Artillery, with four 4.5 inch guns. This was also complemented by the 125 men of the 109th Canadian Light Anti-Aircraft Battery with their eight Bofors guns and 147 men of the RAF Ground Defence Section, who operated four Hispano guns and two four-barrelled Vickers guns at fixed gun positions. The whole defence system was under the command of Major Brown, the Local Defence commander, and Flight Lieutenant Nash in charge of RAF Ground Defence.

Station Commander Group Captain Broadhurst was visited by the famous artist Sir William Rothenstein on 31st May. He had arrived for a sitting with 'Broady' for his RAF series of portraits. Also on this day, a new 'Defence Scheme' began, which consisted of training 100 to 150 airman as a 'Reserve Rifleman Squadron'. The WAAF strength on the station also increased that month from 65 to 176.

Another new Wing Commander Flying arrived at Hornchurch on 2nd June 1941. This was Joseph Robert Kayll, a native of Sunderland. He was an 'ace' pilot who had exceptional qualities, having fought through France and the Battle of Britain.

On 4th June, No.54 Squadron suffered the sad loss of its last pre-war member, when whilst over the French coast Flight Lieutenant George Gribble was lost. He and his wingman Pilot Officer Batchelor had sighted a lone Me109 and had dived to attack, when they were bounced by enemy fighters. Gribble was heard to call over his R/T 'Engine cut, I'm baling out.' His parachute was seen going down into the sea by Pilot Officer Batchelor some 12 miles from the English coast. Batchelor orbited for nearly half-an-hour before he came home. No rescue boat picked Gribble up and he was never found. He is remembered on the Runnymede Memorial Panel 29.

The station received more VIP guests on this day, when Inspector of the RAF Sir William Mitchell arrived along with Lieutenant General Carr, CB, DSO, OBE, the General Officer in Charge of Eastern Command and some of his staff.

On 6th June, No.611 was visited at 3.45 pm by Air Vice-Marshal Trafford Leigh-Mallory and Group Captain Broadhurst, while they were operating down at Rochford. They talked with the pilots and took tea before returning to the Hornchurch Mess for dinner. The squadron officers were invited en masse as guests at Hornchurch for the dinner and attended a very enjoyable function. The only other incident of the day concerned Pilot Officer Johnson of 611, who crashed his Spitfire R2717 on landing in very bad weather conditions, by overshooting the flightpath and colliding with a stationary aircraft of B Flight.

Two pilots of the No.11 Group Anti-Aircraft Co-Operation Flight flew in on the 11th. Pilot Officer Swarsbrick (British) and Pilot Officer Stembrowicz (Polish) arrived with their Westland Lysander aircraft and a small ground crew party to look after them. Hornchurch was visited on the 17th June by Jeffrey Quill, the Supermarine Test Pilot, who gave a quarter of an hour's display of aerobatics, which caused one of Hornchurch's most senior pilots to say 'He flies the machine, I only drive it.'

During the evening of 20th June, Pilot Officer Jack Stokoe of No.54 Squadron was air-testing an aircraft, when the engine suddenly cut, and he was forced to make a crash-landing near Havering. Although the machine was badly damaged, fortunately Pilot Officer Stokoe was not injured. The very next day while on offensive patrol between Gravelines and St Omer, Stokoe claimed an Me109 damaged, when he shot off the enemy aircraft's engine cowling and noticed glycol streaming away.

Group Captain Wilfred Duncan-Smith was a pilot officer with No.611 Squadron at this time, and recalls:

> Keeping morale high at Hornchurch at this time was very largely due to people like Harry Broadhurst and the squadron commanders that we had; they kept us going day after day. I remember coming back one day from flying high escort cover to bombers over Hazebrouck, having myself been shot up by three different 109s. When I got out of my aircraft on landing, I was sick all over the carpet. 'Broady' saw what was going on and came over and said, 'If you can't take your booze, you better not damn well drink any', I said 'It's nothing to do with the booze, it was your leadership, Sir. I think it was bloody awful this morning.' He said, 'You cheeky bastard,' and after that we became good friends.
>
> About this time we were losing pilots quite frequently here and there. I think one sort of shut it out of one's memory, you didn't forget the bloke, but you forgot the incident. We lost some excellent chaps around this time.

News was received in Britain on 22nd June 1941, that Germany had invaded Russia. With the Luftwaffe now flying and fighting on two war fronts, Fighter Command hoped this would stretch them and help cut RAF casualties, which had been mounting over the last six months during the circuses and sweeps. It was estimated by the intelligence section of the RAF, that the Luftwaffe strength across the Channel in northern France now stood at about 500 single and twin-engined fighters.

Another party of ATC cadets visited the aerodrome on the 22nd, this time from Romford. On arrival at 3.00 pm, the 50 cadets led by two of their officers were met by what was called the 'Conducting Officer'. He then took them on a trip to see the Photographic Section where they saw combat film footage. The cadets were then split into three equal smaller parties. One of these went to the Parachute Section, where the officer or airman in charge showed them something of the construction and care of parachutes and dinghies. One went to the Armoury, where there was a similar demonstration of the belt filling machine, tommy guns, etc and one group to the Link Trainer room, where a pilot explained the workings of that. After about 15 minutes, the parties would swop over until everyone had seen all three 'sideshows'. Next the whole party was taken to one of the hangars to see the work in progress on the aircraft. It was then given a treat of seeing a Spitfire up on tressles, firing off at the butts. Finally the cadets were taken to the various dispersal points, after which the Conducting Officer took them to the

Mess for refreshments and a conference. They departed at 6.30 pm.

On 24th June 1941, Hornchurch again was involved in a Circus operation (Circus 21). Twelve Spitfires Vs of No.54 Squadron left Hornchurch in company with No.603 and 611 Squadrons. Group Captain Broadhurst led No.54 and the Wing. The objective of the Wing was to create a diversion at Dunkirk during the inward journey of the bombers' mission and then to cover them on their return over Gravelines. With 54 Squadron leading and the other two squadrons stepped up behind them, the Wing crossed the position of North Foreland at 17,000 feet and flew until the beaches of Dunkirk were sighted. The course was then changed to 90 degrees and within one minute the bombers and their escort were sighted two miles ahead, crossing the coast east of Dunkirk. The Wing turned and followed the bombers inland for three miles.

It was at this time that two Me109s appeared above at 25,000 feet and shadowed the Wing for some considerable time. The Wing then turned out to sea, following the coast west of Dunkirk, then turned inland for ten miles towards Lille. It then turned back to the coast and climbed into the sun, making a wide circle turn to Gravelines. At about 8.53 pm the bombers were seen crossing the coast on their return journey, and the Wing was then split into sections of four aircraft. They were still being shadowed by the two Me109s.

After splitting, Red Section, led by Harry Broadhurst, sighted several lone Me109Es diving to attack the bombers. Red 1 attacked one of these, which was at the same height as himself. He followed it in the dive and fired short bursts from astern from 300 yards. The enemy aircraft belched smoke and turned away in a dive into the haze over France. It was claimed as damaged. Red 1 then collected the section and led it back to the coast in the track of the bombers.

Twelve Me109s were then seen approaching out of the sun on the port bow; they were in loose formation 1,000 feet above Red Section. The enemy fighters tried to swing in behind the section, but Red Section turned to port into them. The enemy went into a line astern formation of loose pairs and turned away. Red 1 attacked the first three enemy aircraft with short bursts, the first from the beam and the other two from astern at 300 yards range. In all cases strikes were seen and the second aircraft belched smoke. The other three members of Red Section attempted to attack, but the rest of the enemy formation dived steeply into the clouds. It had been noticeable that although the enemy were in favourable positions to attack, they refused combat. They all carried the standard German camouflage, with yellow noses.

Yellow Section, which was flying line abreast in a south-westerly direction at 18,000 feet, saw one aircraft approaching from the south-east and slightly above. Pilot Officer Jack Stokoe manoeuvred his aircraft onto the tail of the Me109F now diving past him, he carried out a quarter attack, opening fire at 200 yards and closing to 100 yards. After the enemy fighter had also damaged his starboard mainplane, Pilot Officer Stokoe saw the enemy aircraft take no evasive action and it continued its dive straight into the sea.

Meanwhile Blue Section, led by Flying Officer Jack Charles, was travelling west from Gravelines, and saw Me109Es flying at a height of 18,000 feet over Gris Nez, in a north-easterly direction. Charles attacked the leading enemy aircraft in a quarter head-on attack from slightly below. The enemy aircraft took no evasive action and went down with black and white smoke pouring out of it. Blue 2, Sergeant Harry Knight, made a quarter astern attack on a second Me109, which dived into the sea off Gris Nez. Pilot Officer Sewell, Blue 3, also claimed an Me109 destroyed. The Wing returned to Hornchurch soon after with another successful operation under its belt.

The following day, 25th June, Wing Commander Joe Kayll was shot down on a sweep over France in Spitfire R7259; he remembers that day vividly:

My time at Hornchurch was very short unfortunately. A raid was scheduled for June 25th and just before take-off Group Captain Broadhurst said that he would like to lead the Wing, I said I would go as his No.2.

It was a clear day as the Wing went into northern France. The bombers dropped their stuff and then the Wing headed for home. 'Broady' then handed the Wing to one of the other squadron commanders and turned his section back into France and started to climb steeply. We were flying into the sun and after a few minutes we were still climbing when we were attacked out of the sun by a flight of Me109s. My engine was stopped and my No.3 and 4 were both shot down. I could see the Channel and had a slight hope that I might be able to glide to over half way across. This was frustrated by frequent attacks by the 109s, and I had to dive steeply and manoeuvre to avoid them, I tried to bale out, but as I slowed down so that I could open my hood, they attacked again. There was no other option left but to force-land the aircraft.

I landed in a field wheels up, between two canals. Once I had landed, I tried to smash up the instrument panel, which I found quite indestructible. Suddenly I heard a bullet pass me quite close, and then a second bullet. I decided to run across the field to the nearest house. However the shooting continued for some time, not at me, but at the aircraft. I later learnt that there had been two guards, one on each canal and the aircraft landed right between them. The first guard shot at me, but his bullet just missed the guard opposite who naturally fired back, and this continued for some time.

I was eventually captured, found hiding in a cornfield.

There was an interesting sequel to the shooting by the two German guards. It was reported to the Luftwaffe at St Omer, where I was eventually taken, that after my forced-landing, I had used my revolver to shoot at German soldiers.

In consequence, I was not invited to supper at their Mess, which I understand was the custom for wing commanders or above. This story got back to the United Kingdom about ten days later, where our intelligence officer was interrogating a German pilot shot down from St Omer. I didn't carry a revolver anyway. It was unfortunate for my family; they had been told I had been shot down in flames, however owing to the German pilot's story, they knew I was safe quite quickly.

Wing Commander Joe Kayll was sent to Spangenberg Castle PoW Camp and later to Wartburg. He escaped during a break-out in September 1942, but was recaptured and sent to Stalag Luft 3 at Sagan, where he was involved in organising escape activity. He remained in captivity until release in May 1945, and was awarded the OBE for his work in this respect.

On 26th June, Flying Officer Peter Dexter DFC returned to Hornchurch after his time spent in hospital recovering from wounds he collected during October 1940; he was posted to No.611 Squadron. On the 27th, Wing Commander F.S. Stapleton, the commanding officer of 611 Squadron was promoted to Wing Commander Flying, to take the place of Joe Kyall. Another promotion and posting that day was of Pilot Officer Eric Lock, who had been wounded in action with No.41 Squadron in late 1940. He returned to operations at Hornchurch as an Acting Flight Lieutenant to serve with 611 Squadron.

Squadron Leader 'Joe' Leigh remembers Eric Lock:

He was my flight commander. I always remember that in my log-book I used to write little notes if something happened. But one of the chaps in the flight, he used to write down massive amounts on what had occurred either about weather or whatever.

When 'Lockie' came in as flight commander, he wrote in this chap's log-book 'enough of this bull-shit.' But unfortunately Lock was only with us a few weeks before he was shot down. After this had happened, the pilot wrote in his log-book:

'Flight Commander shot down, bull-shit starts again.'

It was a fine day on Sunday 29th June, when the station was visited by Air Officer Commanding-in-Chief Fighter Command, Air Marshal Sholto Douglas. He stayed for lunch and was introduced to squadron and flight commanders; some pilots were also presented to him. Meanwhile one of Hornchurch's squadrons was mentioned in the newspaper headlines titled *'Weekend airmen bag 18 in 10 days', 'The City of Liverpool Auxiliary Squadron (No.611) RAF in the last 10 days has destroyed 18 Me109s, probably destroyed nine more and damaged several others for the loss of only two aircraft and two pilots.'* Sir Archibald Sinclair, Air Minister, Secretary of State for Air, sent a telegram to the squadron saying: 'Many congratulations on the magnificent results which you have achieved during the hard fighting in offensive action against the enemy this week.'

The Station Operations Book, under the title of General Notes for June 1941, reads:

Defence – 'The Reserve Rifle Squadron' or 'Backers-up' numbering about 150 have made progress. Many of them have now fired at the annual rifle practices. In addition there have been lectures for all senior NCO's on defence subjects. There is promise of a good stock of Tommy guns.

WAAF – Strength has gone up to over 200, and still they come. But there are continual screams from Operations, of shortage of skilled plotters.

The 1st July started with a morning haze, which instead of dispersing continued throughout the rest of the day. This somewhat complicated the show that had been laid on for a party of visitors from South America. The party of representatives of the fighting services of various South American states included General Bilbao of Bolivia, Wing Commander Gana, Squadron Leader Contreras and Squadron Leader Garcia from Chile, Lieutenant Commander Marengo of Argentina, Lieutenant Commander Panay and Lieutenant Fuller de Costa of Peru.

After lunch and in spite of the difficult visibility, a flypast by the Wing was carried out successfully, and was marred only by one belly-landing by a pilot of 611 Squadron, who was obliged to go round again when attempting a section landing and in his haste to get down forgot his undercarriage on the second approach. During the evening the station was visited by 50 cadets from No.227 Squadron, Dagenham.

It was announced on 2nd July, that Wing Commander Frederick Stapleton, now Wing Commander Flying, and Flying Officer Jack Charles, a Canadian pilot of No.54 Squadron, had both been awarded the Distinguished Flying Cross. Each had shot down three enemy aircraft and several probables; their courage and dash were highly commended. No.611 Squadron received a new commanding officer in early July, when Flight Lieutenant James Hayter arrived.

On 4th July, Group Captain Harry Broadhurst led the Wing on a Circus operation over Béthune. 'Broady' Broadhurst recalls the following events:

> I was leading 54 Squadron and the Wing, as target support to Circus 32 over Béthune. As we crossed the French coast at Gravelines at 14,000 feet, the Wing loosened formation and shortly afterwards an Me109F flew across the formation from west to east, slightly below.
>
> I turned after him firing a short burst with cannon and machine gun from 400 yards, 20 degrees on quarter. I observed no results of my fire. I then rejoined the formation and led it to Béthune, where it broke up into sections of four aircraft. Red Section in the centre immediately engaged a number of Me109s above and split up.
>
> I was Red 1 and after chasing two enemy aircraft without bringing them into combat as they half rolled and dived away, I engaged a yellow-nosed Me109 on the top of its climb, as it pulled up after a dive attack on the bombers. I fired 20 rounds

from each cannon with slight deflection from astern, and saw smoke appear from the starboard wing root and the enemy aircraft disappeared into cloud. This aircraft I claimed as destroyed.

After two more successful skirmishes with Me109s, I got my sights on another 109 from 250 yards and slightly below. I fired 30 rounds from each cannon. The starboard wing fell off the enemy aircraft and it fell into a vicious spin and disappeared into clouds. I also claimed this as destroyed. There were still several enemy aircraft about and I got into combat with another 109, as my cannon ammunition was finished. I fired all my 0.303 from 300 yards astern, but saw no results.

All of a sudden I was then hit by cannon shells from an Me109 which must have got onto my tail. My port aileron controls were damaged and the control column was knocked out of my hand and the aircraft went into a spin. I recovered from the spin when I passed through cloud at 4/5,000 feet, and from the resulting dive came out at 1,000 feet over Béthune. The aircraft appeared to be still flyable, though very left wing low on account of the damage to the controls. In addition the port wing flap and undercarriage mechanism was damaged, and large parts of the panelling had been shot away from the upper and lower surfaces of the port main plane. Splinters of cannon-shell had damaged the reflector gun-sight and windscreen and splinters had entered my left arm and thigh. The oil pressure gauge only registered 10lbs per square inch, but as the temperature remained normal, I assumed that the gauge was damaged. This proved eventually to be the case. I re-climbed into cloud, flying towards Gravelines and remained in cloud until it ended over St Omer, where I was immediately attacked by intense and accurate heavy 3-inch anti-aircraft flak. I evaded this by losing height from 4/3,000 feet and saw no signs of any activity.

I crossed the French coast at Cap Gris Nez at zero feet and continued at the same height across the Channel. Owing to the damage to my undercarriage, I decided to crash-land back at Hornchurch, which I did successfully. After landing I was taken to the hospital in Romford, to have my splinter wounds seen too. I woke up in hospital the next morning, a junior doctor came and sat on the end of my bed and talked to me. I said, 'How long have I got to stay here, there's nothing wrong with me.' He then told me a story about an old lady who had come in; she'd been bombed out and shot up. She complained of a headache, she had just been one of a queue of people waiting, so the doctor prescribed her some aspirins and sent her home and said, 'if that doesn't get rid of your headache come back and see us again.'

A few days later she returned, saying that the pain was

intolerable, so they did a x-ray and found a 'bloody bullet' inside her. That's a true story. Well after the doctor told me this story, I said, 'Well you can't keep me here, the worst I've got is a bullet in the backside.' I got out of hospital that day.

At 1.20 am, on 7th July, a Beaufighter of No.29 Squadron operating from Manston airfield and controlled by Hornchurch, shot down a Junkers Ju88 bomber that was laying mines in the Thames estuary. This was the first sortie made in connection with the experimental use of Beaufighters under Hornchurch's control to combat night mine-laying. During the day, Harry Broadhurst was back in action again, leading the Wing on Circus operation 36. The Spitfires were escort cover to Blenheims bombing a target over St Omer.

Flying that day with Broadhurst was Wilfred Duncan-Smith, who remembers:

> Over the target area, about 15 to 20 enemy fighters began a determined attack on the Blenheim bombers. We went into the attack and during the affray, 'Broady' and his No.2 'Streak' Harris became separated from the rest of the Wing. While they were separated, six Me109s launched an attack on the two of them. They dived down to 6,000 feet and fought a defensive battle all the way back to the French coast, during which 'Streak' Harris was shot down and killed. I heard Broady's voice over the radio shouting his call sign 'Taipan', asking for assistance. Some of us saw the 109s and started to fly to his aid. Unfortunately we didn't see the two 109s which had positioned themselves above and either side of Broady's aircraft, while another 109 came into attack from a head-on position. With guns blazing, both aircraft continued their collision course.

Harry Broadhurst continues:

> One enemy aircraft attacked me at the same level, dead ahead and firing. I fired with both cannon and machine guns, opening fire at 200 yards; we passed within a few feet of one another. The enemy aircraft, which I hit with cannon, exploded in front of me and pieces of it were brought back on the port wingtip. Another 109 in the meantime got onto my tail and fired a burst of cannon and gunfire. One of his shells entered the fuselage by the wireless aerial, making a large hole and severing one elevator control and a harness cable, which caused further damage inside the fuselage. An armour-piercing bullet put the port cannon out of action, buckling it like a hairpin. After successfully losing my attacker, I flew due west at zero feet for North Foreland and headed for home.

After landing, his Spitfire was more or less a write-off. On further inspection the Spitfire's propeller and wing fronts were found to be covered with small deposits of oil and human blood remains from the aircraft that had blown up during the head-on attack. After this episode, he gave instructions that the oil-splashed spinner be fitted to his new aircraft when it was ready, to remind him of the fight and how lucky he was to survive. Wing Commander Frank Dowling who was Station Adjutant recalls:

> 'Broady' came back from that trip and walked into my office and flung a piece of cloth onto my desk. He said 'There's a bit of Hun for you.' It was a bit of the German pilot's battledress from the 109 that had blown up in front of him.

The Wing carried out a sweep on the morning of the 8th, and was very successful in shooting down four enemy aircraft, two probably destroyed and four damaged. One pilot of No.611 Squadron, the Dutchman Flight Lieutenant Bruinier, was unlucky in that the seat of his Spitfire collapsed, so that he was unable to see over his instrument panel. He overshot on landing and his aircraft was written off, but he was unhurt. Flight Lieutenant Eric Lock added to his score that day. His combat report states:

> I was leading Charlie Section and having crossed the French Coast at 18,500 feet.
> Saw 5 Me109 Es a few miles north of the target, up sun and above. We turned to get behind them when I was attacked from astern by some more 109s. Evading these, I attacked the last one of that formation, giving a short burst of cannon fire, but missed.
> I then observed that I was boxed in by 109s, so I spun down in aileron turn.
> When pulling out of my dive at 4,000 feet. I observed an Me109 converging on me and did a beam attack with cannon. The enemy aircraft belched smoke and I continued to follow him down to 2,000 feet. I saw him go into the ground near a wood.
> As there were some troops in the vicinity, I kept on diving and sprayed them with machine gun fire. On climbing back I was attacked by 3 more so pulled the plug and came home at zero feet.

In the afternoon, the Chief of Air Staff, Air Chief Marshal Sir Charles Portal came to the station to see a Circus operation from as near the front line as possible. The Circus consisted of an attack by one Stirling on Lille power station, and two on the Kuhlman chemical works at Béthune. During the operation 15 to 20 Me109s were encountered and five were destroyed, two probable and one damaged. Unfortunately one pilot of 611 Squadron failed to return. The Wing was considerably split up during the action and pilots landed back at airfields far and wide, from Coltishall in Norfolk to Detling in Sussex.

# CHAPTER 2

# THE HORNCHURCH WING
## July – December 1941

During this period, Fighter Command's losses of experienced Wing Leaders and pilots were beginning to tell. As with the Germans in 1940, the role was being reversed. Our boys were now on the receiving end. The Germans had learnt a valuable lesson in the Battle of Britain and now their use of radar on the French side of the Channel was paying off. Many squadrons were being bounced by high flying Me109s who had been given the time to climb above the Allied fighters and bombers coming over to northern France. Allied pilots shot down over enemy territory had very little chance of escaping back to Britain once captured, unless picked up first by the French Resistance and then smuggled through various routes to a neutral country.

On 9th July, No.54 Squadron lost Pilot Officer Gordon Herbert Batchelor on a Circus operation. He had joined No.54 at Catterick in October 1940. The following account is taken from Pilot Officer Batchelor's own diary that he kept after being captured as a prisoner of war.

> *July 9th:* I was shot down presumably by an Me109. I heard some shells hit the underside of my aircraft. One came in through the bottom of the cockpit, the next thing I remember was trying to pull out of a spin, but my elevator and rudder cables had been severed. I decided to bale out, and in doing so my wireless plug got caught in the aircraft and gave me such an abrupt jerk, after which I must have fallen several thousand feet before pulling my ripcord.
>
> It seemed ages before I reached the ground, but was told later, it was 10-15 minutes.
>
> I came down in a cornfield, and as I had been shot in the legs, I could not stand.
>
> I was surrounded by Huns in about five minutes, who took me on horseback to an armoured car, where they gave me a drink and bandaged my legs.
>
> I was taken to an Army HQ in Vitry, and after being searched and questioned, I was taken to hospital at Arras. When I arrived, they X-rayed my legs and found two pieces of shrapnel in the left leg and one in the right; as they were only about as big as peas, they decided not take them out. They pricked out very small pieces that were just under the surface

of the skin. I came round after the operation, during the evening. I slept in the hospital with very little to report. The doctors were very good to me and found a couple of English books for me to read. The food was pretty awful, the tea and coffee worse.

*29th July:* I was taken by ambulance from Arras to Brussels. The hospital was much larger, here the food a little better, but the doctors not so friendly. They again X-rayed my legs, but decided not to operate. A guard was placed by the window and the door was locked, but it was of little account as I was unable to walk. I had my watch, cigarette case and lighter given to me here, also my fountain pen. I wrote my second letter home.

Gordon Batchelor was to spend the rest of his time undergoing more tests and x-rays in hospital. The reason was that when he had baled out his parachute had been slightly damaged causing his descent to be faster than normal. On hitting the ground he had badly damaged his legs, hips and spine. Infection set in and he died of Ewing's septicaemia on 15th April 1942, aged 23 years. He is buried at Ohlsdorf British Military Cemetery at Hamburg, Grave 9, Row H, Plot 5.

Bernard Batchelor remembers his older brother:

We were both brought up on our father's farm at Higham in Kent. We had a very happy family upbringing; there were five of us. I expect if war had not come, Gordon would have continued and eventually taken over the running of the farm.

I remember he went and joined the RAF Volunteer Reserve at Rochester, before the outbreak of war. He did some training at St. Leonard's, near Hastings and from there he went to Catterick. Once he had joined the RAF, his whole heart was in it, and he was very delighted when he was posted to a Spitfire squadron, No.54 at Catterick. He did not have any real apprehension about the task he was given. He had great faith in God and did not fear death in that way.

He would escort the bombers over to France on daylight raids. On several occasions, if he had enough petrol in the tank, he would on return, do three low sweeps over the farm and family home, to let us know that he was safe. On one occasion, there was a village conference being held in the garden, which was to raise money through the church. Unbeknown to him, he flew low over the garden, where 200 people had gathered, all looking up as he flew by.

When he arrived back at Hornchurch, he immediately telephoned to apologise for the disturbance. My mother and father were very proud of him. After he had been shot down, it was a good six weeks before we received his first letter. In fact we heard that he was safe, when listening to Germany's Lord 'Haw Haw' on the radio. The next day we received an official telegram from the Air Ministry.

While 611 Squadron was on a sweep over France on 10th July, Flight Lieutenant James Hayter destroyed an Me109, but on the return trip his aircraft was badly damaged by enemy flak and he was forced to make a crash-landing near Southend. Squadron Leader A.C. 'Joe' Leigh, then a sergeant pilot, was flying with Flight Lieutenant Hayter that day and remembers:

> We had done our stuff, and were crossing back over the French coast in cloud. I was formating on Hayter when I suddenly lost him. I felt a bit lonely up there on my own, so I went down to see if he was below. I suddenly found Hayter and stayed with him on his tail. His aircraft was full of holes and his radio had been damaged by the flak, but he managed to make it back. It had been fortunate that Hayter had not turned into me when he had been hit or we might have collided. He later told me I had done a very good job of sticking with him.

On the ground, Captain G.H. Rawlins and Lieutenant A.H. Farland of the Royal Tank Regiment arrived with 12 other ranks and three light tanks as an addition to the already varied defences.

On 14th July, Flying Officer Peter Dexter was killed when his Spitfire collided with another Spitfire of No.54 Squadron while over Boulogne. He was seen to bale out, but it was reported later by the Red Cross that he had been picked up by the Germans dead in his parachute.

A signal was received at RAF Hornchurch on the 15th, from Headquarters Fighter Command to pass on to the Station Commander, which read:

> Please pass the following information to Group Captain Broadhurst:-
>
> On 10/7/41, a German communiqué announced that Wilhelm Balthasar had been shot down in combat on the western front.
>
> He was the leader of the most important unit JG2 and is credited with 44 victories. He has all the usual decorations for a person of his importance.
>
> He is ex-Richthofen and Air Condor Legion in Spain.
>
> Should further information come to hand it will be forwarded directly.

This communication confirmed the identity of the pilot whom Harry Broadhurst had vanquished in the head-on attack, several days earlier.

Although Hornchurch and most of Fighter Command's squadrons were now flying the Spitfire MkV variant, some of the main commanders still felt that the aircraft was not being used to its maximum potential against the German fighters. Harry Broadhurst sent the following signal to Fighter Command, who in turn passed on these observations to Rolls-Royce:

It is essential that fighter aircraft should attain their maximum speed at the greatest possible height, but a comparatively small increase in ceiling would not justify any substantial reduction of speed at medium heights. It is, therefore, considered that the superiority in speed at medium heights is more important than superiority in ceiling with a consequent sacrifice in speed.

Diving attacks are always the most effective as the element of surprise is achieved, but turning radius and quick initial acceleration are equally important. At all heights a Spitfire can turn inside a Bf109, but the 109 appears to have quicker initial acceleration in a dive and also in climbing. The greatest disadvantage in this respect is the cutting out of the Merlin engine on application of negative G force. The diving attack is probably of greater importance, as it cannot easily be evaded, whereas it is usually comparatively easy to avoid a circling attack.

Light ailerons at high speed are absolutely essential. This is one of the greatest advantages the Spitfire has over the 109. It is impossible to bring guns to bear on an aircraft that is diving fast and aileron turning at the same time. Quick turns either level or diving is a sure method of evasion against a less manoeuvrable aircraft.

Reserve of power and manoeuvrability are the foremost requirements for efficient fighting at great heights. The superiority in this respect of the Bf109, particularly the Bf109F, must to a large extent, be due to its light weight. At present the Spitfire V has insufficient reserves of power to stay in combat with the Bf109 at 35,000 feet. The latter definitely had greater speed at that height on the level, climb or dive.

Pilot Officer Duncan-Smith of 611 Squadron volunteered to inspect an aircraft factory at Deptford on 16th July. Afterwards he was entertained by Messrs Rootes & Company at a champagne dinner at Claridges, where a cheque for £8,000 was handed to him for the Spitfire Fund. 'Smithy' afterwards made a speech to the workers, which was most appreciated by those attending.

Squadron Leader Robert Finlay Boyd, No.54 Squadron's commanding officer, was posted away on 19th July, to take up a position as an instructor at 58 OTU, Grangemouth. His place was to be taken by Squadron Leader Newell Orton, known to his friends as 'Fanny'. He had distinguished himself during the Battle of France and had already claimed five enemy aircraft destroyed by 10th May 1940, while with No.73 Squadron flying Hawker Hurricanes.

A visit by 30 Air Training Corps Cadets of No.437 Squadron from Poplar also arrived this day, along with BBC broadcaster Alan Melville and a representative of the *Liverpool Daily Post* to cover a story on 611 Squadron. Another group of 50 cadets from No.6 and 374 ATC-Romford arrived for a tour of the station on 20th July.

Road re-surfacing work on the station and along Sutton's Lane was started on the 23rd. This had been cancelled at previous times due to the shortage of tarmac. On this occasion the work was carried out by the Essex County Council, not the Ministry of Works and Bricks and was completed by 31st July. Visits by local ATC continued on the 26th, when 50 cadets from 106 Squadron, Grays arrived, commanded by Flight Lieutenant Algie DSO, DFC. He had served at Sutton's Farm as a flight commander during the First World War.

The morning of 3rd August started with slight cloud, but after a few hours turned into a beautiful sunny afternoon. No.611 Squadron was heavily involved in Rhubarb sorties that day. Twelve aircraft split into pairs flew one sortie during the morning, and five pairs flew in the afternoon. Cloud cover over France was minimal, so everyone returned except for one. The loss of Flight Lieutenant Eric 'Lockie' Lock, DSO, DFC, was extremely hard on his fellow pilots. 'Lockie' had recovered from his injuries after being shot down in 1940, and after undergoing 16 operations on his legs, he undertook on behalf of the RAF, to visit the workers in aircraft factories and do radio interviews for the BBC.

During the flight, Lock had seen German troops marching on a road and had decided to give them a squirt. He had gone into the attack and was last seen streaking down a road at the back of Boulogne, causing soldiers on bicycles to disperse and seek cover in all directions, while shouting over the Spitfire's R/T: 'Ha-ha, look at the bastards running.'

In the 611 Operations Record Book, it records: 'It seems a ruddy awful waste to lose so great a pilot on so trivial an expedition. It is anticipated that the German Press will make much of Lock's capture or death.' His Spitfire W3257 was never recovered, and he has remained to this day as listed 'Missing in Action'. Flight Lieutenant Eric Lock died aged 21 years, and is remembered on the Runnymede Memorial, Panel 29. He was the top scoring pilot during the Battle of Britain, with 20 aircraft destroyed, although his final tally was 26 enemy destroyed and 8 probable.

On 4th August 1941, No.54 Squadron was moved to Martlesham Heath for a well-earned rest. Its place at Hornchurch was taken by one of the recently formed Canadian squadrons, No.403 'Wolf' Squadron, which flew in from Ternhill, replacing its Spitfire Mk1s for Spitfire Vbs. Their commanding officer was Squadron Leader B.G. Morris. A detachment of 20 men of the Pioneer Corps also arrived, to assist with the work of wiring the station defence system.

No.611 Squadron received another flight commander on 7th August, this was Flight Lieutenant George Barclay, an 'ace' pilot who had spent some months in hospital after being wounded in action in November 1940 with No.249 Squadron, but had recently been instructing at No.52 OTU at Debden.

On the 8th, No.611 Squadron were involved in combat with 109s over St Omer; Pilot Officer George Mason became separated from the rest of the squadron and recalls:

> I suddenly became detached from the rest of the chaps and found myself accompanied by a Staffel (Sqdn) of Me109s. In

the ensuing battle I was hit in the starboard cannon magazine, which fortunately was empty by then. I then flew flat out for England, home and beauty and ran out of fuel half way across the Channel. I glided and crash-landed on a beach at Walmer only to find that I had landed in a minefield.

I was rescued by a Corporal Chick of the Royal West Kent Regiment who threaded his way through the mines to get to me. He was awarded the British Empire Medal for this gallant act, about which I knew nothing at the time. After a spell in hospital I returned to Hornchurch and worked in Station Flight as Duty Pilot until I was fit enough to return to operations.

Sergeant Mason's Spitfire W3523 was a write-off, while he suffered a deeply lacerated left leg and a compound fracture of the right tibia.

The following day, the Canadian squadron No.403, claimed its first success during the morning while on a Circus sweep over St Omer. Pilot Officer Anthony claimed a probable. In the afternoon however, they also suffered their first casualty when the squadron was jumped near Gravelines and Pilot Officer Walden was listed as missing.

On the morning of 12th August, a Circus operation at St Omer was staged as part of a diversion to cover the first big daylight raid over Germany by Bomber Command. No.403 was scrambled in flights to cover the withdrawal of a striking force of Blenheims. In the evening, the Wing made another fighter sweep, which resulted in a probable being claimed by Sergeant McKelvie of 603 Squadron. Pilot Officer Van de Honert of 611 made a sensational landing, finishing up in a tree bordering the western hangar of the airfield, with a wounded arm, no rudder controls and a flat tyre.

A Defence Exercise had been held that day between 4.00 pm and 8.00 pm. The mock attack was by the 10th Essex Battalion, and defended by the 70th Essex, RAF ground defence and a small representative body of 20 backers-up. There was also a visit by Godfrey Wynn of the *Sunday Express*, who was there to write an article on fighter sweeps.

On 18th August, personnel from Hornchurch, under the command of Squadron Leader H.G.P. Ovendon arrived to prepare squadron billets and an orderly office at Hornchurch's new satellite airfield at Fairlop, near Barkingside, Essex.

Pilot Officer Chapman was given the appointment of RAF Defence Officer. The new airfield had been under construction since December 1940, when construction engineer Mr J.B. Hoyle was given control of the site. Delays due to the bad winter had held up construction, but the three concrete runways were fully completed by June. The lengths of the runways were as follows: north-east to south-west was 1,300 yards, north to south was 1,100 yards, and east to west, 1,100 yards.

The 19th August was to be one of the most successful days that the Hornchurch Wing would record. It would also include a mission that was unusual.

The morning was fine, but misty. This caused the operation to be postponed from 7.30 am until 10.00 am, when the Wing took off on Circus

81. In this operation, 6 Bristol Blenheims were to bomb a target at Cosnay, but on the outbound trip they were also tasked with the unusual job of dropping a new artificial leg for Wing Commander Douglas Bader, who was now a prisoner of war after baling out over St Omer on 9th August. During his frantic escape from his spinning aircraft, he had to leave behind one of his tin legs when the supporting straps broke. Once one of the Blenheims had dropped Bader's new limb they continued onto their target.

The Hornchurch Wing as Target Support Wing was scheduled to go in east of Dunkirk, and arrive over Cosnay, five minutes before the bombers. But the Wing did not reach Cosnay. By the time it had gone as far as the Poperinge/Cassel area, all three squadrons had found enemy fighters to engage. No.611 Squadron was leading with Wing Commander Stapleton and engaged some 109s, which were seen below approaching from the south and to the east. This was not a very successful action in that no enemy fighters were shot down, but all 611 Squadron returned to base, and the enemy fighters were prevented from intercepting the British bombers.

No.403 Squadron, which had returned to operations at Hornchurch, was more fortunate. At 30,000 feet they saw 15 Me109s to the west flying in a north-westerly direction at 15,000 feet. The squadron dived to engage them and destroyed four Me109s, one probable and damaged two others, for the loss of one pilot (Pilot Officer Anthony who was listed as missing), and the aircraft of Pilot Officer Dick, who destroyed two Me109s before baling out over the Channel. He was picked up by the Air Sea Rescue and was flying again next day. Sergeant MacDonald landed his Spitfire at Orsett, near Grays in Essex, short of petrol; his machine was damaged (Category 2).

Circus 82 took place in the afternoon. The Wing left Hornchurch at 5.45pm led by Group Captain 'Broady' Broadhurst with Wing Commander Stapleton leading 403 Squadron. The plan was to sweep the area between St Omer and Gravelines to cover the return of bombers from a raid on Hazebrouck. No.603 was leading at 28,000 feet, 403 was in the middle at 29,000 feet and 611 was top cover at 31,000 feet.

Several small formations of 109s were seen and chased, but 611 Squadron was the only squadron to inflict casualties. They intercepted some 109s about 15,000 feet over Gravelines and shot two of them into the sea, both shared by Pilot Officer Smith and Sergeant A.C. Leigh. No.403 Squadron suffered three casualties on the 21st, while on a escort to a raid on Chocques. Squadron Leader Morris in Spitfire P8740 and Sergeant MacDonald in R7279 were listed as missing, while Flying Officer McKenna baled out over France. Later, it was confirmed that Morris and MacDonald were prisoners of war, but McKenna remained listed as missing.

The airfield was visited by Major Mechling, a United States Army observer specialising in ordnance matters, on the 22nd. In the early evening, a glider towed by a Hawker Hector aircraft appeared. Practice attacks were made on this by 10 aircraft of No.603 Squadron and the pilots hugely enjoyed themselves, shooting the thing up when it was about to land on the aerodrome.

In the evening, Pilot Officer Wood of 403 Squadron came into land in a Tiger Moth aircraft with one of its wheels useless. A variety of Very lights were fired to warn the pilot, but to no effect, so Pilot Officer J.F. 'Teddy' Reeves of 611 took up the Miles Magister with large letters painted on the side of the fuselage reading 'Your undercarriage is u/s.' The landing, on one wheel, caused the aircraft to slew round sharply, but no one was injured. An Army officer, who was passenger in the back seat of the Tiger Moth, thought that the flares fired had been part of a firework display for his benefit and had waved back.

No.403 Squadron departed for Debden on the 25th, to be replaced by 54 Squadron from Martlesham Heath. A fatal flying accident occurred on the 26th, when Pilot Officer E.W. Swarsbrick, who was in charge of a detachment from No.11 Group Flight, was killed. He crashed in a Blenheim that he had taken on a test flight and spun in while trying to land; he was killed instantly.

No. 603 Squadron received two new pilots, Sergeants Harold Bennett and Alan Otto who was a Canadian. They both reported for duty on 28th August, transfered from No.122 Squadron based at Ouston, near Newcastle.

Another ground defence exercise took place at the aerodrome on 29th August. Starting at 5.00 am, a battalion of the Suffolk Regiment attacked and partly broke in along the southern edge of the station. The 10th Essex, now camped at Hacton House, was thereupon called in to fulfil its role as a counter-atttack battalion, and recaptured the aerodrome. All of the full-time defence personnel of the 70th Essex and RAF Ground Defence took part as well. The ATC Cadets in camp here were also roused earlier than usual, and attached as 'backers-up,' in a dual role of runners and friendly 'Fifth Columnists'. They enjoyed themselves, and some of them even decided to forego their breakfast to see more of the exercise.

On the 30th, Pilot Officer Swarsbrick, who had been killed a few days earlier, was given a full military funeral at St Andrew's Church, Hornchurch and laid to rest there.

Harry Broadhurst took off from Hornchurch to fly over to the new Fairlop aerodrome on 1st September 1941, to make a trial landing on each of the new runways and give his views of the new facility. By the 3rd, all electrical power, telephone systems and operational necessities had been installed. Fairlop was declared fully operational on 10th September. Another arrow in Hornchurch's offensive armoury against the enemy was ready at hand.

Back at Hornchurch, the Emergency Ops Room at Rainham was almost completed, built on waste ground in Wennington Road. Hornchurch's other alternative emergency Operations Room was at the Coombe Lodge in Brentwood.

Flying Officer David Walter Hunt, a Battle of Britain pilot who had been severely burnt when his Hurricane was shot down on 3rd September 1940 and had undergone plastic surgery, arrived at Hornchurch. He was posted as Officer-in-Charge of No.11 Group Flight. The unit had a Hurricane, which he flew, also a Lysander and a Blenheim. Their work entailed the calibration of radar, searchlights and anti-aircraft defences, which involved flying on set courses at known height and speeds to co-ordinate the defence system.

A Fairey Fulmar aircraft landed mistakenly at Fairlop on 7th September, and then crashed into a steamroller while attempting to take off. The day was marked by fog and poor visibility on the 8th, which effectively prevented any sweeps that day, but an American Aircobra aircraft did arrive and land at Hornchurch, flown by a pilot of No.601 Squadron, for the purpose of being demonstrated to groundcrews and pilots.

Various service members from Hornchurch were guests of the Mayor of Romford on 11th September. A lunch was held at the Town Hall. The officers representing the station were Squadron Leaders Johnston, Ovendon, Adams and Davies and Flight Lieutenant Birley. On the 12th, Wing Commander F.S. Stapleton assumed command of RAF Hornchurch, while Group Captain Harry Broadhurst went on a well-deserved break. 'Broady' would resume command again on the 18th.

The Hornchurch Wing carried out two Circus operations on 17th September. Although the day started with a very heavy ground mist, soon after breakfast time brilliant sunshine was to dominate the rest of the day.

Circus 95, which had been cancelled previously, was to take place early after lunch. The Hornchurch Wing was heavily engaged by enemy fighters on reaching the French coast and never saw the target, which was a pity as by all accounts the bombers really made a good job on the installation. Unfortunately three pilots were lost, Squadron Leader Orton, Sergeants Draper and Overson, all of 54 Squadron. The Wing claimed only two probable enemy aircraft, one by Squadron Leader Orton, the other by Wing Commander Stapleton and two damaged by No.611 Squadron. The Wing landed piece meal in various airfields in the south-east, and had barely re-assembled, when they received orders to escort six Hampden bombers on Circus 96.

Thirty-six aircraft took off at 5.00 pm, the target being the shell manufacturing factory at Marquise. The French coast was crossed at Hardelt at 16,000 feet, then on to Marquise. Due to faulty navigation by the Hampdens, who did no bombing, the Spitfires were led into a hornet's nest of aggressive 109s, who were up-sun of the British fighters. During the engagement, 54 Squadron got three 'probables' and the Wing were lucky to lose only two aircraft, which also belonged to No.54. Sergeant H. Preece ditched his aircraft in the sea, and was very quickly picked up by rescue launch. Sergeant W. Batchelor did a high-speed crash-landing back at Hornchurch, damaging his aircraft which was already considerably shot up. Sergeant Pilot Hurst of No.603 claimed a probable Me109E and Pilot Officer Fawkes, also of No.603 Squadron, shot up an ack-ack post on the coast near Boulogne.

On 18th September, 12 Spitfires of No.603 flew as part of a Target Support Wing to Abbeville. Taking off from base at 2.05 pm, they crossed the French coast at Calais, and then turned south to a position east of Le Touquet.

The Wing then orbited the target, while the bombers did their work. Enemy fighters were sighted and engaged over Le Touquet; Flight Lieutenant David Scott-Malden and Sergeant Ruchwaldy each claimed an Me109 as a probable. All the aircraft landed back at Hornchurch safely at 3.45 pm. On his return, Scott-Malden was told he had been given command of No.54 Squadron.

The station was also visited this day by Mr Eugene Meyer, the proprietor of the *Washington Post*. He was evidently impressed with what he saw, and unexpectedly presented £5.00 to each of the three squadrons for the benefit of their pilots.

On 20th September Flight Lieutenant George Barclay of No.611 Squadron, was attacked by Me109s and his aircraft was badly damaged; he was able to make a forced-landing at Buyschoeure, although he hit high tension cables while landing. He evaded capture and with the help of the local French Resistance, he made his way over the border into Spain. On 7th November he reached Barcelona and by 11th November he had arrived at the British Embassy. He was flown back to Britain by Catalina aircraft on 9th December 1941.

While the Royal Air Force continued to take the fight to the enemy, what view did the citizen onlookers on the ground make of the increasing activity? Robert Ballard was 14 years old, he lived just a few miles east of Hornchurch in Grays. He recalls:

> One could clearly hear the aircraft engines as they were all getting airborne, then over they would come, upwards of 24 or 36 or more all heading east. It was an unforgettable sight for those of us who lived through those momentous times.
>
> One incident I recall during this period of the war was the regular appearance of a certain Spitfire. I suppose the pilot, whoever he was, had parents, wife or girlfriend living close by and was simply heralding his safe return from action, acknowledged by doing a couple or so turns which appeared to be over the house.
>
> For my part, when able, I rushed into the garden frantically waving a towel in excitement. I could see the scorchlike marks along the leading edges of the wings indicating where the machine guns had been fired. The aircraft was quite low, but I never thought to read or note the squadron code letters.
>
> I often wonder if the pilot survived the war. I like to think he did, rather than becoming the victim of an enemy bullet, like happened to so many of the Hornchurch boys.

An outbreak of acute stomach trouble attacked the officers on Tuesday, 24th September; approximately 80% of the pilots were quite unfit to fly. The cause was suspected to be a certain steak and kidney pudding, which was consumed at lunch-time on the Monday. The sickness also affected personnel who had gone to Buckingham Palace for an investiture. Some received their decoration and withdrew in haste.

On 27th September, No.603 took off from Hornchurch at 1.35 pm on an escort and fighter sweep. It was to close escort 12 Blenheim aircraft whose target was at Marzingarbe. They crossed the French coast at 17,000 feet over the Mardyke area. The bombers went to Lille, Mazingarbe and then out over Le Touquet, and heavy flak was encountered while over Hazebrouck. The squadron was heavily engaged by Me109s and many dog-fights took place. Flight Lieutenant Innes claimed an Me109 damaged and

Pilot Officer Marland one Me109 probable, Sergeant McKelvie destroyed one and damaged another. Sergeants Allard and Archibald did not return and were posted as officially missing, Allard was last seen in the Hazebrouck area. On the return trip Pilot Officer Marland ran out of fuel and crash-landed on the beach at Dungeness, while Sergeant Harold Bennett, also running short of petrol, crash-landed at Lympne. Sergeant McKelvie's Spitfire lost most of its rudder and had his tail-plane damaged, but he managed to return safely, claiming two destroyed and one probable. The rest of the squadron had landed by 3.20 pm. Harold Bennett remembers that operation:

> The worst thing that happened as far as I was concerned, was that Harry Broadhurst of course was the CO at the time, and they were so short of aircraft on this occasion that I was given his own personal aircraft with HB painted on the side of the fuselage. Of course being Harold Bennett, I was as pleased as punch. But unfortunately the trip they sent me on was across to Lille, which was about the maximum distance we could do at around this time and when we came back, I ran out of fuel just as we came up over the coast. I crash-landed at some woods near Lympne. I was not very popular as you can imagine, when I returned to the airfield.

It was also on the 27th, that RAF pilot combat reports were telling of encounters with a new German radial-engined aeroplane, that seemed to have advantage over our own Spitfires. This was in fact Germany's new fighter, the Focke-Wulf 190A-1. The aircraft was superior to the Spitfire MkV in every aspect except the turning circle. It was faster, it could outclimb the MkV and its firepower was greater. Flight Lieutenant Wilfred Duncan-Smith, who was leading 'B' Flight of 603 Squadron that day in Spitfire P8784, wrote in his logbook:

> We ran into a packet of trouble, Me109s everywhere. I was flying as No.2 to Harry Broadhurst on this occasion. When we were attacked by 10 or 12 at once, I had got one of them in my gunsight, but I had to break away as I was attacked by another.
> One of our Sergeant pilots shot down a Curtis Hawk (Focke-Wulf). The 109s definitely played with us this time [written in red ink] First contact with FW190.

Air Commodore His Royal Highness The Duke of Kent, paid a visit to the station on 30th September. He visited the dispersal points of No.54, 603 and 611 Squadrons, where all available pilots were presented to him. At one point, when Sergeant Shuckburgh of 603 Squadron was introduced, he was surprised when the Duke said 'You have a brother in 54, true?' Indeed, Pilot Officer Shuckburgh of that squadron had been introduced a few minutes earlier. Besides meeting the pilots the Duke inspected the ATC Cadets of 106 Squadron from Grays. The Duke lunched at the Officers' Mess before proceeding onwards to visit Southend.

Squadron Leader Tollemache, who worked in Ops, was not amused while landing his Hurricane that day. He observed two pilot officers about to land in Spitfires and overheard over the R/T one saying to the other, 'Look out for that clot on the ground.'

Squadron Leader H.G.P. Ovendon was awarded the Order of the British Empire on 1st October 1941. He had been the Civilian Station Adjutant at Hornchurch for nearly five years before the outbreak of war. He had then been promoted to Squadron Leader Admin from the autumn of 1939, until he was posted to Fairlop in June 1941.

Another posting arrived at Hornchurch on the 2nd, in the shape of Pilot Officer Len Harvey. Harvey had been a famous British pre-war boxer, and he was now attached as Hornchurch's physical training instructor. 'Ricky' Richardson recalls:

> I remember on one occasion, I had just run up a couple of aircraft checking the engines etc, I was really feeling tired and the squadron CO said, 'You better go and get some bed.' I went back to the billet and no sooner had I got into bed when Len Harvey walked in and told everybody to get out for PT instruction. You can imagine how I felt, having worked 24-hours straight off. I wasn't very nice to him and I went to Harry Broadhurst and told him. Len Harvey wasn't very happy about it and after that if ever he could get me on PT he did, because he'd had a rollicking from 'Broady'.
>
> Another little incident that happened was that we had general duty men, who would go around helping in the billets, making the beds and things. One of them was a big lad and Len Harvey had him boxing in the ring one day. Harvey was boxing with him and talking to somebody at the same time, all of a sudden the lad landed an almighty punch, probably the biggest punch Len Harvey ever received. I think he was a little bit shocked.

On 13th October, Group Captain Harry Broadhurst left Hornchurch for a four to five week goodwill trip to the United States. During his absence, Wing Commander Stapleton was left in command. The trip to America was laid on by the Air Ministry, and involved a chosen party of RAF officers to talk to thousands of trained pilots about the latest combat information, as well as themselves trying out new American aircraft, that were coming on line. Along with Broadhurst in the group, there were some notable ex-Hornchurch people: Sailor Malan and Robert Stanford-Tuck, who were representing Fighter Command. Representing Bomber Command were Wing Commander Charles Whitworth, Group Captain John Boothman and Wing Commander Hughie Edwards vc.

On the 15th, Hornchurch witnessed the arrival of the most strange flying machine. One can imagine pilots' and groundcrew's first words, when seeing it arrive: 'What the hell is that?' probably greeted the arrival of one of the first experimental helicopters. Much interest was shown in the new machine, but it proved to have a very disappointingly long take-off run.

No.54, 603 and 611 Squadrons took part in an offensive sweep on 21st October. They were airborne at 11.00 am, and met up with squadrons from North Weald. Their route was to take them over Dungeness, Mardyck, Gravelines, St Omer and Hardelot. During the sweep only two enemy aircraft were sighted, but not engaged. Unfortunately No.603 suffered two casualties as, when five miles south of Calais, Pilot Officer Fawkes and Sergeant McKelvie collided; McKelvie's aircraft was seen going down, and he was heard over the R/T to be baling out. Pilot Officer Fawkes' Spitfire had lost about four feet off one of its wings, but he managed somehow to land at Lympne, on the south coast of Kent.

Harold Bennett was a sergeant pilot with No.603 Squadron during this time, and remembers some of the operations that he flew on:

> When on convoy patrols, this meant taking off, crossing the Thames to the south side, passing over the large chalk pits at Stone to join the shipping in the Thames Estuary. This time of year there was often a considerable amount of haze in this area.
>
> Approching the convoy was always a period of concern. We had to approach at about 100 feet, so that the Naval escort could recognise us. We did have IFF which was fine so long as it worked. Identification, Friend or Foe was a small electrical device which sent out a special signal. As we made the first circuit of the escort and convoy, every gun of the Navy and Merchant ships would follow you around. Some of those muzzles looked as big as houses. On the return trip, we would cross to the north of the Thames. When the mist was really thick you hoped that those coming on patrol would remember the one-way circuit. Only on one occasion did this happen to me, when two aircraft coming out, passed between us going home in line astern.

The special event on 23rd October was a visit from officers of the United States Navy. Captain Wentworth, Chief of Staff to Admiral Chormly (Head of the US Naval Mission) arrived with Lieutenant Commanders Leppert, Austin and MacDonald and Lieutenant Commander Morehouse, the Assistant Air Attaché to the US Ambassador in England.

Arriving at 11.30 am, they were greeted at the Officers' Mess by Wing Commander Frederick Stapleton and other officers. They were then taken to see a Spitfire Vb fire its cannon at the firing butts. Then on to 54 Squadron's dispersal (known as Rose Cottage) and also to No.603. The Wing took off and gave a display of formation flying, not quite up to Hendon standard, but nevertheless very good owing to wartime procedure. After lunch, they visited the Operations Room and before leaving they were presented with a polished cannon-shell mounted on a wooden base, as a memento. By all accounts they enjoyed themselves, for the Foreign Office rang the station later in the evening to tell the Station Commander that they were very grateful.

On October 31st, Nos.603 and 611 Squadron were given orders to escort

Hurricane fighter-bombers on a raid against the power station at Halques. Sergeant Harold Bennett remembers the raid:

> Both squadrons put up twelve aircraft, flying in fours inline astern. The Hurricane squadron of six aircraft in the centre. In order to maintain surprise we crossed the Channel at sea level, literally. I was one of the 'Tail-end Charlies.' The propeller was picking up spray from the wave tops. Flight orders were to cross at 300 feet and lift to 1000 feet over the French coast. Our return was to be by the same route – 'Ha bloody Ha.' After seeing the Hurricanes to their target we then broke away in pairs. I accompanied Pilot Officer Fawkes as his No.2.
>
> We then followed the canals, attacking barges, several being sunk according to photo reconnaissance later on. Trains and all military looking articles were attacked. Radio silence was maintained from the time we rendezvoused until we crossed the French coast on the way back. With Pilot Officer Fawkes leading we came out to the French coast at roof-top height and saw people waving in the streets below. At this point, I was in very close formation on Fawkes' starboard wing. We flew straight over the top of a heavy anti-aircraft battery; looking down, we could see right down the barrels and then suddenly they all went off together. One shell went through the centre of Pilot Officer Fawkes' starboard wing, ballooning the metal out like a flower, fortunately it did not explode or impact or we would have both have disintegrated, it was so close. The journey from there back to the Kent coast was very slow and thankfully uneventful. We both landed back at Lympne, Pilot Officer Fawkes with great difficulty. Evidently the power station was well and truly clobbered and left burning, as were a train, carriages and a warehouse. The rest of the squadron landed back at Hornchurch at 2.00 pm.

The Hornchurch Operations Book for this period does make some interesting reading, especially the summary of events. It reads:

> The difference between fighting over one's own country on the defensive and carrying the war into the 'other man's land', is effectively demonstrated by the figures of casualties suffered by the squadrons operating from this sector.
>
> Between 1st January 1941, when offensive operations began, to 31st October 1941, we have destroyed 154 aircraft for the loss of 95 pilots.
>
> Bearing in mind that probably a fair proportion of the enemy pilots shot down over their own territory will be able to fly again, whereas those of our own people who were shot down over enemy territory, and survived are now prisoners, our losses must have been something like equal. From the beginning of the war up to 31st December 1940, we destroyed

517 aircraft and lost 103 pilots; that is we inflicted losses at a rate of five to one. A statement of the figures is given below. It is not possible to give figures for damaged enemy aircraft, because for a long period no record was kept of this.

### From 1st January 1941 to 31st October 1941

| Own Casualties | | Enemy Casualties | |
|---|---|---|---|
| Aircraft | Pilots | Destroyed | Probable |
| 116 | 95 | 154 | 94 |

### From 3rd September 1939 to 31st December 1940

| Aircraft | Pilots | Destroyed | Probable |
|---|---|---|---|
| 202 | 103 | 517 | 285 |

### Total for the war so far:

| Aircraft | Pilots | Destroyed | Probable |
|---|---|---|---|
| 318 | 198 | 671 | 379 |

### Other General Notes at Hornchurch for October 1941

Over 1,800 ATC Cadets, from 17 different squadrons had now visited the station on half-day visits, while 9 parties, totalling 320 cadets had spent time at camp here.

With the approach of winter, a more extensive programme of entertainment had been started. Dances were now held at Sutton's Institute every week. The Station Headquarters, squadrons and the Army garrison took it in turns to play host.

Films were shown twice a week and ENSA Concerts were held every fortnight.

Other concerts, plays, lectures and choral society shows were also available.

Four new Institutes were now open on the station, including the Corporals' Club, which was a new room at Sutton's; there was also a canteen and a games room with two billiard tables, table tennis, skittles and darts.

The WAAFs started to use the new Dining Hall and the NAAFI Building which had just been completed.

Two amusing conversation pieces were noted in the Station Diary: The first that a Duty Pilot had just phoned Hornchurch Ops with 'Hello, Ops, one Tiger Moth has just taken off from Martlesham Heath.' The WAAF in Ops replied, 'OK thank you,' she then hastily rang back, 'Oh, yes! What call sign is that Tiger Moth using. The exasperated Duty Pilot replied, 'Have you ever seen a Tiger Moth?

The other occurence was when six airman appeared on the flightpath and proceeded to lay out a target drogue, whilst disentangling the towing rope. Having completed the operation, which was observed by those in the Watch Office, they abandoned the drogue temporarily. At this point the aerodrome look-out apparently awoke. He telephoned the Watch Office and announced 'The windsock from No.54 dispersal has been blown away and is now lying in the middle of the aerodrome.'

On the evening of 1st November, London suffered its first air-raid since July. The following day, a visit by 50 cadets of No.53 Squadron from Hackney took place, and the departure of 50 campers of No.452 Squadron, Upminster. In the air, two pairs of Spitfires from 603 Squadron and one pair of No.611 carried out a convoy patrol, 20 miles east of Clacton. During the patrol, they sighted the first enemy aircraft they had seen for a while, in this sort of operation. A couple of Dornier 215s were seen diving out of cloud at 2,000 feet to bomb a convoy. Only two aircraft from 603 Squadron were within range to be able to fire at the enemy, and claimed some damage, before they were lost in cloud.

RAF Fairlop was officially opened as operational on 12th November, and on the same day, No.603 Squadron moved to Fairlop to operate from there. No.611 Squadron left for Drem in Scotland, they would not return to Hornchurch again.

On 17th November, the station bade farewell to No.54 Squadron, the longest serving squadron to be based at Hornchurch. First arriving in January 1930, they now took off for the final time, to their next base at Castletown. Old friends, No.64 Squadron, returned from Scotland for another tour at Hornchurch on 19th November, under Squadron Leader D. Kain as commanding officer.

Hornchurch received another new squadron on 22nd November – No.411 'Grizzly Bear' Canadian Squadron who flew in from Digby. They were led by Squadron Leader Paul Brooks Pitcher, a Canadian from Montreal, who had flown with No.1 (RCAF) Squadron during the Battle of Britain and claimed one enemy aircraft destroyed and three damaged. One of the pilots who flew down with No.411 was William 'Tex' Ash, who recalls:

> I was born in Texas and shortly after the outbreak of war, I decided to travel over the border to Canada and try to enlist in the Royal Canadian Air Force. I was accepted and trained there and arrived in England at the end of 1940. I was sent straight away to an Operational Training Unit and was shortly with a Royal Air Force squadron, No.234, but about this time, in mid 1941, they were forming some new Canadian fighter squadrons, one of them No.411. So I was a founder member of 411 Squadron, this was at Digby. We did some more training here and once we had become operational we were then moved down to Hornchurch.
>
> The main thing about Hornchurch was it had such a reputation that when we heard in Digby that we were being sent to Hornchurch, of course we were thrilled. When we got

there it seemed such a well established fighter base. It was there that I paid my first visit to a control room and watched all the people there pushing the aircraft plots on the giant table. It really gave us a sense of actually belonging to this great British Air Corps with all its great traditions, which nothing else could have done.

The accommodation at Hornchurch was rather good. To begin with I was in with a load of other pilots in the Officers' Mess, but then I was fortunate to be moved into married quarters where I had a very nice room, bath and everything else to myself, so that was very pleasant indeed. I liked listening to classical music and this way with my old crank up gramophone, I could listen to the music I wanted to, without disturbing my mates who preferred other types of music.

When we moved to the satellite drome at Rochford, we moved into somebody's country house which was situated nearby and I always think about those people whose country house we were using, because by the time we had finished using it, the house wasn't worth much. I can remember one night, we even took a motorbike inside, so that didn't do much for the house either.

One of my friends in the squadron was Robert 'Buck' McNair; he hailed from Nova Scotia. He was a very good pilot and became an 'ace' later when flying in the defence of Malta, where he became one of the most notable pilots in the campaign. Don Blakeslee was another, I knew Don very well, but he was only with the squadron briefly. Later on he rejoined the American Army Air Force and had a very good record indeed leading the 335th Fighter Group over Europe, flying Thunderbolt and Mustang aircraft.

One of the things that practically changed my life was that Hornchurch was so close to London, so that if we were off flying we could be in the centre of London within 40 minutes by underground tube. Throughout the blitz on London, all the theatres were running, there was lots of good music, the Proms were running. Everyday in the National Gallery there was a recital where you could hear the famous names of the day like Myra Hess and it didn't cost anything. But it was the theatre that really got me and on several occasions we did have Leslie Henson and other entertainers from the West End who came out to Hornchurch to put on shows for us.

One thing I recall is the cartoonist Bill Hooper, who helped produce the magazine *Tee-Emm*. He drew a picture of me flying a Spitfire as a cowboy would ride a bronco and I valued that very much, but somewhere along the line I lost it.

Crown Prince Paul of Greece visited the station at 3.15 pm on 22nd November with a number of Greek naval and air-force officers and remained for tea. Later a dance was held at the Officers' Mess, attended by some of the more illustrious people from Group Headquarters.

On 24th November, Hornchurch played host to a visit by a party of five isolationist United States congressmen, who were at present touring the country, and were very much against America entering the war. They arrived at 12 midday along with a representative of the Prime Minister, a newsreel cameraman and a press photographer. Unfortunately, low cloud and poor visibility prevented a fly-past, though after lunch they were treated by one pilot of No. 411 Squadron beating up the airfield at very low altitude. The were also duly impressed with the parachute dinghy and the film record of one of the squadron's exploits. In fact, for all their isolationism, the guests were flat out for all possible aid for Great Britain. They themselves gave some interesting details of the production of one US aero-engine factory and its working procedure.

After his tour of the United States, 'Broady' Broadhurst arrived back at Hornchurch on 30th November. During his trip back across the Atlantic, he had flown as co-pilot and taken control of the Liberator bomber which had brought them home. The weather on this day suffered from poor visibility in the Thames estuary as far west as London, and made flying difficult. But there were lots of convoy patrols and practice flying.

One aircraft of 411 Squadron broke a left leg of its undercarriage as it touched down. Some observers thought it landed rather 'high' and therefore dropped unduly hard. It skidded along the ground and did really very little damage to itself. Sergeant Harper of No.64 Squadron came to grief rather more seriously. Coming into land after a rather tight circuit, he appeared to stall in the turn, and the nose was the first part of the aircraft to hit the ground in the beginning of a dive-cum-slide slip from a height of 20 feet. The Spitfire AD312 broke its back, just behind the pilot, who suffered considerable cuts and other minor injuries.

Group Captain Broadhurst appeared in the Mess on 1st December for the first time since arriving back from the USA. He was welcomed by junior officers with great enthusiasm. The award of his second Distinguished Service Order was announced and there was much celebrating.

The station took part in the Eastern Command exercise 'Scorch' on 6th and 7th December 1941. In order to bring the station to the requisite state of readiness by the time the exercise proper was due to commence, a state of 'Alert 2' had been put in force at 3.40 pm on 3rd December. As dusk approached, the station presented a scene of intense activity as the various preparations were put in hand. Special anti-sabotage measures were put into force, and so effective were these that even the station commander had great difficulty in getting onto the base.

At 8.40 am on 4th December, 'Stand to' was ordered, defensive positions were manned and final preparations for the exercise were made. This state of alert was continued until 10.00 pm on the 5th, when the station reverted to 'Alert 1'. At 12.30 pm on the 6th, 'Action Stations' was ordered, which continued for the next 30 hours. The weather conditions turned out as bad as they could possibly be, with a steady rain setting in for most of the day and night. It failed, however, to dampen the keenness and enthusiasm of all ranks, who carried out their duties in an atmosphere of reality.

Soon messages and reports soon began to flow into Battle Headquarters, and Intelligence was kept busy sifting through information, much of it proving to be false or exaggerated. One report indicated that the aerodrome was to all intents and purposes surrounded already, but patrols checking up the situation proved this to be entirely fictitious. The first real threat in the exercise came at 11.55 pm, when authenticated reports were received that a consderable enemy force was advancing south-west from Chelmsford, had already captured Ingatestone and Mountnessing, and were advancing on Brentwood, just 7 miles from the aerodrome.

At 12.35 am on 7th December, information was received that No.223 Infantry Brigade was being relieved of its aerodrome responsibilities and was being concentrated to meet this threat. This entailed the withdrawal of the 10th Battalion Essex Regiment, from Hacton Ridge, which left the aerodrome defences to their own resources. Communication was maintained with the 10th Essex by wireless for a time after they moved, but reception was bad and eventually they lost touch. In view of the known proximity of the enemy forces and absence of information, morning 'Stand to' was ordered at 6.30 am. At 7.30 am however, reports were received from the 'Home Guard' of an enemy landing at Purfleet. By 8.15 am, this report was proved correct, and the position then was that an enemy force strength of one battalion had successfully landed from the river at Purfleet and was advancing north-west along the Rainham Road. At 8.20, the 'Attack Alarm' was broadcast.

It now became difficult to follow the progress of this enemy force, for it turned aside to destroy industrial premises during its advance. A light tank reconnaissance as far as Wennington, failed to make contact. But on a subsequent recce at 12 pm, a troop of light tanks encountered the advance guard. It was clear that the enemy was moving on to Hacton Ridge and orders to repel the attack from this direction were given.

The attack did not materialise till 2 pm, when under the cover of smoke, a company attack was launched, which was easily repelled. The survivors moved off in a northerly direction. Many useful lessons were learned as a result of the exercise. The all round keeness and enthusiasm displayed was most encouraging.

The Smith light-weight guns, manned by the Service Police, endured the vigil throughout the exercise. Their first and only chance of action came when they received a report that a tank and 50 men were approaching from the direction of the Cherry Tree, Rainham, early that Sunday morning. They went briskly into action as soon as the tank appeared. Their claims, made to an umpire close at hand, that they had scored four direct hits on the vehicle and knocked it out, were unhesitatingly allowed. They later discovered that the tank was one of their own, but this did not diminish their faith in their accuracy of aim.

The 8th December was the first day in several weeks on which the weather had been suitable for large scale flying operations. An operation was laid on in which No.607 Squadron with two squadrons of Spitfires would bomb a factory target at Hesdin in northern France. The Hornchurch Wing would provide close escort, with the Biggin Hill Wing above; the rendezvous was over Dungeness at and above 14,000 feet.

The bombers were to start diving to ground level, when about 5 miles off the French coast, the Hornchurch Wing with No.64 Squadron leading with Wing Commander Stapleton and 603 Squadron in the middle and 411 Squadron positioned on top. They started to dive with the intention of being over the target at 10,000 feet, while the bombers did their work. No.603 for some reason went astray; instead of going in, they lost the other two squadrons and orbited Le Touquet at 10,000 feet. Without any top cover, they soon became the target for Me109s and Focke Wulf 190s.

During the following combat, three of 603's pilots were shot down, Flying Officer Fawkes, Pilot Officer Falconer and Sergeant Harold Bennett. No.411 followed No.64 Squadron in, and they too were jumped by enemy fighters, losing Pilot Officer Coleman and Sergeant Court. 64 Squadron was unmolested. The only redeeming feature was the effort of Sergeant Lamb, who shot down an Me109, during 603 Squadron's turmoil. It had been a bad day. Harold Bennett recalls the day he was shot down:

> We had taken the Hurri-bombers in, when we had a warning from HQ that there were aircraft approaching from some direction, the next thing we knew the German fighters were in among us and then bang, bang, bang, and I was gone. As tail end Charlie, you usually copped it anyway. I baled out and went into the drink, the Channel. I was picked up by a German armed trawler. I can't praise them enough for what they did for me. I think they were regular Navy. From there I went to the normal prisoner-of-war collecting area at Frankfurt. There were about 120 of us to be moved; they started to move us, when all of a sudden there was a typhus scare, so they put us in a large French work camp at Mooseberg, near Munich. We were there for about 18 months, digging gravel and screeding. I eventually ended up in a camp in Poland. During the final months of the war, the Germans marched us back towards Berlin, but we were overtaken by the advancing Russian Army and liberated.

There was no flying due to bad weather on the 9th, and instead Group Captain Broadhurst held a talk in the briefing room to all the pilots of the three squadrons. He described the fundamental principles of air-tactics, so far as fighters were concerned, the need for top cover and mutual support, and the necessity to study the performance of the Messerschmitt 109F in comparison with that of the Spitfire. It was by all accounts a truly illuminating and inspiring talk; 'Broady' was at his wonderful best.

The news that filtered through to Hornchurch on the 10th December was not so good. The sinking by the Japanese of the battleship *Prince of Wales* and the battle-cruiser *Repulse* came as a great shock. Everybody was getting well accustomed to hearing that the Army had suffered a defeat, but the Navy had always been regarded as invincible.

Over the two days of 12th and 13th December, Hornchurch played host to the Swiss Attaché, Captain Charles Schlegal, and Captain Boldt-

Christmas of the Swedish Navy, acting as Swedish press war correspondent. On 15th December, No.603 'City of Edinburgh' Squadron left the Hornchurch Sector for the last time and flew up to Dyce. The squadron had one of the most distinguished records of any unit that flew from this airfield. They would now go on to fly in the defence of Malta and continue their proud record.

No.313 (Czech) Squadron arrived to take up their new posting, led by their new commanding officer Squadron Leader Karel Mrazek. Mrazek had fought his way across Europe after the German invasion of his homeland, then Poland and France, where he had joined the Foreign Legion, the only unit open to foreigners.He then joined the French Air Force until France's collapse; from there he sailed to Casablanca, and finally made his way to England. During the summer of 1940, he had flown with the RAF in Nos.43 and 46 Squadrons.

WAAF Ada Hewitt worked in the Hornchurch Operations Room during this period and she remembers the Czechs:

> The Czechs had their own controller in the Ops Room, in case the pilots reverted to their own language when things got hectic. They also had their own doctor when they first arrived. He knew only one word of English – strip – at least that's what some of our fellow WAAFs said. They evidently sent for an English-speaking nurse to help him.
>
> I remember that when the weather was bad and they couldn't get across the Channel, they would just get airborne and 'buzz' the 'drome.

On 19th December, a Boxing Tournament was held at the Sutton's Cinema at Hornchurch. RAF Hornchurch contestants were winners by 10 points to 8, against RAF Hunsdon.

On Christmas Day the weather first thing was good, but by 10.00 am the visibility had fallen to about 1,000 yards and stopped any convoy patrols that had been sanctioned. One of the Czech pilots of No.313 had to land at Southend on account of this, and on landing bumped into the hangar; luckily the aircraft was undamaged. The rest of the day was apparently enjoyed by everyone. A church service was held in the morning and airmen's dinners were served in two sessions; the officers and senior NCOs acting as waiters in the accepted fashion. Thanks to the exertions of Hornchurch's new Catering Officer, Pilot Officer Prince, the airmen's Christmas dinners were almost up to pre-war standard. There was a set meal of soup, turkey and plum pudding. The Station Commander attended both sessions and was greeted by 'For he's a jolly good fellow', and tremendous cheering on each occasion; he also had to sign a large number of menus. Harry Broadhurst recalls:

> During that year, I had been given a couple of baby piglets and had kept them in the back garden of my headquarters; the batman fed and looked after them. During Christmas 1941, I had them killed off and cut up, and sent round to all the

various messes, nice fresh pork. Incidentally, I didn't eat any myself. I couldn't bear the thought of eating the pigs which I'd had since babies.

Late that afternoon the weather had improved sufficiently for No.313 Squadron to carry out two convoy patrols, each with four aircraft, while 64 Squadron made one patrol, again four aircraft were involved.

The officers and sergeants had their turkey and plum pudding in the evening, when the Officers' Mess was host to the WAAF officers as well. This was not the sum total of the day's festivities by any means. The WAAFs were waited on by their officers and the Station Commander visited them also. To wind up the day's events, there was a dance held at Sutton's in the evening.

On Boxing Day, there was no operational flying at all. The event of the day was a party put on by the WAAF officers in the evening. The Group Captain and senior officers were in attendance, and after a very cheery dinner, fun and games were enjoyed by all. On New Year's Eve, there were other parties held in the various messes to herald in the year of 1942. For the aerodrome and its personnel, 1941 had been an extremely hectic and demanding year. However it had been a year when the spirit of the country had been lifted and the fight was at last being taken to the enemy. Now with the United States of America entering the war, with all its massive arms production geared up to the pursuit of victory, Britain no longer stood alone.

# CHAPTER 3

# BIG FRIENDS AND LITTLE FRIENDS
**1942**

The new year came in quietly, and on 1st January the persistent fog precluded any possibilities of flying that day; all pilots were occupied with lectures held in the Intelligence Block during that morning. Pilot Officer Cookson arrived, posted from the Officers' School, Uxbridge, as Education Officer for Bradwell Bay and Fairlop as well as Hornchurch. This meant the end of visits by Flight Lieutenant A.C. 'Professor' Williams, whose fortnightly two-day visits had been a regular feature. During the evening of 1st January, officers and pilots of No.313 (Czech) Squadron were invited and entertained by the management and staff at the Bata shoe factory at East Tilbury. Despite the obvious language problem, a splendid evening was had by all.

It was a cold and frosty morning on 8th January, but by mid-morning the mist had lifted. The Commander-in-Chief of Fighter Command, Air Marshal Sir William Sholto Douglas, paid an official visit to the station that morning and inspected the squadrons out at dispersal. Nos.411 and 313 Squadrons carried out patrols from Manston. One of 411 Squadron's pilots pranged his aircraft while coming into land at Manston, and another did the same coming in at Hornchurch. Both pilots escaped serious injury, but their machines were written off. Another accident occurred during the afternoon, when two pilots of No.64 Squadron, who were practising dog-fighting, touched wingtips and damaged each aircraft. They both landed safely, but somewhat shaken. As if things couldn't get worse, a pilot of No.411 borrowed No.64 Squadron's Miles Magister and crashed it near base. He too was not injured. As one RAF officer was heard to comment, 'A very successful day for shareholders of aircraft companies.'

Ada Hewitt, who worked in the Operations Room, recalls Sholto Douglas's visit that day:

> I remember that day we had to use a field-kitchen instead of the Mess for some reason or other. We had to line up to get a plate of soup, a plate for dinner and one for pudding. And guess what? It started raining. So by the time we got back to our tables, our meals had increased somewhat. Sholto Douglas was there and he accidentally bumped into me. How I didn't tip any of my meal down his uniform I'll never know.
>
> Later on he tried to enter the Ops Room, but he hadn't got his pass. So he was kept out. I don't think he was very happy about that.

Four aircraft of the Czech squadron, No.313, took off at 9.50 am on 11th January, for convoy patrol. The weather started to deteriorate and they were told to head to Rochford. Only three arrived, for Blue 4, Sergeant Pilot Joseph Valenta, for reasons unknown crashed into a field near the anti-aircraft gun positions, adjoining the southern perimeter of the airfield and was killed. This happened at 10.05 am. The funeral of Sergeant Valenta took place in the morning of 14th January at 11.30 am at St Andrew's Parish Church. The chief mourner was Squadron Leader Mrazek and the assisting party was commanded by Flight Lieutenant F. Fajtl. Sergeant Valenta was buried in the military plot of St Andrew's Church, Hornchurch Cemetery.

On 17th January 1942, Robin Peter Reginald Powell was promoted to Acting Wing Commander and appointed as leader of the Hornchurch Wing. Later that month, on 22nd January, Pilot Officer Blazej Konvalina of No.313 (Czech) Squadron was killed, when his Spitfire crashed and burnt out just in front of the offices of the Vandenburgh & Jurgens Margarine Company in Purfleet, Essex. He was buried at St Andrew's, Hornchurch Cemetery with full military honours.

No encouragement was needed in the ranks to attend another show put on by the Windmill Theatre cast, when they visited again on 25th January. Arriving at teatime, they were entertained to a splendid display of aerobatics by Flight Lieutenant Leon Prevot, a Belgian serving in No.64 Squadron. The subsequent show that evening at the Sutton's Institute was enthusiastically received by a packed house. Afterwards the girls were entertained in the Officers' Mess, where fun and games continued into the early hours. One officer was reported to have made the following remark, which aptly summarised the show put on by Mr Van Damm's young ladies. 'Never has so much been shown, by so few to so many'; this was particularly relevant to the young woman who performed the 'fan dance' and gave extremely good value, since she gave an encore.

A visit by a Major Del Gardo, of the Portuguese Embassy was conducted on 7th February, during which he was shown round the 'drome by the Sector Intelligence Officer of No.11 Group.

### 'The Channel Dash'
On 12th February, news arrived at Hornchurch that the two German battle-cruisers, the *Scharnhorst* and *Gneisenau*, and the cruiser *Prinz Eugen* were trying to breakout from the French port of Brest, back up the Channel to the German port of Wilhelmshaven. Since mid-1941, the RAF had kept a close eye on the enemy ships who posed a great threat to Allied shipping, if they were allowed to break out into the Atlantic, since much needed material and armament could be lost coming across from America. Air Chief Marshal Harry Broadhurst remembers:

> I remember when the call came about the *Scharnhorst* and the Channel Dash. I was in bed at the time with a cold, when the news arrived we were fog bound at Hornchurch. Leigh-Mallory telephoned me and shouted down the phone that *Scharnhorst* and *Prinz Eugen* were loose. Victor Beamish who

was working from Kenley, had spotted the two ships through a hole in the clouds. I eventually got our squadrons off just after lunchtime, but Spitfires were not exactly the right weapon to use against battle cruisers.

They sent a Fairey Swordfish squadron led by Lieutenant Commander Eugene Esmonde, but during their attack, the slow vulnerable biplanes were cut to pieces by the heavy German fighter air cover and the ships' guns. I think only one or two of the Swordfish airman survived from the mission. Esmonde was awarded the Victoria Cross posthumously.

The following is the combat report of that day's events over the Channel, made out by Harry Broadhurst on his return to Hornchurch:

The Hornchurch Wing having left from Fairlop at 12.25 hours with orders to rendezvous with Swordfish aircraft and the Biggin Hill Wing at Manston, and carry out attacks on 'E' boats accompanying the *Scharnhorst* and *Gneisenau*.

I took off from Hornchurch at 12.45 hours and flew straight to Dungeness hoping to catch up with the Wing, and if not, to see the enemy naval force. I crossed towards Boulogne hugging cloud base at 3,000 feet. Over Boulogne I found the cloud broken at up to 6,000 feet, where there was another layer of broken cloud. I climbed to 6,000 feet mid-Channel towards Calais and then saw several pairs of small boats of the 'E' boat variety, stretching as far as the Gravelines-Dunkirk area. I also saw several destroyers near the English coast heading for Boulogne.

When at 6,000 feet over Gravelines, still hugging broken cloud, I sighted a gaggle of five to six Me109s at 3,000 feet about a quarter of a mile away from me, going round in a wide circle. I watched them for two to three minutes whilst speaking to the Controller in order to ascertain the activity of the Wing. I then dived down on the rearmost of the 109s which proved to be an Me109F. I opened fire at about 100 yards from slightly below without deflection, firing one short burst of two seconds with cannon and machine-guns; almost immediately I saw the enemy pull up in a right hand turn and spin to the right emitting a cloud of black smoke. As the Me109F was at less than 3,000 feet and had obviously been hit, I did not consider he could possibly recover from the spin.

I could not wait to watch him as whilst I was firing, I caught sight of several other Me109s diving towards me from the direction of the French coast. I therefore pulled up into a thin layer of cloud at 3,000 feet in order to escape, and was followed by two or three Me109s. I nipped in and out of the cloud, but as some was so thin, I eventually decided to spiral down to sea level, amidst about twenty-four Spitfires, who were flying east between Dover and Calais. I followed them

for a few seconds at 1,500 feet, and when they turned towards
Dover, I returned towards Manston and met another two
squadrons of Spitfires, also at sea-level flying in the direction
of Dunkirk.

I landed back at Hornchurch at 14.20 hours.

The two squadrons, Nos.64 and 411, which had taken off from Fairlop had
patrolled along the coast of Calais and Mardyck, but had not encountered
any enemy fighters, or seen the battle-cruisers or the attacking Swordfish
squadron No.825. The Wing landed back at Fairlop at 2.15 pm. The other
Hornchurch-based squadron, No.313 (Czech), had been designated that
day to provide escort on convoy duty. The German ships finally reached
their destination, but they did not arrive unscathed. *Scharnhorst* and
*Gneisenau* were both damaged by British mines, although the damage was
only superficial. Out of a total of eighteen airmen who had bravely
attacked the battle-cruisers only three survived. The sea gave up Eugene
Esmonde's body two months later, when it was washed ashore on a Kent
beach. His remains were taken to his home town of Tipperary to be laid to
rest.

On 24th March, the Texan, William Ash of No.411 Squadron, was shot
down. 'Tex' recalls the events that followed:

I was shot down by a Focke-Wulf 190. I had just shot down
one of his fellow comrades when I was hit. I mention this, as
many a pilot who has been shot down will be found to have
been doing rather well before the enemy got him.

Although my engine had stopped and my machine out of
action, I still had flying control so I didn't bale out, I crash-
landed. I picked a place that did not seem too settled, landed
and did manage to get away from my aircraft and eventually
made contact with the French Resistance.

For about three months I was being pushed around France,
while they were getting ready to try and get me out across the
Spanish frontier. Unfortunately while in Paris, where I was
hiding for a time, some French people had told the Gestapo
and we were all rounded up. I had been wearing civilian
clothes when I had been picked up and the Gestapo was using
this against me as a threat, to get me to tell them the names of
all the French people who had helped me and that also I could
be shot as a spy. I pointed out to them that surely the British
wouldn't be so silly as to send in as a spy, somebody who
spoke very bad French and didn't know a word of German.
Anyway that was a most unpleasant experience and after that
I was sent off to prison camp, Stalag Luft 3.

Once there I met other Hornchurch people. There was Bill
Stapleton who had been there since 1940. I knew Roger
Bushell, because he like myself was an active escapist. I
missed the famous 'Great Escape' operation, because some
sergeant pilots were being sent off to another camp in

Lithuania, and I thought it would be easier to get out of there than Stalag Luft 3. So I changed identity with one of the sergeants and spent a year in Lithuania, so was away when the escape took place. But a lot of people who took part in the escape I personally knew, like Squadron Leader Cross, Bushell and a number of others who were murdered later by the Gestapo.

The Belgian Michael Donnet was flying with No.64 Squadron, and remembers his first combat:

My first combat was on 27th March 1942, when escorting 12 Douglas Bostons which were bombing the Ostend docks. I was flying as No.3 in the Vaxine Blue Section on the port side of the Wing Commander when crossing the Belgian coast at Ostend. I saw five FW190s diving out of the sun. I called up over the R/T, but my message must have been jammed. I turned to meet the enemy aircraft, who immediately turned away, two of them climbing up, two diving back to Ostend and one diving down in the sea direction.

I started weaving violently and noticed that my No.2, Pilot Officer Divoy, was not with me. I then observed four aircraft coming behind and below me, and realising they were FW190s, I turned to attack them head-on. As I started firing on the first one, I saw strikes going into his aircraft and opened up again at 200 yards. The FW190 pulled out just three feet above my cockpit. I fired then on the No.3 as there were four aircraft in a large echelon, and saw strikes and incendiary bullets going into his engine.

I closed range to 40 yards and fired on No.4 with a very short burst of fire. I had no time to observe the results of my bursts and passing on my back, I dived down from 8,000 feet to the deck, where I found a pilot of No.411 Squadron and came back with him.

The action that had ensued resulted in a good bag for the Hornchurch Wing with the following results: one Me109 destroyed by Pilot Officer Green, one Me109 probably destroyed by Pilot Officer Long and one FW190 damaged by Pilot Officer Connolly, all of No.411 Squadron, while No.313 Squadron claimed an Me109 damaged each by Flying Officer Vancl and Sergeant Dohnal. Unfortunately Pilot Officer V. Michalek of 313 was listed as missing; his aircraft had been seen spinning down.

Michael Donnet had joined the RAF after a daring escape from occupied Belgium. Born in 1917, he entered the Belgian Air Force as an officer cadet on 1st March 1938. He then served with the 9th Reconnaissance Squadron during the early part of the war, but was captured on 1st June 1940 and repatriated to Belgium on 10th January 1941. Wishing to carry on the fight against the Nazis, he and fellow countryman Leon Divoy made plans to escape by stealing a Stampe biplane from a heavily guarded occupied airfield. The aircraft unfortunately had several parts missing, making it unflyable. They spent three months replacing the missing parts by making new ones themselves and then re-fitting them under the noses of the Germans.

They managed to attain enough petrol for the aircraft by buying it on the black market. After a couple of false starts due to the Germans changing the locks on the hangar doors and a petrol leak, they finally succeeded on the night of 4th/5th July 1941. They crept into the airfield and wheeled out the aircraft, started the engine, took off and set course for England. After arriving in England and joining the RAF, Donnet and Divoy undertook operational training and joined No.64 Squadron on 6th September 1941.

It was again fair and warm weather on 28th March, when four sections of 313 Czech Squadron took off from Manston at 11.39 am to escort four Hurricane bombers on a raid to attack Berck aerodrome. An aerodrome was attacked, but it was Le Touquet owing to inaccurate navigation. On the return trip, machine gun posts, barges and huts were fired at and no enemy aircraft were seen. The sections landed back at Hornchurch at 12.50 pm.

During the afternoon eight Spitfires of 313 and ten of No.64 Squadron took off to rendezvous with the Biggin Hill Wing at 5.05 pm for a fighter sweep over Calais, Gravelines and St Omer. Just after crossing the French coast a large force of Focke-Wulf 190s were sighted and a general melee took place with individual dogfights. Wing Commander Farquhar claimed a probable after he saw large pieces falling from the enemy aircraft he had attacked. Squadron Leader Mrazek of 313 Squadron claimed an Me109 as did Pilot Officer Jecha who saw the FW190 he had attacked dive into the sea. Sergeant Vancl left a FW190 emitting black smoke and rocking from side to side. Other probable claims were made by Sergeant Reznick of 313 and Pilot Officer Conard, Sergeant Walker and Sergeant Stewart of No.64 Squadron. Hornchurch's only casualty was Sergeant K. Robinson of 64 Squadron who was listed as missing.

On this day Station Commander Group Captain Harry Broadhurst left for Headquarters No.11 Group for duty as Senior Air Staff Officer. While he was away, Wing Commander David de Clarke assumed temporary command, arriving from RAF Hunsdon.

On 4th April, No.64 Squadron lost Pilot Officer Leon Divoy. The squadron had been on an escort mission over St Omer, when an unknown Spitfire was seen to collide with Divoy, cutting the whole of the rear part of his fuselage in two. He was reported as missing, but information received later reported him as a prisoner of war.

The weather had changed yet again by 10th April, when squally showers and poor visibility covered most of the south-east during the early morning. The Wing took part in a practice sweep at 10.50 am and landed at 12.35 pm. Later in the afternoon a combined Rodeo operation by the Biggin Hill, Kenley and Hornchurch Wings was laid on. The Hornchurch Wing took to the air at 4.55 pm, and rendezvoused over the French coast at Hardelot. No.313 became heavily engaged with enemy fighters and although claiming one Me109 destroyed and two damaged, they lost two pilots, Sergeants Truhlar and Pokorny who were reported as missing.

By the 12th, fine weather had returned, warm and sunny with no cloud and good visibility. Squadrons Nos.64 and 313 led by Wing Commander Powell took part in Circus operation No.122, taking off at 12.40 pm. They met the bombers over Clacton at 1,000 feet along with the North Weald and Debden Wings. Once over the enemy coast, inaccurate enemy anti-aircraft fire was experienced over Gravelines and soon afterwards enemy fighters appeared at the same height as the Wing. These aircraft appeared to dive on the North Weald Wing, but they disappeared as quickly as they had arrived. Wing Commander Powell was told that the North Weald Wing was in need of help, so Powell took 313 Squadron down to 1,000 feet above the bombers. As enemy fighters appeared, Powell got in a short burst on an FW190. Flight Lieutenant Fatjl and Sergeant Brazda destroyed an Me109 between them, watching it fall out of control in flames. Squadron Leader Mrazek claimed an Me109 damaged.

In the meantime No.64 Squadron had engaged about a dozen 109s and 190s which resulted in Squadron Leader Duncan-Smith claiming an Me109 as probably destroyed.

On return to base it was reported that Sergeant Kresta of 313 was missing.

The need for station personnel to unwind and keep their spirits up was always important. The addition of Walt Disney's *Pluto* to the programme in the camp cinema seemed to have great effect on the personnel; their laughter was spontaneous when the film was shown.

During the afternoon of 18th April, two sections of No.64 Squadron were tasked with a Rhubarb operation. This consisted of Pilot Officer R.A. Mitchell, who was Yellow 1 and Pilot Officer D.A.S. Colvin, Yellow 2, while Pilot Officer D.P. Lamb was Red 1 with Pilot Officer W. de Wolff, Red 2. They took off from Hornchurch at 2.14 pm to attack the marshalling yards and army barrack blocks at Etaples. Once they had crossed the French coast, they attacked a single steam locomotive and tender at Merlimont-Plage, then three goods trains were strafed near Etaples.

Pilot Officer Mitchell shot up an army lorry, which lurched to the side of the road. All the pilots, with the exception of Pilot Officer Colvin, who overshot the target, fired at German army Nissen huts. The two sections encountered slight flak as they left and headed for home; all arrived safely back at Hornchurch at 3.20 pm.

As the pilots of 64 landed, another Rhubarb consisting of pilots of 313 Squadron took off to attack railway targets between Boulogne and Le Touquet. Sergeants Spacek and Zauf both fired short bursts at a factory south-east of Condette. About 50 German soldiers were drilling in front of the factory and they were sent scattering in all directions. Sergeant Spacek then turned out to sea and called up Sergeant Zauf over the R/T, but he received no reply. Sergeant Zauf was listed as missing after this operation.

On 25th April, Frantisek Fajtl, a Czechoslovakian who had flown with No.310 and No.17 Squadrons during the summer of 1940, was given command of No.122 Squadron. The station again played host to VIPs when on 28th April, the President of the Czechoslovak National Committee in exile, Doctor Eduard Benes and his wife, arrived here to present medals to the pilots of No.313 (Czech) Squadron.

One visitor that was always welcomed by squadron pilots at Hornchurch was a gentleman who was named 'Doc' Corner. Group Captain Wilfred Duncan-Smith remembers:

> We had this chap called 'Doc' H.W. Corner who was a flying doctor. We saw a lot of him for various reasons, he'd suddenly appear with a new make of Mae-West life jacket, oxygen masks or boots; he'd pick one of the squadron boys out and ask them to try them out for evaluation. He himself was about fifty years of age and a fully qualified pilot, though he wasn't allowed to fly on operations. He'd go as far as the Channel, then have to turn back. I did take him over the Channel once, on a sweep and we got involved with some 109s. I looked around for 'Doc' and found him sitting on my tail. When we landed I asked him if he had fired at anything. He said, he hadn't seen any 109s, he had been to busy trying to keep up with me. But I think as a doctor, he had no intention of taking anyone's life, and I respected him for that. Sadly he was killed in July 1942, when he was shot down off Folkestone by a Focke-Wulf 190.

In May 1942, Squadron Leader Leon Prevot, a Belgian who had fought with No.235 Squadron during the Battle of Britain, was given command of No.122 Squadron at Hornchurch. On 17th May, he shot down a FW190, and on the 30th July, he claimed another, but was himself shot down in return. He managed to evade capture from the Germans and successfully escaped back to England by way of Spain.

He also commanded No.350 Belgian Squadron at Hornchurch from January to March 1944. On 5th May, No.122 Squadron lost their commanding officer, the Czech, Frantisek Fajtl. He was shot down during a sweep over Lille, along with six other pilots from the Wing. Squadron Leader Fajtl landed safely and avoided capture; through the network of the French Resistance he managed to get back across the Channel and resume the fight. He was later awarded the DFC.

On the same day, ten South American Naval observers, escorted by Lieutenant Commander P.W.F. Stubbs, Royal Navy, and Lieutenant S. Arlington of the Royal Navy Volunteer Reserve, visited RAF Hornchurch to obtain a view of procedure at an operational fighter station.

The RAF Film Production Unit under the guidance of the Air Ministry of Information, arrived at the station on 7th May, to film general scenes of Nos.64 and 122 Squadrons at dispersal, taking off, landing and formation flying. There were also some air to air shots taken from Tiger Moth KJ7777. The film unit consisted of all RAF personnel. The film director was Flight Lieutenant P. Moyna with five cameramen, Pilot Officers Hatchard, Pollard, Pilgrim and Sergeants Challis and Towler. Lieutenant General Baron Michael Donnet recalls:

> The filming was carried out at the squadron's dispersal, as for
> the air-to-air filming of No.122 Squadron taking off from

Hornchurch. It happened that I was flying the aircraft on which the cameraman shot the sequence.

Another squadron, new to Hornchurch, took up its operational role on 14th May. No.81 Squadron arrived after receiving Spitfire VBs at Turnhouse, Scotland; led by their commanding officer Flight Lieutenant Ronald 'Raz' Berry, who had flown with No.603 Squadron at Hornchurch in 1940.

On 15th May, RAF Hornchurch received a new Station Commander. Group Captain George Charles Lott, DSO, DFC, arrived from No.13 Group at Newcastle, where he had been Wing Commander Training. He had fought with No.43 Squadron over Dunkirk, but was shot down and wounded on 9th July 1940. Forced to bale out of his Hurricane aircraft, he was taken to hospital, where he was operated on, losing the sight of his right eye, which had been damaged by glass splinters. This ended his operational career. The renowned Harry Broadhurst had now been posted as Deputy Senior Air Staff Officer at 11 Group Headquarters.

On the 30th, Hornchurch's own Physical Training Instructor, Sergeant Leslie Smith who was an ex-Brentford professional footballer, was again playing for Brentford, when the team reached the final of the London War Cup at Wembley Stadium. Smith's talent showed through, when he scored the only two goals of the match against Portsmouth. Some 72,000 spectators watched the exciting game.

On 2nd June, Wing Commander Robin Peter Powell was leading the Wing over France. During the sweep he claimed a FW190 as a probable just west of Le Touquet, but he was himself wounded in the head and neck. On landing he was rushed to hospital where it was discovered he had suffered a fracture to the base of his skull. It was a sad end to his flying career; his score stood at seven enemy aircraft destroyed. He was awarded a Bar to his DFC on 24th July 1942.

No.81 Squadron sadly lost two pilots in an air collision over Hastings, Sussex on 2nd June. Flight Sergeant Victor Reed in Spitfire BL811 and Sergeant Robert Guillermin in BM463 were both killed while on Circus operation 182.

As the air war intensified and the search for better and faster aircraft continued, the Luftwaffe had been given the advantage over the Spitfire MkVs with their Focke-Wulf 190. But at Supermarine, the designers and engineers had developed a new engine for the Spitfire with the two-stage Merlin 61. The new Spitfire would be Fighter Command's answer to the FW190, and the new aircraft would be designated as the MkIX.

On 7th June 1942, Jeffery Quill, Test Pilot from Supermarine, decided to visit Hornchurch with the prototype Spitfire MkIX (R6700) and meet his old friend Harry Broadhurst to ask him to fly it and give his appraisal of the aircraft's performance. The test flight was arranged for just after lunch. Air Chief Marshal Harry Broadhurst reflects on the events that followed:

> After lunch I said to Jeffrey Quill, 'You go off to the Operations Room at Romford, we've got the Wing going off over to France, you can watch that, I'll fly your Spitfire IX while that's going on.'

So he went off to the Ops Room and he saw the Hornchurch
Wing, after a while he said, 'What's that single aircraft plot
doing near the Hornchurch Wing.' Someone called out, 'That's
Broady', 'Christ,' Quill shouted 'that's my aeroplane.' It was
the only Spit IX they had, so I was in the doghouse.

Another thing, I didn't realise of course at the time, was that
the aircraft didn't have any ammunition, it had everything else.
That was my first experience of the MkIX. It was very
impressive.

With everybody duly impressed with the new fighter, the Spitfire MkIXs
started to arrive at No.11 Group fighter squadrons in late June.

Major General Liardet, Commander of the Royal Air Force Regiment,
visited the station on 19th June, to inspect No. 2718 and 2726 Defence
Squadrons at training.

On 21st June, the Irish 'ace' Squadron Leader Brendan 'Paddy'
Finucane, DSO, DFC was appointed to the acting rank of Wing Commander
Flying at Hornchurch. Finucane, who had achieved 26 enemy aircraft
victories, was at the time commanding No.602 'City of Glasgow' Squadron
at Kenley; he had started his RAF career at Hornchurch in July 1940 with
65 Squadron. He was now running second place to Wing Commander A.G.
'Sailor' Malan, who was then top scoring fighter pilot.

Finucane soon settled in to the scheme of things at Hornchurch. He
picked up his Spitfire BM308 from the station flight and proceeded to have
the lucky shamrock painted on the side of the cowling just in front of the
cockpit and his initials as the identification code letters.

Wing Commander Finucane briefed the Hornchurch Wing for a Ramrod
operation on 15th July, against the German army camp at Etaples near Le
Touquet. The Wing was scheduled for take-off at 11.50 am. No.122
Squadron, which was based at Fairlop, left ten minutes earlier to meet
Nos.81 and 154 Squadrons over Hornchurch. Group Captain George Lott
was to act as radio transmission linkman between Hornchurch Operations
Room and the Wing. He took off five minutes after the Wing was airborne
and was told to operate from 20,000 feet.

As the Wing crossed the French coast at Le Touquet at 12.22 pm, Wing
Commander Finucane's aircraft was hit in the starboard wing by German
small calibre machine-gun fire from the ground. Straightaway white glycol
vapour was seen coming from his Spitfire's damaged radiator. Finucane
was supported by his No.2, Pilot Officer Alan Aikman, a Canadian from
Toronto. Aikman gave his leader's aircraft a quick look over and told him
the bad news; Finucane knew he would have to turn back for home. Back
over the beach, where they had crossed, Aikman dived down and strafed the
machine-gun nest that had done the damage. Several miles out across the
Channel, Finucane had no option but to ditch his aircraft. With his engine
overheating and no glycol, he would not make it back to England. Alan
Aikman recalled what happened next:

He jettisoned the cockpit canopy and radioed, 'This is it,
Butch.' It was a textbook ditching, but the Spitfire suddenly

disappeared in a wall of water; it nosed down and sank instantly. There was no sign of Finucane. He had gone down with his aircraft. When ditching in the sea, aircraft usually stayed on the surface long enough for the pilot or crew to escape, but not in this case.

Later speculation was that Finucane had been knocked unconscious when hitting the water. Aikman circled the crash spot and signalled a mayday message. The rest of the squadrons arrived on their return trip and also circled the area, but were forced to return to Hornchurch due to low fuel. So died one of the RAF's most notable 'aces' and fighter leaders. He was twenty-one years old.

Finucane, who had been elevated to 'legend' status through the newspaper media, was such a great loss that a memorial requiem mass was held at Westminster Cathedral, which was attended by 2,500 people. A telegram of sympathy was also received from two of Russia's ace fighter pilots, Eugenyi Gorbatyuk and Ivan Kholodar.

Hornchurch received another new Wing Leader on 18th July, in the shape of Squadron Leader Petrus Hendrik Hugo, a South African. But he left after only a short spell, on 31st August 1942.

A visit took place on the 25th, by Mr George Allen, head of the American Red Cross Organisation. Also arriving that day for an inspection was Brigadier C. Britten MC, the Command Defence Officer, together with a defence officer from No.11 Group. They watched the RAF Regiment at their training and also visited the satellite airfield at Fairlop to inspect Defence Squadrons Nos.2797 and 2737. This day saw also the arrival of another new squadron to Hornchurch. Led by their commanding officer Squadron Leader Bernard Duperier, No.340 (Ile de France) Squadron arrived from Westhampnett, Sussex to take up their new posting. Ada Hewitt remembers the French:

> When the Free French arrived, things were made difficult for us WAAFs. We were not allowed to go across the drome, in less than threes, better still by bike.
>
> I can see them now, their round hats (berets) with the red pom-pom, and every other tooth a gold one and the leery grins they gave us, as you passed by. We just kept on going. The Free French pilots' uniform was very smart indeed, not unlike a naval uniform; it was dark blue in colour with gold braid around the bottom of the cuffs. The French groundcrew's uniform again looked like a sailor's.

The first squadron to be equipped with the MkIX was No.64 Squadron at Hornchurch, and Flying Officer Michael Donnet was the first pilot to fly the squadron's new aircraft. They were declared operational on the new variant on 28th July. Two days later on the 30th, Flight Lieutenant Don Kingaby claimed the first enemy aircraft destroyed by the new MkIX when he downed a Focke-Wulf 190 over Boulogne. Flying Officer Michael Donnet of No.64 Squadron also destroyed an enemy aircraft later that day, flying the new MkIX:

> I was flying as Blue 1, when over the north of St Omer Forest, my section dived down on 15 Focke-Wulf 190s. I got a squirt at the last three of a section of six, who were flying in line astern, but did not observe any results. When I pulled out, I sighted two FW190s at 4,000 feet. I dived down from 14,000 feet onto the two enemy aircraft who were climbing. I closed very quick on them and opened fire on the No.2 aircraft at 800 yards. The two FW190s rolled over on their backs on sighting me and as I closed to 200 yards, I saw strikes around the cockpit of the second 190, which burst into flames.
>
> I did not see the pilot baling out, but the aircraft was out of control. I claimed this as destroyed. My attack took place at 7.15 pm.

George Mason, also with No.64 Squadron, remembers the arrival of the Spitfire IXs:

> My first flight in the Spit IX was on 12th July, I reached 40,000 feet. The squadron then deployed to Martlesham Heath for air to air firing practice and to work up. My first op on MkIXs was a rodeo on the 28th, but we had no action. The first action was on the 30th July. My flight commander 'Tommy' Thomas and I had to turn back before the engagement because our drop tanks were not working.
>
> Don Kingaby got a 190 and the squadron accounted for three others destroyed and one damaged. We had experienced quite a lot of trouble with our drop tanks at that time; one pilot actually ditched when his engine failed to pick up after changing from main to drop tanks. The MkIX made all the difference in the world. For the first time we were on the tactical offensive. Up to then both the Messerschmitt 109 and the 190 were always above and could choose their moment to attack, but now we could be on top. This joyous freedom was short-lived because the USAAF B17s began operations and being the only squadron that could fly high enough and fast enough, we were mainly used as close escort and confined to 25,000 feet. However even then, we could always climb out of trouble if need be. Later when more squadrons got the MkIX we had more freedom of action and the fun began again.

Also in action on the 30th July was No.340 'Ile de France' Squadron. Sous Lieutenant A. Moynet was flying that day, and records:

> I was flying as Yellow 4 in 340 Squadron, and took off from Hornchurch at 18.25 hours, to take part in a Ramrod operation. I flew via Clacton and Marck to St Omer, and while near the latter place on the way back, I was attacked twice by some

sections of FW190s. As a result I became separated from my section, and while I was losing height from about 6,000 feet, I saw one Spitfire turning towards the east followed by two FW190s. The first enemy aircraft, which was firing at the Spitfire, was flying towards me at an angle of 30 degrees and about 200 yards. In front, I fired a burst of about 1½ seconds, cannon and machine guns and could see my bullets and shells hit the aircraft; some flames and black smoke came out of the rear and bottom part of the engine. At the same time the FW190 rolled onto its back and went towards the ground in a vertical dive from about 3,000 feet, the height at which the combat had taken place.

When I last saw him diving and smoking, I think he could not have recovered in time, considering the height, and I claimed this aircraft as probably destroyed.

Hornchurch's satellite, RAF Fairlop, played host to numerous important VIPs on 6th August, when the Right Honourable Sir John Laurie, The Lord Mayor of London, arrived, accompanied by Sheriff Sir Howard Button and Rupert de la Bere MP. They were greeted by other notables such as Captain Balfour MP (The Under Secretary of State for Air) and Mr W.P. Hildred, the Director General of Civil Aviation, and Air Marshal Trafford Leigh-Mallory, CB, DSO (Air Officer Commanding No.11 Group). There were also members of the City Corporation as well as the Officer Commanding RAF Hornchurch and his Wing Commander (Flying). After a fitting lunch, the Lord Mayor inspected a Guard of Honour provided by No.2797 Squadron, RAF Regiment, and then toured the aerodrome meeting the officers of No.154 Squadron. He witnessed a demonstration of some of the equipment used by the pilots in the squadron, and afterwards watched a formation flight of 12 Spitfires, with which he was duly impressed.

On the morning of the 9th, 64 Squadron carried out a practice close escort to 12 American B17 bombers. Many lessons were learnt, the chief of which was that the formation flown by the bombers must be greatly improved, if they were to be adequately guarded. Many of our aircraft landed at various 'dromes within the Lincoln and Norfolk area, with scarcely any petrol to spare.

During the afternoon, the Wing undertook a Rodeo operation, being airborne at 4.34 pm. Making landfall east of Dunkirk, they swept over St Omer and then out over Sangatte, near Calais where heavy anti-aircraft flak was experienced. During this time, Sergeant J.J. Matthews of No.122 Squadron was forced to bale out. He was seen to descend inland in the Calais area. The Wing landed back at base at 6.01 pm.

On Sunday, 16th August, exercise 'Humbug' was held to test the station defences.

There was the usual conflict of opinion as to who had been killed by whom, the attacking force claiming the liquidation of the defenders.

### The Dieppe Raid
On 19th August, Operation 'Jubilee', the raid against the harbour town of

Dieppe, was put into action. The plan consisted of landing British and Canadian troops in a large force of over 6,000 to attack and destroy local defences, power stations and aerodrome installations near the town. To cover the ground forces during the attack and withdrawal, air cover was provided by RAF fighters and bombers, and some American B17s.

The raid was launched early morning at 3.05 am. Back at Hornchurch, the pilots of the three squadrons Nos. 64, 122 and 340 were all up busy preparing for the day ahead. At Fairlop No.81 Squadron led by Squadron Leader 'Raz' Berry was at readiness by 4.20 am and was airborne at 4.42 am, as was No.154 Squadron led by Squadron Leader D.C. Carlson.

Once airborne, the squadrons met up with No.71 (Eagle) Squadron and No.124 from Gravesend. Once reaching Dieppe the squadrons spread out to cover the British ships below. Three Focke-Wulf 190s were sighted. Pilot Officer J.G. Buiron, a Frenchmen with No.154, fired at one of these aircraft, but no hits were seen. No.340 had better luck, when Lieutenant Michael Boudier claimed hits on another FW190. However No.340 did suffer one casualty when Lieutenant Kerlan's aircraft was hit and he was forced to ditch into the sea; fortunately a Royal Navy vessel rescued him safely. After patrolling for over 30 minutes the Wing headed back for home at 5.50 am, landing at Hornchurch and Fairlop around 6.30 pm.

Now fully aware of what was happening, the Germans sent out orders to all their Luftwaffe units to engage the RAF force covering Dieppe, as well as sending bombers to attack the ground troops and ships.

At 9.15 am Wing Commander 'Dutch' Hugo led the Hornchurch Wing from base for their second sortie, consisting of Nos. 122, 154 and 340. Once again over Dieppe, the squadrons split up to cover more airspace. During the patrol Flight Lieutenant L.P. Griffiths sighted six Dornier 217 bombers at 4,000 feet. Both Flight Lieutenant Griffiths and Pilot Officer B.J. Bland attacked the last bomber of the formation from astern, and claimed it as damaged. Meanwhile another of the enemy bombers was attacked by Squadron Leader Kilian, Sergeant W. Peet, Pilot Officer L.C. Collington and Sergeant A. Williams, and was later confirmed as destroyed.

No.340 (Free French) Squadron had better luck, for they found some Dorniers over the harbour, and claimed four damaged and two destroyed, one by Capitaine François de Labouchere DFC, the other by Second Lieutenant Pierre Laureys. Their only loss was Adjutant René Gerard Darbin in Spitfire BL262, who was seen shot down into the sea.

Sergeant M. Bouguen of No.340 reported:

> I was Yellow 2 in 340 Squadron, three aircraft being in the section. I saw two Dornier 217s flying in close formation towards the convoy about three miles north of Dieppe bearing on an easterly course. I heard a ship calling, 'Dive bombers coming towards me' and I saw the two enemy aircraft diving. Yellow 1, Adjutant Guignard attacked the first and I saw this aircraft dropping its bombs.
>
> I attacked the second one, from the beam at about 400 yards range, and I kept firing for about five seconds. I saw strikes on the starboard engine and smoke pouring out.

Owing to heavy flak, I had to pull out at about 1,500 feet. Yellow 4, behind me, saw the bomber being hit and I thinking it was finished did not open fire; he followed it down to 200 feet and said it appeared to be badly damaged. I claimed the Dornier as damaged.

At 9.35 am, No.64 Squadron led by their commanding officer Squadron Leader Wilfred Duncan-Smith, took off on their first mission of the day, to escort 24 B17 bombers of the 97th Bombardment Group to their target, the aerodrome of Abbeville/Drucat. The B17s were based at Polebrook and Grafton Underwood and came from the 340th, 341st, 342nd and 414th Squadrons.

The mission was named Circus No.205, and also included as fighter escort along with No.64 Squadron, No.411 Squadron from Lympne, No.402 flying from Kenley and No.611 based at Redhill. The B17s reached their target at 10.32 am, without interference from enemy fighters and dropped their bombs down on the enemy airfield, hits being observed on two of the three runways and dispersal areas. The bombers headed back to England without loss, escorted by No.64 Squadron, and landed at times between 11.25 am and 12.00 mid-day, while the other fighter squadrons remained over Dieppe to carry out a sweep.

Air Commodore George Mason DFC, DFC (US) was a flight sergeant with No.64, and recalls:

Yes, the first Op was escorting B17s to bomb Abbeville, which annoyed us because we would have preferred to have been over the beachead. However once the B17s were safely on their way home, 'Kingo' Kingaby spotted some Dorniers about 15,000 feet below. We dived on them but just as we were coming within range a voice over the R/T warned that they were friendly, so we broke off in disarray, but not before Don Kingaby who knew a Dornier when he saw one, sent one down. We never did establish whose voice it was, but it was an expensive call.

On the ground, things were going from bad to worse, with the Allied troops suffering heavy casualties, now that the Germans were bringing more troops into the area, to repel the attack. The order to withdraw the British and Canadian troops was given at 11.00 am, with the RAF given instructions to lay smoke and cover the naval ships and small landing craft from German bombers and fighter aircraft. At 12.20 pm, three of Hornchurch's squadrons arrived over the evacuation area.

No. 122 Squadron, on patrol at 10,000 feet, sighted a gaggle of Dorniers, and went into the attack, where it was in turn attacked by eight Focke-Wulf 190s. Squadron Leader Kilian's aircraft BL812 was hit by enemy fire, which smashed his perspex hood, causing him to suffer cuts to his face. One Dornier was shot up by Sergeant D. Mercer, who chased it inland and saw it trying to crash-land near St Aubin. No.64 Squadron also engaged Dorniers at this time. Squadron Leader Duncan-Smith claimed one destroyed, as did Flight Lieutenant Don Kingaby. Duncan-Smith also claimed a half-share with Flight Sergeant W.J. Batchelor, while Flight Lieutenant T. Thomas claimed an Me109 damaged. The squadron suffered one casualty, Spitfire BR604, flown by Sergeant Eric McQuaig, who was shot down into the sea and killed.

At around the same time No.340 'Ile de France' Squadron were on their third sortie, patrolling shipping off Dieppe. They did this for half an hour at 12,000 feet, but cloud interfered with observation. Several pilots attacked and fired on a Dornier 217, whose crew were seen to bale out. The squadron landed back without loss at Hornchurch at 1.25 pm. Capitaine de Labouchere DFC wrote in his report:

> At 12.45 pm, I was flying as Blue 1, when I heard by R/T a report of one hostile bomber at cloud height. We were at 12,000 feet and the squadron dived down to engage him; when I saw the Dornier, it was already engaged by a lot of aircraft. I did a diving turn to the left to cut off his retreat to the French coast. As the enemy aircraft was not evidently damaged, I decided to attack it. I gave it a five second burst from the rear quarter from 300 to 200 yards. At the end of the burst, the port engine caught fire and he disappeared in a small cloud, smoking. I did not search for him further and I carried on my patrol. One pilot who also fired at the enemy aircraft saw two of the crew bale out. I claimed a half share in the destruction of the Dornier.

At Fairlop, No.81 Squadron took to the air at 1.53 pm to patrol over the homeward bound convoy, led by Squadron Leader Ronald Berry. The sortie was uneventful until it was time for the squadron to return. It was then that one of the Spitfires was badly damaged when a Focke-Wulf 190 attacked suddenly. Pilot Officer W.S. Large, a Canadian, managed to fly his badly shot-up aircraft back across the Channel as far as Shoreham, Kent, where he landed without flaps or brakes. He himself was unhurt, although a cannon-shell had clipped one of his flying boots.

Squadron Leader Wilfred Duncan-Smith was leading No.64 Squadron at 23,000 feet at 3.00 pm, when they spotted two formations of Dorniers at 10,000 feet. He led No.64 down into the attack. Duncan-Smith himself attacked a Dornier from astern and saw strikes on the port engine of the enemy aircraft. Suddenly his aircraft BR581 juddered as he heard four loud bangs from cannon shells hitting his machine. Duncan-Smith recalls:

> I had flown six sorties that day and was feeling deadbeat by the end of it. On the last sortie, which was around 3.00 pm, we attacked some Dorniers and I got clobbered and had to bale out into the sea.
>
> I couldn't work the electronics to get a message out, and I had been separated from the squadron when this had happened. I managed to get out and after I hit the water the next thing I remember was three Spitfires circling overhead. I

splashed my feet and hands in the water and they saw this little white spot in a very blue background. They obviously radioed for the Air Sea Rescue and after about half an hour a rescue boat picked me up.

The Dornier he had attacked was seen to crash into the sea. He was later awarded the Distinguished Service Order for his actions during the Dieppe operation.

Flight Sergeant Mason claimed one FW190 damaged, Flight Lieutenant C. Thomas one FW190 destroyed and Pilot Officer H.F. Withy, one Dornier damaged. The squadron lost one pilot, a Rhodesian, Pilot Officer J.K. Stewart, who was listed as missing in Spitfire BR977. The late Wing Commander Don Kingaby DSO, DFM, **AFC recorded in his flying logbook for that day:

> Combined operations raid on Dieppe. Quite a day. We escorted 24 Fortresses to Abbeville and blasted it, moderate flak, but no huns.
>
> Second trip – Over Dieppe. 4 190s sheered off when we out climbed them.
>
> We went down below and the squadron got 2 Dornier 217s and I got one of them in flames. Tommy damaged a 109. Sgt McQuaig baled out.
>
> Third trip – over withdrawal of ships, Tommy got a 190, CO got a 217 and Mason damaged a 190. The CO baled out, but was picked up immediately happily. Stewart is missing.

One of the last patrols of the day flown over the Channel was undertaken by No.340 Squadron. They took off at 6.10 pm, led by Wing Commander Petrus 'Dutch' Hugo flying with Red Section, while Captain Rene Mouchotte led Yellow Section and Captain de Labouchere led Blue. The squadron's last sortie was carried out to protect returning shipping off Beachy Head. They patrolled at about 4,000 feet with 8/10 cloud at 5,000 feet. During the patrol Captain Bechoff of Red Section in Spitfire EN899 GW-Z, attacked and damaged a Dornier 217. Several of the other pilots chased the enemy aircraft as far as the French coast, but could not catch it. The squadron landed back at base at 7.45 pm.

Also flying that day had been Hornchurch's previous Station Commander Group Captain Harry Broadhurst, who was now Deputy SASO at No.11 Group. He flew four reconnaissance sorties over Dieppe that day, providing valuable information first-hand, and also destroyed a FW190. He remembers:

> After my second trip I accompanied some RAF bombers back to the English coast and landed back at Hornchurch at 11.45 am for refuelling and re-arming. After meeting with the Wing Commander Flying and talking with the pilots around dispersal, I rang up the Air Officer Commanding and told him the situation.

I took off on my third flight at 12.30 pm with Wing Commander Peter Powell and flew direct to Dieppe. It was during this sortie that I shot down a FW190 which had been dive-bombing a destroyer. I then returned to Kenley at 2.40 pm.

Leaving Kenley at 3.15 pm, while over Dieppe at 19,000 feet I was attacked by two FW190s and after shaking them off became entangled with four more FW190s. After losing the enemy fighters I tried to land at Tangmere, but the weather was now turning bad so I landed back at Hornchurch at 4.45 pm. After again reporting back to Group Operations by telephone, I left Hornchurch for Northolt and landed at 7.00 pm. I had flown eight and a quarter hours that day.

Harry Broadhurst was awarded a bar to his DFC for his actions that day.

During the morning of 27th August, there were three Air-Search-Rescue patrols carried out by squadrons from Hornchurch, Nos.81,122 and 154 respectively. Sergeant J. Hall and Flying Officer A.S. Turnbull of 154, were both shot down when the squadron was bounced by enemy fighters. Flying Officer Turnbull crash-landed at Eastleigh, slightly wounded. Sergeant Hall was picked up by high-speed launch seriously wounded. No.154 claimed two FW190s as probably damaged, one by Flight Lieutenant A.F. Eckford, the other by Pilot Officer Aikman. No.122 were jumped by 20 FW190s, ten miles off Gris-Nez. As a result, two pilots were listed as missing, Pilot Officer Shaw and Sergeant Silsand, a Norwegian.

The WAAFs held a 'Cabaret Dance' at the Sutton's Institute on 3rd September. This was held from 8.00 pm until midnight and was very well attended. But unfortunately the officers who had been invited were not able to be present owing to the recent death of His Royal Highness, the Duke of Kent, who had been killed in an air-crash.

The Fighting French held their annual commemoration of Capitaine Guynemer's death during the afternoon of the 11th. Captain Georges Guynemer had been one of France's most famous aces during the First War; he was credited with 66 victories before failing to return from combat on 11th September 1917. A parade was held, at which General Vallin, the Commander-in-Chief of the Fighting French Air Force, was present, together with Hornchurch's Station Commander Group Captain George Lott.

Over the two days of the 12th and 13th, a WAAF section from the camp participated in two sports events. The first at Abbs Cross, the next at the Hornchurch Youth Club, where they played a cricket match and won.

At 10.45 am, on the morning of 15th September 1942, a court martial was assembled at Hornchurch. The defendant, an aircraftman, was charged with two charges of desertion and improper possession of a pistol. Chairing the court martial was Wing Commander G.S. Taylor and senior member Squadron Leader A.J. Butler OBE, MC, AFC. A junior member was supplied by the station, Flight Lieutenant F.E.B. Elsbury. Flight Lieutenant, the Right Honourable Lord Morris was Chief Prosecutor and Pilot Officer D.G. Gluett was defending officer acting on behalf of the accused.

On the 16th, the station received a distinguished visitor in the person of Colonel the Honourable W.P. Mulock KC, Postmaster General of the Dominion of Canada. With him came Wing Commander H.L. Campbell, Director of the Royal Canadian Air Staff and two Canadian Army colonels. They came to study the service methods of dealing with mail in this country. They were very impressed with everything that they saw here and at Fairlop, which they visited with Squadron Leader Frank Dowling, the Station Administrative Officer.

More visitors arrived on the 19th, when No.340 Squadron received Mr G. Parsons of the *New York Herald Tribune*, Mr Kuh of the *Chicago Sun*, Captain Pompei of the Fighting French Headquarters and Monsieur Maudinian, the Fighting French photographer. During the afternoon, Squadron Leader F.W. Dowling and Flight Lieutenant B.M. Conybeare, together with Corporal Ovendon and an airman of the station fire section, went to a National Fire Service display given by No.11 District in Hornchurch Park.

The District Court-Martial against the aircraftsman AC1 which had been held on the 15th September, reached its verdict on the 22nd. The court found him guilty on both charges (to the second of which he had himself pleaded guilty). He was sentenced to undergo detention for six months.

On 23rd September, the Belgian Spitfire squadron No.350 arrived at Hornchurch to operate within the sector from RAF Southend (formerly Rochford), led by Squadron Leader D.A. Guillaume. No.340 (French) Squadron left Hornchurch for Biggin Hill.

September 26th saw the arrival of another new squadron to Hornchurch. No.453 (Australian) Squadron came with their Spitfire Vbs from Drem, Scotland, led by Squadron Leader F.V. Morello.

WAAF Joy Caldwell, (nee York) had worked in Signals in Hornchurch's Operations Room during the Battle of Britain. She had left in 1941, but had returned again to Hornchurch to take up her role. She remembers:

At the Masonic Hall Operations Room in Romford, a Special Intelligence direct line was installed to HQ 11 Group, on the end of the dais next to Ops B. This is where I worked most of my watch and where I came to meet the pilot and author Richard Hillary who had been badly burned during the Battle of Britain while flying with 603 Squadron. I cannot remember quite how long he worked on Ops B, but it was only for a short while. He seemed much older than his years, reserved and very scarred about the face due to the many operations he had undergone for plastic surgery to rebuild his burnt face. His burnt hands, I noticed, were like claws as he handed over the signals.

Giving me his book (*The Last Enemy*) one day, he asked me to read it and let him know what I thought of its content. Unfortunately, due to events, I cannot recall – I didn't get the chance to talk to him again. The book, which Richard signed, I lent to somebody after the war; it was never returned. I learnt later that he had been killed in an air crash in January 1943.

Signals used to be handed directly along the dais from the Controller Ronnie Adams.

They contained all of the up to date information on squadron state, activities and casualties etc, ending up at Ops B to be collated in turn, then handed to me to transmit – pronto!

At Fairlop, the Secretary of State, Sir Archibald Sinclair KT, CMG, MP visited the aerodrome in company with Group Captain Louis Greig KBE, CVO, his personal secretary, at 5.30 pm. They were met and shown around the drome by Wing Commander R.H. Thomas DSO, DFC, Squadron Leader H.G.P. Ovendon OBE and Squadron Leader F.W. Dowling. The party afterwards drove to Hornchurch for tea in the Officers' Mess.

The next day, aircraft never before seen at Hornchurch arrived. Six Westland Whirlwind twin-engine aeroplanes of No.137 Squadron flew in and took off an hour or so later.

Alf Allsopp was a sergeant fitter with No.350 Squadron, and recalls an incident which took place on 26th October while down at Rochford:

The weather that day was very low cloud and poor visibility. The squadron state of readiness was 30 minutes availability. I was at that time in charge of 'B' Flight as a sergeant. I was in the office checking through the paperwork (Form 700's etc), when the telephone rang; it was Flight Sergeant Jackson, the armament chief, who was my best friend in those days – he suggested we go to early lunch for a change as normally we went late and often missed the soup! The method of transport was the bicycle.

We cycled up to the Sergeants' Mess (the golf club house) and sat in the bay window waiting for our soup, it was about mid-day. As the soup arrived, the Hun arrived and dropped a stick of bombs. As soon as I could get out from under the table, I shot out of the Sergeants' Mess, onto my bike and headed for the gap in the hedge leading to dispersal, with one thought in mind: 'Get a Spitfire started up!' The chain came off the bike's gear wheel twice before I actually got onto the airfield. In retrospect this was lucky for me otherwise I would have been a lot nearer to what was about to take place next.

Suddenly a German Dornier 215 crashed into the middle of the airfield and plunged straight through the dispersal buildings. I was told later he was firing all guns as he came down. I don't know if there were any other casualties other than Warrant Officer Dijon, the Belgian engineer officer, who had taken refuge in my office and was killed.

By an amazing coincidence when I emerged from the ruined building after a quick search through, a voice said 'Cup of tea Alf?' and there was my brother in-law, Harry Tracky, a member of the RAF Gang Show, who were going to be putting on a show that night.

Another memory while at Rochford was one late night

while heading across the airfield, I spotted the silhouette of a Lysander aircraft against the skyline, and beside it the easily recognisable well built figure of a warrant officer pilot I had seen in the Sergeants' Mess a few times. Next time I saw him, I commented on his late hours; he said I had been probably drunk and imagined it. We played darts in the Mess with commando daggers when the pilots were not quite sober!

The Hornchurch Operations Book up until 1st October 1942 recorded that the number of enemy aircraft destroyed since the outbreak of war by squadrons operating from Hornchurch was 739. The number of our own casualties, 459 aircraft lost with 345 pilots missing or killed.

During the afternoon of 12th October, Messrs Aldous and Smith arrived from No.10 Works Area at Northwood, to discuss the question of the curved approach lighting system for Hornchurch and Fairlop. Other proposals included the placing of obstruction lights on Sutton's Senior School which was close by, and the removal of the landing obstruction wires between the school and the aerodrome's northern perimeter track.

On the 15th, Hornchurch provided target support for Circus 227 during the afternoon. Wing Commander Flying led 122 and 64 Squadrons. The two squadrons (64 was up from Fairlop) met up with the bombers on the way to Beachy Head, but when half way across the Channel Wing Commander Thomas and three pilots of No.122 had to return owing to jettison tank trouble. The remainder crossed the French coast at St Valéry at 25,000 feet, then flew down the coast to Fécamp, crossing the river east of Le Havre.

The Wing orbited the target and saw 12 bomb bursts on the quay and others in the dockyard. On completion of their orbit, a mixed bunch of about 20 Me109s and FW190s were seen approaching from the east at 28,000 feet trying to overtake 64 Squadron, who turned to attack. Half the enemy aircraft rolled and dived away, and the remainder climbed up sun and shadowed the Wing for 20 miles out to sea. When ten miles north of Le Havre, Squadron Leader Kilian warned the squadron of the shadowing enemy fighters. Unfortunately the squadron did not hear and his No.2 Sergeant Regis turned to attack above. As a result they had to take violent evasive action, and Sergeant Regis was last seen diving steeply with an enemy aircraft on his tail.

With wartime rationing, every spare acreage of ground was put into use for growing crops and vegetables. The field areas in Wood Lane, adjacent to the Station, were used in this way. The start of lifting the potato harvest began on the 19th October, when men of the No.2718 Squadron Regiment lifted some 8 tons. Once this had been completed, they then set about the field opposite the Good Intent public house. The estimated yield per-acre was about 6 ton.

Squadron Leader Frank Dowling, the Station Adminstration Officer, left for a three-month course at RAF Staff College at Buckstrode Park on 26th October. The Operations Book recorded: 'An officer of great capabilities in every direction, he has had a unique career on this station, having been posted in before the war as a Corporal Clerk General Duties, to train

Operations Room crews.' He was commissioned soon after the outbreak of war and became Assistant Adjutant, then Adjutant and later Squadron Leader Admin.

A ceremony of great interest took place on the 29th, when His Excellency Senor Monir de Arago, the Brazilian Ambassador to the Court of St James, visited the station in order to present two Spitfires to No.64 Squadron. He was accompanied by the Second Secretary to the Embassy and eight Brazilian journalists, together with Flight Lieutenant Teeling of the Air Ministry and Messrs O'Brian and Rose, representatives of the British Council. The ambassador was on the station for almost an hour and was met at the main Guard Room entrance by Station Commander Group Captain George Lott, DSO, DFC; and the Air Officer Commanding 11 Group, Air Commodore G. Harcourt-Smith, CBE, MVO. After inspecting the Guard of Honour, provided by 2718 Squadron, RAF Regiment, he proceeded between Nos.2 and 3 hangars, where 64 Squadron was drawn up in a square with the pilots in front. The commanding officer and the pilots were then presented to the ambassador, who made a speech first in Portuguese and then English, during which he named the two aircraft and Air Commodore Harcourt-Smith replied. The BBC made a recording of the ambassador's speech and Paramount News filmed the ceremony.

Southend also had a ceremony that day, when the exiled Belgian Prime Minister, Monsieur Pierlot visited the station to present medals to No.350 Squadron. He was accompanied by General de Viertel, the Belgian General Operations Chief. Squadron Leader Guillaume, the commanding officer of 350 Squadron, was awarded the DFC, and other members of the squadron also received decorations.

Sergeant Alf Allsopp who worked with 350 Squadron remembers some of them:

There was Flight Commander Du Monceau de Bergendael better known as the 'Duke'. He had been born in London in 1915 of Belgian parents and had returned to his native country in 1937 to attend the military academy there. He was initially posted to a cavalry regiment, but decided his future was in aviation. He made his way to France when his country fell to the Germans and escaped to Britain via Morocco in 1940. He had flown with No.609 Squadron before being posted to 350 Squadron. He was the top scoring ace of 350 Squadron with 5 enemy aircraft destroyed and 4 probables.

Flight Lieutenant Henri Picard was a wonderful shot with a 0.22 rifle; he was also a gifted young artist. I remember he came back from a sortie to France with part of the wind indicator from a German airfield stuck in his wing. He was shot down over Dieppe and became a prisoner of war. He was sent to Stalag Luft III, where because of his gift as an artist he became a forger, in charge of passes, passports and permits for the escapees. He took part in the 'Great Escape' from the camp on 24th March 1944. He was recaptured and shot along with other prisoners at Danzig by the Gestapo on 29th March 1944.

Another I remember was Flight Sergeant Jean Ester, who was also shot down over France but was repatriated, and we drank the Sergeants' Mess dry the night he returned. He was an exceptional pilot and after the war, he flew for KLM Airlines.

Sergeant Furlong of No.453 Squadron was lost on 30th October. While on convoy patrol off Margate, he was seen to dive into the sea. The cause of the accident was unknown, but greyish white smoke was seen pouring from the engine.

On 31st October, Monsieur Kanellopoules, the Deputy Prime Minister and Minister of Defence to the Greek Government, visited the base. He was accompanied by Wing Commander Kinatos, the Greek Air Attaché in the Middle East, along with Mr R.B. Meade of the Foreign Office and Flying Officer Lloyd of the Air Ministry. After having lunch, the party was shown combat film footage at the photographic section; they then moved onto the parachute section and the intelligence block. Monsieur Kanellopoules was also shown the Wing Commander's Spitfire and sat in a Spitfire cockpit and fired its guns at the firing butts.

A visit from our allies the Russians took place at Hornchurch on 10th November 1942, when a party arrived to be shown around the airfield. The centre of attention was the famous Soviet girl sniper Lieutenant Pavlichenko, who claimed to have killed more than 300 Germans. She was met and shown around the various points of interest at the station by Station Commander, Group Captain George Lott. A Spitfire MkIX (BS387) of No.122 Squadron and its groundcrew were brought to attention and introduced. Lieutenant Pavlichenko was then helped into the cockpit and told about the various controls, and shown how to fire off a burst of gunfire from the aircraft into the firing butts. She was then escorted with her colleagues Lieutenant Pchelintzev, Captain Diky and Krasavchenko to watch a flying display by a Spitfire, and was also shown Link Trainer flight simulator.

The arrival of the Brazilian Ambassador, His Excellency Senor Monir de Arago took place on 16th December 1942, to present two new Spitfires on behalf of the Brazilian Fellowship. His Excellency, accompanied by Air Commodore Hopwood-Smith, inspected the Guard of Honour and then the new aircraft, signing his name on one of the Spitfires which was named 'Brazil' on the cowling. Afterwards they posed for the usual news and film reporters.

With the year of 1942 drawing to a close, RAF Hornchurch had witnessed many changes in the fortunes of war. The United States of America was now fully involved in the war, fighting alongside the British on all fronts, Europe, Africa and the Far East. Hornchurch had witnessed the disaster of Dieppe, but a great victory had been won in North Africa at El Alamein. In November the Allied Operation 'Torch' saw landings on the North African coast by US and British troops.

Hornchurch had seen the arrival of many squadrons which were made up of Commonwealth or European pilots who had escaped to fight again. The Australians, Belgians, Canadians, Czechoslovakian, French and a few Americans had all flown from the aerodrome. Hornchurch had now truly become a multi-national fighter station.

# CHAPTER 4

# SQUADRONS INTERNATIONAL
## 1943

On 1st January 1943, RAF Hornchurch bade farewell to Group Captain George Lott, DSO, DFC, who left to take over the duties of Senior Air Staff Officer at No.81 Group.

Wing Commander Bentley took over the duties as Station Commander, pending the arrival of the new commanding officer.

Sporting events were still in evidence: on 2nd January teams from RAF Hornchurch participated in a triple event against North Weald in the Inter-Sector Challenge Cup. Unfortunately the station lost all three matches, football, rugby and hockey. The new Station Commander, Group Captain A.G. Adnams, arrived to take up command of the station on 5th January. He had previously been stationed at RAF Northolt.

On 20th January, the Germans carried out the largest daylight raid on the south-east and London area since the Battle of Britain. Soon after 12.30 pm, both 64 and 122 Squadrons were scrambled, while No.350 were sent to north-west London to patrol at 7,000 feet, then to Beachy Head at 5,000 feet after which they patrolled the Channel between Dungeness and Cap Gris Nez. They only saw four aircraft, none of which they were able to close with.

No.122 Squadron were sent to the Dover area at 8,000 feet and sighted four Me109s, one of which Squadron Leader Don Kingaby chased across the Channel and destroyed over a forest, south of Guines. Flight Lieutenant Charlton Haw attacked another, and damaged it, but then lost it in cloud. Two other pilots fired their guns without visible result. During the afternoon, a Rodeo operation, No.155, took place. Nos.64,122 and 350 Squadrons, led by Squadron Leader Kingaby, set course for Calais at 12,000 feet.

After sweeping over St Omer, the squadrons went out by way of Gravelines, where they sighted six enemy aircraft over the Channel, but lost them in cloud.

Meanwhile No.64 Squadron had reached Gris Nez at 13,000 feet and patrolled one mile of shoreline between Gris Nez and Dunkirk for 20 minutes. They then received a report of a ship three miles north-west of Calais and dived down to investigate when the ship was seen to be an 'R' boat, travelling fast towards Calais. The squadron were about to attack, when they saw seven Focke-Wulf 190s flying in two lots of four and three in line astern, coming in at 5,000 feet. The Germans were jumped by the squadron from behind which claimed one destroyed and two damaged.

On 26th January, Pilot Officer George Mason of No.64 was flying as Blue 1, while carrying out Circus Operation 256 over Audruicq. In his report he states:

> After passing over Audruicq and turning towards the coast, the commanding officer reported three enemy aircraft behind us, at our height. Blue section was then flying on the left and could not see any enemy aircraft at my height, but saw a rather straggly formation at about 16,000 feet below flying from north-east to south-west.
>
> I led the section round in two quick orbits to see if there were any enemy about and warned the CO that I was going down. I took the section down from an up-sun position, being fairly confident they wouldn't see me. No.122 Squadron, who were trailing, would divert their attention.
>
> On the final turn, I ordered the section into line abreast and made our approach on the enemy from dead astern, closing rapidly. Blue 4 had to return after reporting engine trouble. The bandits, of which there were about 12, were flying straight and level, but fairly open in two lots of six. I led the section to attack the nearer enemy aircraft, taking one of the middle ones for myself. I opened fire at about 700 yards owing to the rapid closing speed and when I was about 200 yards away the enemy fighter turned very slowly starboard. I then gave him a deflection shot. I finished up dead astern of him and saw flames coming from below the right side of his cockpit and the side of his engine cowling. I broke away upwards and saw my No.2 closing in on his target on the right. He confirmed that he saw flames coming from the fighter I had engaged.
>
> After breaking away we climbed with the section in line abreast, leaving France at 20,000 feet, just east of Dunkirk, climbing rapidly to obtain top cover protection from 122 Squadron, as I could see eight Focke-Wulf 190s behind and about 10,000 feet above us, approaching from the east. They subsequently tried to get up-sun of 122 Squadron, but failed. On return to Hornchurch I claimed one Focke-Wulf destroyed.

One of the first pilot casualties of 1943 was from No.122 Squadron. On 24th January Warrant Officer Samuel Earwaker, who hailed from New Zealand, was killed when his oxygen system failed while flying over Chelmsford, Essex. His flight had been taking part in formation flying practice and cine-gun exercises when the tragedy happened. The Royal Observer Corps report of the incident stated that the Spitfire was seen to glide down from 30,000 feet before spinning into the ground from 5,000 feet. The body of Warrant Officer Earwaker was laid to rest at St. Andrew's Church cemetery.

During February No.122 Squadron were visited by Sir John Colville. A new flightpath extension was opened at Hornchurch in February. Its layout from east to west extended across the South End Road, which had now been sealed off to public access. A new Control Tower had also been built across from the main hangars on the side of the Ingrebourne River near the perimeter track. This gave the control tower personnel full view of both flightpaths.

The Belgian squadron No.350 returned to Hornchurch on 13th March, with Squadron Leader A.L. Boussa in command. Alf Allsopp remembers his time at Hornchurch with No.350 Squadron and some interesting events:

> I was very fond of rifle shooting and always made friends with the station armourers and RAF Regiment NCOs. When I found the giant concrete dome trainer at Hornchurch, I was over the moon! I was in there one day when the station warrant officer came in with his young son. He watched me shoot down three dive bombers that were superimposed on the walls of the building, and said, 'You should join the RAF Regiment.' I said no thank you, that would have cut my wages down.
>
> Romford was bombed whilst we were there one morning. In fact I was coming out of the Sergeants' Mess when German Focke-Wulf 190s went across the end of the airfield. A Regiment sergeant going into the Mess said, 'Are they ours with black crosses on them?' The Spitfires had white stripes painted on them for an invasion exercise at the time and from a distance the fusalage markings did look like crosses. We did hear that a Norwegian squadron from North Weald intercepted the Huns on their way home.
>
> I was friends with a Sergeant Fitter in No.122 Squadron. I was talking to him on an open night in the Mess over a Guinness (Romford Brewery Guinness was very good) when Squadron Leader Don Kingaby, the famous 109 'ace' came over and had a word with us; he took out his hip-flask and proceeded to spike our drinks with something a little stronger.

On Wednesday 24th March, an incident happened that would be indelibly etched in many young schoolchildren's minds for the rest of their lives. At around 10.00 am, Flying Officer Raimund Sanders Draper of No.64 Squadron, an American who had joined the RAF before the United States had entered the war, was scheduled to take his aircraft on a flight that morning. He took off in his Spitfire MkIX, Serial No.EN132, coded SH-F, but almost immediately his aircraft developed engine problems, which caused it to cut out at 200 feet. With no other option but to try to land his aircraft, Sanders Draper was faced with the sight of the Sutton's junior and senior schools in his direct path. He managed to avoid the junior school, but now with no power he was confronted with the two-storied senior school. He put the aircraft down into the playing field in front of the school, the Spitfire careering across the grass and finally bouncing up onto the gravel drive, before coming to rest against the end classroom wall of the school.

By the time the RAF crash-crew had arrived, they found Sanders Draper dead in the cockpit. It was just after 10.45 am. The aircraft did not catch fire fortunately and the only damage to the school was broken windows. One schoolchild, Richard Barton, was injured slightly with a cut leg from flying glass while five other children were treated for shock. Surprisingly, the school had resumed normal classes by 11.15 am.

The official cause of the crash was engine failure due to an ignition fault. The pilot stayed with his aircraft being unable to bale out due to his low altitude of only 200 feet and having seconds only to decide what to do next. The Station Operations Book recorded the crash only briefly:

> Weather was sufficiently good for practice flying. At 10.00 hours F/O Draper went into the deck by Sutton's School in aircraft F, his engine cut when only 200 feet up and he spun in and was killed instantly.

Ken Finding was one of the boys at the school, when the incident occurred. He now reflects on what took place:

> It was a very bright spring day, and there was quite a lot of sunshine because we had the windows slightly open, although they were covered in the protective netting which was used to protect us from flying glass. At that time we thought that all danger was over, we'd had the tip and run raids by the Focke-Wulf 190s, but that was all.
>
> We had heard the sound of a Merlin engine, we were used to hearing them taking off and coming down, but this one, there was something different about this and we just went down under our desks, instinctively. We didn't see anything, but there was a large 'woomph' as it went down into the playing field. Had it not done so, had the pilot attempted to pull of clear of the school with such reduced power, he would have undoubtedly gone into the school.
>
> One of the boys, Henry Short, who was outside in the gardening class, he said, that as the Spitfire was coming round, as it had turned to miss the junior school, then faced with the two-storey school, he could see the pilot had his cockpit open and was waving to those below to get away. When it hit the ground, the aircraft swung around on the gravel drive, the nose pointing towards the airfield and the tail went right up into the air. Henry Short, who was the tallest boy in the school, ran towards the crashed Spitfire to see if he could help, climbed up onto the wing, but the gardening master, Mr Meads threw a clod of earth at him to attract his attention, and said, 'Come away boy,' as he was sure it was going to catch fire at any moment.
>
> The Deputy Headmaster had been in our classroom, he had heard all the noise. I remember he leapt for the door. The door had a thumb catch you had to press, but in his anxiety to get out, he forgot about the catch and could not open the door. One

of the boys shouted out, 'The thumb catch sir!' He opened the door and raced out. Shortly afterwards he came back and said, 'Unfortunately the pilot is dead.' The RAF crash-crew had arrived by then. They then thought it best that we evacuate, we went out through a side entrance to the shelters. When it was obvious that nothing was going to happen and the RAF gave the OK, the Deputy Head assembled us in the hall and told everyone the tragic news that the pilot was dead.

The RAF took the wreckage away and later one of my schoolboy chums, Alf Goodnew, told me that the RAF had asked some of the older boys to help them by picking up any pieces of aircraft debris they could find.

Sanders Draper's sacrifice had saved many lives; it can only be speculated on the devastation that would have occurred had the Spitfire crashed into the main part of the school, which was full of children. Raimund Sanders Draper was given a military funeral and buried at St Andrew's Church military graveyard plot at Hornchurch. Ken Finding:

When we heard when the funeral was going to take place, of course everybody wanted to go. What they did was, they drew lots, so they let two pupils from each class, two boys from the boys' class, two from the girls to attend. The two boys from my class were David Seaman and Ron Ives.

In March 1946, Ruth Draper, the aunt of Sanders Draper, visited his grave and Sutton's School. While there she also entertained the children with songs, as she was an actress and entertainer of some repute who had travelled the world with her own solo stage show. The school decided to keep the memory of this brave pilot alive by awarding an annual Sanders Draper prize for 'displaying qualities of reliability, unselfishness, helpfulness and steadfast attention to duty'. In 1973, Sutton's school was turned into a mixed comprehensive school, and a new name was suggested for the school. Many names were suggested, but the most voted name put forward was that of Sanders Draper, in honour of the wartime pilot. So it was that in September 1973 Sanders Draper school was officially opened. On the anniversary of Sanders Draper's death, a service is held at his grave every year, which is attended by men and women who were pupils there over 50 years ago, along with the children of today. During the service, flowers and wreaths are laid in memory of the 25-year-old American who gave his life for others.

Wing Commander A.M. Bentley, Wing Commander Flying, was posted to No.12 Group Headquarters on 26th March. Wing Commander John Ignatius Kilmartin DFC was posted here in his place. He arrived at Hornchurch on the 30th. He had fought with No.1 Squadron during the French Campaign in May 1940 and then with No.43 Squadron during the Battle of Britain. Wing Commander Kilmartin remembers:

The Wing Leader at Hornchurch was a chap named Bentley,

whom I didn't know; he had finished his tour of duty and they needed another Wing Leader, so I was posted in.

There were two squadrons at Hornchurch at that time: one was 122, commanded by Squadron Leader Pete Wickham and an Australian squadron, No.453 I think it was, commanded by Jack Ratten. The Australian pilots were excellent, they were very game and No.122 was one of the finest squadrons in RAF Fighter Command at that time.

We did bomber escorts, mainly high altitude. The Spitfires we had at that time were MkIXAs with a two-stage supercharger engine which gave us a plus boost to 25,000 feet, which was almost unheard of and took us up to a level 30,000 feet. It was absolutely marvellous up there, because for the first time in my fighting experience we could get above the Germans. Before invariably, they were always above us. We did some escorts for the American bombers, but mostly aggressive sweeps over northern France, Belgium and Holland.

The Focke-Wulf 190s were the ones to look out for. Most of the 190 squadrons as far as I can remember were strategically positioned to intercept the American or RAF bomber formations on their way to the Ruhr or Berlin, Hamburg or whatever. So it was always like a hornet's nest up there, once the bombers went in.

Of course we could only go so far. We could just about fly to the German frontier from Holland, which was our limit. We had no long-range escort like the Americans had. We did use jettison-fuel tanks which did help, but hampered the Spitfire's flying ability.

To relax, the boys of the Hornchurch Wing used to travel up to the Savoy Hotel in London to let off steam, which was great fun. Of course this was only allowed if there were no operations the following day, but we were always pre-briefed anyway.

One of the most interesting stories I recall while I was at Hornchurch, was when one day I was telephoned by Peter Townsend, who was commanding West Malling at the time. He said, 'Come on down, I've something to show you,' so I hopped into my Spitfire and flew down, just over the river to West Malling. And there I was amazed to see four Focke-Wulf 190s parked up on the runway. They had landed the night before, thinking they had crossed the Channel onto the French side. The four pilots were taken off for interrogation, while the RAF had four 190s in perfect condition to play with; they were later taken to Farnborough for testing and evaluation.

The 1st April marked the 25th anniversary of the founding of the Royal Air Force in 1918. At Hornchurch, the day opened with a colour-hoisting parade, the largest parade on the station since the war had begun. There were 400 airmen, 300 airwomen and 50 officers. The salute was taken by

Group Captain A.G. Adnams. The airmen and airwomen were entertained to a special dinner at midday and each received a free beer.

The BBC arrived that day to conduct interviews with a couple of the pilots. Broadcaster Gilbert Harding, accompanied by two engineers, set equipment up for a radio broadcast. Squadron Leader Don Kingaby, Flight Lieutenant Prest and Flying Officer Hull, all of No.122 Squadron, were interviewed. The interviews were broadcast nationwide. Three Spitfires took off and dropped three chamber pots attached by small parachutes over the aerodrome of Biggin Hill. On each of the pots was painted a Zeppelin airship. This was just a cheeky joke to remind Biggin Hill of Hornchurch's long start as an aerodrome, before theirs.

Hornchurch was once again put in the spotlight by visiting press reporters on the 11th April. Mr Bishop of *Sport and General* arrived to take photographs of No.453 Squadron. A Swedish reporter Mr Kristian, was shown around the station and also took many shots for use in Swedish newspapers. Mr Alfred Wagg, an American journalist, arrived one hour late, and in spite of every effort made, he did not appear to show much interest in anything.

At 7.30 am on 12th April, No.122 Squadron was scrambled to intercept 12 enemy aircraft that had been reported coming in from the north-east at a height of 5,000 feet. When the squadron was airborne and climbing they saw FW190s at zero feet, bombing and strafing the Romford and Ilford area. The interception now became a chase at roof-top height, but the squadron was unable to catch the enemy; although Pilot Officer Edwards and Sergeant Livesey both fired from long-range, only Edwards claimed an FW190 damaged. All the squadron's aircraft landed safely back at Hornchurch at 8.35 am.

Hornchurch was visited by several VIPs on 23rd April, when a presentation Spitfire named 'Spithead Billy' was handed over to No.122 Squadron.

Viscount Knollys, the Governor of Bermuda, accompanied by Admiral Harcourt arrived to do the presentation. After lunch in the Mess and an inspection of the ante-room, they proceeded to No.2 hangar where the Spitfire was standing, surrounded by a Guard of Honour. Viscount Knollys made a short but impressive speech to the pilot, Pilot Officer Bernard, a Bermudan, and presented him with a wristwatch in memory of the occasion, as the first pilot to fly the new aircraft. Also in attendance at the ceremony was Flight Lieutenant Wyatt who escorted Major Cerwell, the Swedish Air Attaché and Colonel Mossberg. Air Officer Commander of No.11 Group. Air Vice-Marshal H.S. Saunders CBE, DSO, MC was also present. After the ceremony Viscount Knollys climbed into the cockpit of 'Spitfire Billy' and was shown its detail by the station commander. The guests finally left the station at 5.30 pm.

The children living in the local vicinity of the aerodrome took every opportunity to try and get as close as possible to see the Spitfires coming and going. John Cox was just seven years of age, and remembers one particular day:

I remember that my brother Peter and I, along with a friend,

Brian Olley walked down past St.Georges's Hospital, then we climbed through a hole in a hedge at the back of the airfield. There were airman standing around, but they didn't say anything to us. We then went around the perimeter track where we met some more airmen who stood and had a chat with us. Then luckily some Spitfires came out and taxied past us. I'll always remember one of the pilots turned and waved at us. I remember that I thought he was wearing glasses at the time, but obviously they were his goggles. They then took off.

On the 24th, Squadron Leader Donald Kingaby left Hornchurch to take up the position of Station Commander at RAF Southend. No.222 (Natal) Squadron returned for their fourth stay at Hornchurch on 29th April 1943, led by their commanding officer Squadron Leader E.J. Harrington. Among the pilots arriving with No.222 Squadron was Pilot Officer Gordon Braidwood, who remembers his time at Hornchurch:

I had joined the squadron on 4th March, and in April we moved to Hornchurch. The commanding officer was Squadron Leader E.J. Harrington and I served in A Flight under Flight Lieutenant Lardner-Burke. We were flying Spitfire VBs until the end of May, when they were replaced by Spitfire IXAs. The IXAs were turbo-charged for high altitudes, which was just the job as No.222 flew top cover at around 35,000 feet plus, whereas the other squadrons were layered down to 20,000 feet, the height of the bombers.

This high altitude flying was rather stressful, as with an outside temperature of –40°C; the aircraft had no heating and we the pilots had only electrically heated slippers and Irvin jackets to counter the cold. The oxygen mask would freeze to your face, and the reduced pressure at this altitude would cause your body to balloon with the expansion of inner body gasses.

During May and June our squadron and the Hornchurch Wing were involved mainly in the following types of operations: routine convoy escorts over the east coast; sometimes escorting naval motor torpedo boats attacking targets off the coast of Holland; and also acting as rearguard escort for American B17 bombers (Flying Fortress) bombing targets in Germany, Belgium and France, which sometimes involved up to six squadrons of Spitfires from Hornchurch, Biggin Hill and North Weald.

On 4th May, No.222 Squadron flew close forward escort to 12 Ventura bombers on a bombing raid to Abbeville to bomb the marshalling yards. No flak was encountered but Focke-Wulf 190 fighters were sighted and two destroyed, for no loss of Allied aircraft. The next day, 35 Turkish officials escorted by a Flight Lieutenant Salter arrived at 3.00 pm. Owing to the fact that these officers had just completed a course at a fighter station, it was most difficult to show them anything new. However, they were kept interested until 5.00 pm, then given an excellent tea before leaving.

Squadron Leader Jack Ratten, officer commanding No.453 Australian Squadron, was appointed Wing Commander Flying at Hornchurch on 7th May, while Flight Lieutenant K.M. Barclay was appointed to take over command of the squadron. Wing Commander John Kilmartin DFC, whose position Ratten had taken, was posted to No.61 Operational Training Unit.

On 8th May, German bombers taking advantage of low cloud cover, operated over the Thames estuary at about 7.00 am. A section of No.122 Squadron was ordered off to intercept. During the encounter Sergeant Williams destroyed a Junkers Ju88 which crashed near Pitsea, Essex. Pilot Officer Burt damaged another Ju88. Later that morning Squadron Leader Barton took several pilots over to the crash-site and some of the aircraft's material was brought back to the Intelligence Office. Visitors streamed in and out of the office most of the day to examine the remains of the enemy aircraft.

The station was paid a visit by Sergeant P.Waring, ex-616 Squadron, on 10th May. He arrived to give a talk on his experiences of escaping from a German prison camp. In the afternoon, a dinghy practice for the pilots was held at the Dagenham baths. Also on the 10th, one of RAF Hornchurch's most respected officers, Ronald Adam, had been promoted to the rank of wing commander and posted to become Senior Sector Controller. He had worked in Hornchurch's Operations Room since November 1939.

It was while at Hornchurch, that Adam had been inspired to write his two novels based on characters he had seen and met at the station. The two books, *Readiness at Dawn* and *We Rendezvous at Ten*, were both well received. Due to wartime restrictions RAF pilots' names could not be used, so they were given pseudonyms: Bo'sun Spritt was 'Sailor' Malan, 'Squadron Leader Diamond' was James Leathart, 'Johnny Orwell' was Johnny Allen, 'Group Captain Faversham' Harry Broadhurst and 'Bill Sharp' was Al Deere.

The Station Commander, Group Captain A.G. Adnams, took the salute and gave an address at the Dagenham Civic Centre on the 11th, as part of the Dagenham 'Wings for Victory' Week. A contingent of RAF and WAAF personnel numbering 100 headed the services parade. Although a downpour of rain spoiled the event, the smartness of the contingent was well received by the local population who turned out to watch it. There was also a visit by a small party of Hornchurch airmen to the Victoria Plant of Briggs Motor Company in Dagenham, in aid of the same appeal, where 1,500 workers listened to the talk.

Hornchurch was honoured with a visit from Air Marshal Lord Trenchard on 13th May, and during his stay No.222 Squadron provided the Air Marshal with a flypast comprising a Squadron Balbo formation. A visit by eight officers and MPs from Australia also arrived at 11.00 am; during their visit, films were taken by the Movietone News cameraman. The Wing was busy later that day when it provided escort cover for 80 Flying Fortresses along with ten other fighter squadrons to bomb targets in Amiens and Albert, while another 40 bombers attacked Courtrai aerodrome in Belgium. Nos.122 and 453 Squadrons provided high cover, No.222 operated as withdrawal cover. During the raid they encountered over 40 Me109s and 50 FW190s. The final tally after the raid was five bombers lost, 12 enemy aircraft destroyed.

Pilot Officer Haldo of 122 claimed an FW190 damaged, and an Me109 was also claimed damaged by Squadron Leader Crawford-Compton. Later that evening, two sections of No.453 Squadron flew down to Manston in Kent, to escort Lancaster bombers on a special operation.

On the 15th No.222 provided forward escort to six Mitchell bombers who attacked Caen aerodrome in France. Flak and 190s were encountered but no casualties were suffered by either side. It was on this day that Hornchurch learned of Biggin Hill's pilots scoring their 1,000th enemy victory. They had needed two more claims for the 1,000th and one of these was shot down by ex-No.54 Squadron Hornchurch pilot Squadron Leader Jack Charles, now flying with 611 Squadron. The other enemy aircraft was accounted for by Frenchman Captain Rene Mouchotte, who had also flown from Hornchurch with No.340 Squadron in 1942.

The newspaper press descended on Biggin and a large celebration party was laid on at the Grosvenor House hotel in Park Lane, London, on 9th June, where guests invited from all over No.11 Group partied into the early hours. The cost of the party was so extreme by wartime standards that Biggin Hill could not pay all the expenses. With the help of the Air Officer Commanding 11 Group and financial donation help from other airfields, the bill was paid. Hornchurch drew up a cheque for £600, which helped considerably.

No.222 Squadron also again provided escort the next day, 16th May, to a formation of Mitchell bombers on a raid against Tricqueville aerodrome at 1,200 feet; 12 Me109Fs were seen but no combat took place.

The station's 'Wings for Victory' week concluded in a blaze of glory. The total collection was £33,000 of which £8,000 was received in small savings from station personnel. The station was well represented in a parade which opened the campaign. The contingent was led by Flight Lieutenant C.A. Mackay, the Station Adjutant, and Section Officer Perkins. The Lord Lieutenant of Essex, Lieutenant Colonel Sir Francis Whitmore, took the salute accompanied by Group Captain Adnams.

On 27th May 1943, Operation Ramrod 79 was arranged, then suffered postponement, but during the afternoon, Rodeo 224 took place. The Wing led by Wing Commander Jack Ratten swept the area between Ostend, Ypres and Knocke. Enemy aircraft were seen but not engaged. Strangely, Flying Officer LeBlanc of 222 Squadron was seen at 5.22 pm to break away, 15 miles north-west of Ostend at 28,000 feet. He waggled his wings and dived steeply. A pilot of No.453 Squadron saw a parachute at around this time at 25,000 feet, ten miles off Ostend. Whether this was LeBlanc no one could tell. Flight Lieutenant A. Gaze had to force-land his Spitfire at Tilbury, but was unhurt.

The Wing landed at 6.30 pm, and was airborne again as an air-search-rescue patrol at 8.00 pm; it landed 50 minutes later owing to bad weather. The Hornchurch Wing was required to take part in Rodeo 225 on 1st June 1943. The pilots were briefed at 11.00 hours and were airborne at 11.35. Led by Squadron Leader Barclay, the sweep took them over Gravelines,

Hazebrouck, Desvres and Boulogne, where they sighted 15 Focke-Wulf 190s above and behind them, ready to pounce. The Wing outmanoeuvred the enemy aircraft, and the Germans finding themselves at a disadvantage sped off inland.

Flying Officers Ewins and Thornley of No.453 Squadron both fired at the German fighters, but made no claim. Back at Hornchurch, the Air Officer Commander in Chief of Fighter Command had arrived and was given lunch. Once the Wing had landed, he was introduced to some of the pilots at dispersal. Wing Commander J. Ratten, commanding officer of the Australian 453 Squadron, was awarded his DFC.

The weather in the afternoon and early evening deteriorated so much that visibility over the French coast was nil, but 11 Group insisted that Rodeo 82 take place at 8.30 pm. Wing Commander Flying at Hornchurch protested in vain, and at 8.15 the Wing took off. Needless to say, after a shambles at the rendezvous, the whole formation, while flying at zero feet, turned around in mid-Channel and headed home, all aircraft landing at 9.15 pm.

On the ground, a party of six from the station visited the Thames Board Mill Company at Purfleet, Essex, in connection with the 'Wings for Victory' campaign. While there they were taken on a very interesting tour of the works. Flight Lieutenant C.A. Mackay and the 'Flying Squad' also visited the two large cinemas in North and South Chingford, where they made an appeal to the audience on behalf of the 'Wings' campaign.

The following day, the weather was so bad that no flying was possible, but once again the 'Wings for Victory' Flying Squad from Hornchurch visited the Stork Margarine Works at Purfleet in connection with the Thurrock 'Wings for Victory' week. Their appeal to the works was very well received.

A representative party of airmen and airwomen from Hornchurch took part in a Drum Head Service on 6th June. Held at the Harrow Lodge Park in Hornchurch, it was conducted by the local clergy. An address was given by the Station Chaplain Squadron Leader Davies and the salute by Station Adjutant Flight Lieutenant C.A. Mackay.

Two days later, on the 8th, Flight Lieutenant Mackay was again in demand, when he gave an address to 2,000 schoolchildren who gathered at the Tower Cinema in Hornchurch during the 'Wings for Victory' campaign. He also introduced a number of Spitfire pilots and WAAF personnel.

It was during this month that the station was visited by the Fighter Command Demonstration Rifle Flight No.2713 Squadron, RAF Regiment. Stan Reynolds was an LAC with the unit and recalls their function in visiting various airfields including Hornchurch:

> We toured every Fighter Command aerodrome twice prior to the invasion in 1944, spending between two and three days on each airfield. Our demonstration programme consisted of a severe drill and discipline course, field work, tactics and unarmed combat including how to approach a sentry unseen. Other exercises included attacking enemy positions on airfields before they could consolidate it.

Hornchurch was a good airfield to demonstrate at, mainly because 60% of us were Londoners or southerners, or in my case from Essex. After we had demonstrated on the camp, our time was our own, we were free to leave the airfield and catch a bus or train. While we were at Hornchurch, we were alerted to enemy aircraft approaching. I was amazed to hear a running commentary over the Tannoy system. Fortunately for us we had no direct involvement on the station defence and on this occasion we never took shelter.

We demonstrated to most of the pilots, because all personnel were detailed to attend our demos. One noticeable officer I remember at Hornchurch was Flight Lieutenant Len Harvey, the boxer. It was a regular thing to talk to the station personnel and get the name and rank of any particular unpopular airman; they were usually called out at the demonstration to either take part or receive an ear bashing from the sentry in the particular 'approaching a sentry demonstration,' much to the amusement of station personnel. Sometimes the padre or one or two WAAFs would attend the demos; the flight sergeant had the job of speaking to people when the language got a bit strong; the language was added for authenticity. Most of them took it in good part, but usually WAAFs were not invited. It was on our second tour of Hornchurch that our commanding officer, Flight Lieutenant Black, negotiated with the flight-training officer and arranged for us all to have a session on the Link Trainer. Quite an experience!

The Hornchurch Wing acted as 'high cover' to a force of 12 Mitchell bombers attacking the Dornier Airframe Factory at Flushing, Belgium, on 13th June. Led by Wing Commander Ratten, they took off at 8.30 am, and on the way out to the target No.222 Squadron were attacked and Flight Lieutenant Hall was shot down. No other casualties were suffered.

On 28th June, No.129 'Mysore' Squadron moved to Hornchurch from Ibsley; their commanding officer was Squadron Leader Henri Alphonse Clement Gonay, a Belgian who had flown in the Battle of Britain, after arriving in Britain by Dutch cargo ship from Bayonne following the fall of France. Mervyn Young had joined No.129 Squadron as a pilot officer at Westhampnett airfield in Sussex. He recalls:

When we arrived at Hornchurch, my first impression of the airfield was that it wasn't very modern, but the best impression was that they had Spitfire IXs. When I had joined 129, the squadron was using Spitfire Vs; Flight Lieutenant Bourne had taken me into his flight office and told me to forget everything about the Spitfire being superior. The Focke-Wulf 190 can out-climb you, out-dive and out-roll you, the only thing you can do is turn inside it. So when we arrived at Hornchurch which had Spit IXs, we were very happy. They cancelled out all the advantages that the 190 had; it was a very different ball game.

With an improvement in the weather conditions on 13th July, a Rodeo mission was laid on for that morning with the briefing taking place at 8.00 am. Nos.129 and 222 were led by Wing Commander Flying and were to meet up with Spitfires from the Kenley Wing as they crossed the English coast over Hastings. They climbed up to 27,000 feet with both Wings crossing the French coast at Cayeux. They continued their sweep from Poix to the west of Amiens and came back across the Channel south of Boulogne without incident.

Later that morning, after 129 Squadron had landed, they were visited at dispersal by Sir Orme Sargent, the Deputy Under-Secretary of State for Foreign Affairs, together with Mr Victor Perrone of the Foreign Office and Sir John Dashwood, the Inspector of Security at the Foreign Office. They were escorted by Flight Lieutenant Lloyd who presented the CO and Flight Lieutenant Watson to the guest party, whose visit was to observe procedure at an operational fighter station. Later in the day another Rodeo operation had been planned to take place, but due to a bad weather front closing in, this had to be cancelled. Instructions were received from No.11 Group Headquarters however, that the Hornchurch Wing was to proceed to Tangmere airfield in Sussex for an early start the following day.

Early next morning the Wing operating out of Tangmere took off to escort a force of B17 Flying Fortresses which were to bomb targets in Paris. Earlier at the briefing, the pilots were urged that every effort should be used to get the bombers through for the good psychological effect it would have on the rest of the American bomber groups. Flying towards Fécamp at 22,000 feet, the Wing saw the first box of B17s and took up position left of the bombers. Aircraft were reported by our fighters in front of the American formation and were first thought to be friendly, but they were then seen to attack the bombers. No.129 Squadron dived across to the right and broke up the German attack; unfortunately two of the American bombers were seen to be shot down, while another was losing height. Two Me109s were also reported shot down, one in flames.

Pilot Officer G.R. Dickson (Blue 3), a New Zealander of 129, reported his aircraft was having engine trouble as he climbed out towards the French coast. He was accompanied by Blue 4, who observed black smoke coming from Dickson's engine. They continued together until Dickson was heard over the R/T, 'I am baling out.' Meanwhile Flight Lieutenant Watson found himself alone with a B17 trying to evade six enemy fighters. Watson dived down to 16,000 feet and attacked a Focke-Wulf 190 flying to the right of the B17; he gave a 5-second burst at 400 yards and saw the Focke-Wulf start to spin with a long stream of white smoke coming from its engine. Watson claimed the aircraft as probably destroyed.

Back at Hornchurch during that afternoon, the pilots were given a talk by Major Egerton Smith on Tactical Air Force Training with particular reference to the experience gained in North Africa and the value of tactical air support to ground forces.

During the morning of 15th July, the commanding officer and army liaison officer of No.239 Squadron based at Fairlop, came to the

Intelligence Office at Hornchurch to meet with Wing Commander Ratten. A large operation had been arranged for the afternoon, but this was cancelled later as the weather had become unsuitable. However a smaller Rodeo was laid on. The Wing, led by Squadron Leader Crawford-Compton would take part in Rodeo 245. However, when all the aircraft were about to take off, Crawford-Compton's aircraft's engine stopped and Sergeant Lunn of No.129 unfortunately crashed into the squadron leader's machine. Luckly the squadron leader had jumped out, otherwise he would have certainly been killed. Fortunately neither pilot was hurt and neither aircraft caught fire.

The Wing took off at 4.10 am and flew as instructed below 500 feet. However, the misfortunes were not quite over. Squadron Leader Gonay of 129 and the deputy leader had to return with engine trouble. Flight Lieutenant Tripe of 222 Squadron then took command of Wing and proceeded to sweep over Le Treport, Corteville and Crécy at 23,000 feet, when enemy aircraft were reported over Cayeux.

These enemy aircraft, which proved to be FW190s, were engaged. One was destroyed by Flying Officer Smik, a Czech flying with 222 Squadron and one was damaged by Flying Officer Mason, also of 222. The Wing landed back safely at 5.35 pm.

During the afternoon of 19th July, Colonel M.C. Woodbury, the commanding officer of the United States Air Corps 5th Defence Wing at Duxford, visited the station. He was escorted on his visit by 1st Lieutenant Ellis, who was on detachment at Hornchurch from Duxford.

Hornchurch's Station Commander Group Captain Adnams was posted away on the 20th, to proceed to the United States to take on special duties. His post was taken by Wing Commander H.L. Maxwell who was appointed Acting Group Captain. On the same day, more of our American cousins arrived, when five American Mercantile Marine Officers, accompanied by Flight Lieutenant Ferrier, paid a visit. They were shown over a dispersal, a Spitfire IX, the Intelligence Office and Parachute section and in the afternoon they were taken for a flight.

The Wing participated in Ramrod 165 on 28th July, as 'fighter cover withdrawal' for a large force of B17 Fortresses attacking targets in north-west Germany. The Wing met at Bradwell Bay at 11.45 am, then set course at 11.50 am to rendezvous eight miles south of Amsterdam. When at 15,000 feet, 15 minutes after leaving the English coast, they were diverted to Rotterdam, where they sighted the first box formation of approximately 60 Flying Fortresses at 21,000 feet. The Wing ensured that the Fortresses were unmolested, and then penetrated further inland, north-east, to look for stragglers. When south of Rotterdam at 24,000 feet, they sighted a mixed bag of 20 Me109s and FW190 fighters coming in from the south-east at 4,000 feet higher and on loose finger-four formation.

At that precise moment, the Wing sighted a second box of Fortresses coming out over Rotterdam. The action of the Wing prevented the enemy aircraft from attacking the second box and no further enemy aircraft were sighted. The Wing then took up position on either side of the B17s, escorting them back to the Dutch coast, north of Orfordness.

July 29th was another fine day, but there was thick ground haze. No.129

Squadron led by Wing Commander Compton took off for Manston at 7.48 am, to provide withdrawal cover to Marauder bombers. On arrival at Manston, Flight Lieutenant George Mason burst a tyre and in trying to save the aircraft, broke up the oleo-leg. It was here at Manston that they learned that the mission was cancelled and they returned to Hornchurch. With the operation cancelled, the rest of the afternoon was devoted to recreation; many of the pilots took advantage of the opportunity and went swimming at the Romford Baths.

On 4th August 1943, Pilot Officer Gurmukh Singh Kohli and Pilot Officer Gurdial Singh Paul of the Indian Air Force arrived to take up general instruction duties. They stayed until 10th August and were then posted to RAF Colerne.

A new security procedure was brought into effect at Hornchurch on 9th August. It was decided that it would be wiser from a security point of view to cease referring to the squadrons over the Tannoy system by their R/T code names and that from now on the squadrons would be referred to as 'Jan' for 129 Squadron and 'Cupee' for No.222.

A delegation from our allies in the Far East arrived on this day to be given a tour of the aerodrome. Air Commodore Beamont arrived with the following distinguished Chinese visitors: Dr T.V. Soong, the Chinese Foreign Minister and brother-in-law to General Chiang Kai Shek, Dr Ze, advisor to Dr Soong, Major General Kiang, Major General Tsai-Wen-Tch and Lieutenant Colonel Huang, the Chinese Air Attaché.

American-built Mustang P51A fighter aircraft of No.239 Squadron arrived at Hornchurch from Fairlop on 14th August. The squadron, which was an army co-operation unit, was commanded by Squadron Leader P.M. Evans. Their role at this time was reconnaissance of enemy shipping and army movements.

A familiar sight to many pilots brought a worried look to those on the ground when a Focke-Wulf 190 flew low over the aerodrome at 11.00 am on 18th August. Their fears however were eased when the aircraft carrying British markings lowered its undercarriage and landed. The pilot of the aircraft had arrived to give a demonstration to the Hornchurch pilots. A large number of ground personnel also gathered around the German warbird to see the workings of the machine. During the afternoon the pilot gave a fine flying demonstration over the airfield before heading back to Farnborough.

On 23rd August, the Hornchurch Wing was airborne at 7.45 am to act as high cover for 24 Martin Marauder bombers who were sent to bomb the St Omer railway marshalling yards. The Wing was led by Squadron Leader Gonay, who had taken over command while Wing Commander Crawford-Compton was away on leave. The operation as far as the Wing was concerned was uneventful; as was the second sortie that day at 4.30 pm, which swept over Bethune, Ypres and St Omer. The only hiccup was that Squadron Leader Gonay had to break off and return early with engine trouble. The leadership was taken over by Squadron Leader G.J. Stonehill of 222 Squadron. Later, two Mustangs of 239 Squadron went on a shipping recco, and took photographs of Zeebrugge harbour.

At Hornchurch, later that evening, orders came through that the Wing

*Top left*: RAF Hornchurch Station Commander, Group Captain Harry 'Broady' Broadhurst, led the Hornchurch Wing squadrons on many sweeps into France during early 1941.

*(Broadhurst collection)*

*Top right*: Four pilots of No.41 Squadron at Hornchurch, February 1941. Left to right:

Sgt Hopkinson, P/O Le Roux, Sgt Healey and Sgt Beardsley. *(Author via Beardsley)*

*Bottom*: Spitfire MkII P7618 was presented by the Observer Corps to No.41 Squadron in November 1940. It is here at Hornchurch in February 1941, wearing the codeletters KL of No.54 Squadron after the squadrons had exchanged aircraft. *(Author's collection)*

*Top*: Sergeant Robert Angus of No.41 Squadron survived the Battle of Britain, but would become a victim of German ace Werner Mölders when he was shot down on 20th February 1941. *(Author via Beardsley)*

*Above*: Group Captain 'Broady' Broadhurst with Flight Lieutenant Frank Dowling, the Station Adjutant. *(Author via Dowling)*

*Right*: Sergeant John Gilders of No.41 Squadron. He was reported missing on 21st February 1941 after his aircraft was seen to dive out of formation. Gilders remained missing until 1994.

*(Author via Beardsley)*

*Top left*: Aircraft rigger Max Bygraves aged 19 years, served with No. 611 Squadron.

*Top right*: Flying Officer Peter Brown joined No.41 Squadron during the Battle of Britain, and became one of the squadron's finest stalwarts. *(Author via P. Brown)*

*Bottom left*: The legendary ace Brendon 'Paddy' Finucane, who first flew from Hornchurch in 1940, was given command of the Wing in July 1942 but was tragically killed, when his aircraft sank immediately whilst ditching in the Channel, due to enemy groundfire damaging his Spitfire.

*Bottom right*: Pilot Officer Jack Stokoe flew with both 603 and 54 Squadrons during his time at Hornchurch, and finally returned as a squadron leader. He was awarded the DFC on 6th June 1944 for his outstanding achievements during operational service.

*(D.Ross collection)*

*Top left*: Pilot Officer Jack Stokoe being fished out of the North Sea after being shot down on 17th April 1941. This amazing photo was snapped by one of the sailors aboard the navy minesweeper which rescued him. *(Author via Stokoe)*

*Top right*: A Spitfire MkII of No.54 Squadron comes into land at Hornchurch. *(Author via Broadhurst)*

*Middle*: Pilots of No.54 Squadron gather for a group photograph May 1941. Left to right: 3 unknown Sgt Pilots, F/O Baxter, F/O Knox, F/Lt Sewell, F/O Harris, Sgt Black, F/Lt Gribble, P/O Batchelor, P/O Powell, F/O Bailey, Sgt Panter, S/Ldr Finlay-Boyd, P/O Allen, F/O Jones, P/O

Stokoe and Sgt Cordell. The squadron dog was named 'Crash'.

*Above*: Spitfire MkII P7742, which was a presentation aircraft bought from funds raised by N.E.I. The aircraft was sent to No.603 Squadron at Hornchurch on 17th May 1941. *(Author's collection)*

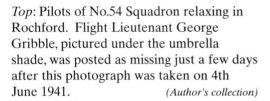

*Top*: Pilots of No.54 Squadron relaxing in Rochford. Flight Lieutenant George Gribble, pictured under the umbrella shade, was posted as missing just a few days after this photograph was taken on 4th June 1941. *(Author's collection)*

*Middle left*: Wing Commander Joe Kayll, who became Wing Commander Flying at Hornchurch on 2nd June 1941. This portrait was done by the artist Eric Kennington in 1941. *(Kayll)*

*Middle right*: Flaps down! A Spitfire MkV of No.611 Squadron is watched by groundcrew on its approach to landing at Hornchurch, June 1941. *(Author via Broadhurst)*

*Bottom right*: Flight Lieutenant Eric Lock after his return to RAF Hornchurch, holding 'Scruffy' the squadron mascot. 'Lockie' was the top scoring pilot during the Battle of Britain with No.41 Squadron. After recovering from wounds, he returned to Hornchurch joining No.611 Squadron. He was reported as missing on 3rd August 1941.

*(Author via Mrs. J Statham)*

*Top left*: Pilots of No.54 Squadron discuss flying manoeuvres after returning from another sweep. Pictured centre is Squadron Leader Robert Finlay-Boyd, CO of No.54; to his left is Pilot Officer Jack Charles, July 1941.  *(Author via Broadhurst)*

*Top right*: What a bloody great hole! Harry Broadhurst's battle-damaged Spitfire. On 4th July 'Broady' was leading the Wing on Circus 32 over Béthune, when he was badly hit by cannon fire from a Me109.  *(Author via Broadhurst)*

*Bottom left*: Pilot Officer Gordon Herbert Batchelor of No.54 Squadron. He was shot down on 9th July 1941 and became a prisoner of war. He died in April 1942 from injuries sustained from a heavy landing by parachute. He was aged 23 years.

*(Author via B. Batchelor)*

*Bottom right*: The original grave marker of Pilot Officer Gordon Batchelor who died on 15th April 1942. He now has a recognised RAF headstone which is looked after by the War Graves Commission.

*(Author via B. Batchelor)*

*Top left*: Sergeant Pilot Harold Bennett of No.603 Squadron stands for the cameraman with Harry Broadhurst's Spitfire, the code letters of which also spelt Harold Bennett's initials HB.

*Top right*: Pilot Officer William 'Tex' Ash of No.411 Canadian Squadron is congratulated by Mr Mackenzie King the Canadian Premier, after a successful combat over France in late 1941. Ash was one of the early Texan volunteers to join the RCAF. *(Author via W. Ash)*

*Above*: The groundcrew of No.122 'City of Bombay' Squadron at Hornchurch, April 1942.

*Right*: WAAF Ada Hewitt worked in the Hornchurch Operations Room at the converted Masonic Hall in Romford, where she was a Plotter on the large operations table in 1941/42. *(Author via A. Hewitt)*

*Top left*: May 1942. Pilots of No.64 Squadron prepare to go on a sweep. S/Ldr Duncan-Smith with hand in air, gives final instructions to his men before they prepare to take off. *(Crown copyright)*

*Top right*: Officers of the South American delegation who visited RAF Hornchurch on 1st July 1942, seen with S/Ldr Robert Finlay-Boyd, wearing mae-west. *(Author via Dowling)*

*Middle*: The Hornchurch Wing, a group photograph taken outside the main hangar in 1942. Front row from right: F/Lt Don Kingaby 3rd, S/Ldr Petrus Hugo 4th, S/Ldr Duncan-Smith 5th, G/Capt Harry Broadhurst 6th, W/Cdr Peter Powell 7th, S/Ldr Leon Prevot 8th, F/Lt Jim Hallowes 9th, S/Ldr Eric Thomas 11th. Second row

7th from right S/Ldr Pat Jameson. *(Broadhurst collection)*

*Above*: Pilot Officer Michael Donnet seated in the Stampe biplane at Hornchurch. This was the aircraft that Donnet and Leon Divoy flew when they escaped from Belgium in 1941. *(Donnet)*

*Top left*: Sptifire Mk Vs of No.122 Squadron take off on another sortie in 1942. *(IWM)*

*Top right*: Group Captain George Lott took over as Station Commander from Harry Broadhurst in 1942. Here he is seen in the garden of the Station Commander's house with the pigs that he continued to keep and feed, after Harry Broadhurst first thought of the idea. *(Dowling/ Lott)*

*Middle left*: A Spitfire of No.64 Squadron comes to grief on landing back at Hornchurch in 1942. While taxiing it nosed over, but fortunately very little damage was done and the pilot was unhurt. *(IWM)*

*Bottom*: Pilots of No.64 Squadron gather at dispersal and discuss the operation they have just returned from. F/Lt Clive Mellersh, the intelligence officer takes down their reports, July 1942. *(Duncan-Smith)*

*Top*: Pilots of No.122 Squadron line up for a photograph in front of one of their Spitfire MkIXs, September 1942. S/Ldr Don Kingaby stands at centre with folded arms, to his right is F/Lt Charlton Haw DFM. *(Author via R. Kingaby)*

*Middle left*: Groundcrew of No.350 Belgian Squadron take a break from servicing a Spitfire MkV, 1942. *(A. Allsopp)*

*Middle right*: Prisoners of War. Three of RAF Hornchurch's pilots photographed at Stalag Luft III in 1943. Left to right: Pilot Officer Bill Stapleton 2nd, No.41 Squadron, 'Tex' Ash 3rd, No.411 Squadron, F/Lt 'Paddy' Barthropp No.122 Squadron.

*Right*: Flying Officer Raimund Sanders Draper, the American who sacrificed himself on 24th March 1943, and in doing so saved the lives of many school children. *(Sanders Draper School)*

*Top left*: The military plot at St. Andrew's Church, Hornchurch. This photograph was taken in the late 1940s; the grave of Raimund Sanders Draper is pictured centre with flowers. Today all the graves have the standard war grave headstones.

*Top right*: LAC Stan Reynolds visited RAF Hornchurch in April 1943 with No.2713 Squadron Demonstration Rifle Flight, RAF Regiment. *(Author via S. Reynolds)*

*Middle right*: Men of No.2713 Demonstration Rifle Flight demonstrate the art of unarmed combat, April 1943.

*(Author via S. Reynolds)*

*Bottom*: May 1943. Two pilots of No.222 Natal Squadron relax outside the squadron's dispersal hut, with the squadron's crest seen in the background. Seated on the right is Pilot Officer Gordon Braidwood.

*(Author via Braidwood)*

*Top left*: Pilot Officer Gordon Braidwood of No.222 Natal Squadron. *(Author via Braidwood)*

*Top right*: Flight Lieutenant George Mason of No.129 Squadron with his two groundcrew at Hornchurch in 1943.

*(Author via A. C. Leigh)*

*Bottom*: Flight Lieutenant Arthur 'Joe' Leigh DFM, DFC of No.129 Squadron seated on the cowling of presentation Spitfire 'Kamba Meru', September 1943. *(Author via A. C. Leigh)*

*Top left*: The Operations Room staff seen outside the Masonic Hall at Romford during 1943. WAAF Joy Caldwell (nee York) is seated far right.　*(Author via J. Caldwell)*

*Top right*: Squadron Leader Philip Tripe (left) and Flight Lieutenant 'Wag' Haw of No.129 Squadron pictured at Hornchurch just before Haw took over command of the squadron in mid-September '43.　*(A. C. Leigh)*

*Middle left*: Pilot Officer Mervyn Young of No.129 Squadron seated in his Spitfire with his mascot of Disney's 'Jimini Cricket' painted on the side.　*(Author via M. Young)*

*Bottom*: Sergeant R. A. Alexandre of No.350 Belgian Squadron in his Spitfire, September 1943.　*(Author via A. Allsopp)*

*Top left*: Wing Commander David Scott-Malden became Station Commander in October 1943. This portrait was drawn by artist Eric Kennington in 1942.

*(Author via Scott-Malden)*

*Top right*: Sgt Pilot Tony Bradshaw of 129 'Mysore' Squadron seen with squadron mascot 'Jannie Bush' out on dispersal, 1943.

*(M. Young)*

*Bottom*: Pilots of No.485 New Zealand Squadron at Hornchurch, November 1943. Left to right front row: F/Lt Gaskin, F/Lt Black, F/O Tucker, Medical Officer, P/O Dasent, Ashworth, P/O Houlton. Middle row standing: F/Lt Lee, White, F/Sgt Strahan, W/Cdr Flying Crawford-Compton, F/O Yeatman, F/O Strachan, P/O Bern, P/O Roberts, P/O Van Dyk, P/O Griffith, and Adjutant. Standing on aircraft: F/Sgts Clarke, Patterson, Robinson, Esdaile, F/O Stead and Frehner.

*(Sport & General)*

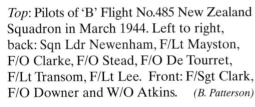

*Top*: Pilots of 'B' Flight No.485 New Zealand Squadron in March 1944. Left to right, back: Sqn Ldr Newenham, F/Lt Mayston, F/O Clarke, F/O Stead, F/O De Tourret, F/Lt Transom, F/Lt Lee. Front: F/Sgt Clark, F/O Downer and W/O Atkins. *(B. Patterson)*

*Bottom left*: Standing on the mainplane of his Spitfire, Squadron Leader Du Monceau De Bergendael (The Duke) of No.350 Squadron at Hornchurch, March 1944. *(Author via A. Allsopp)*

*Bottom right*: Flight Mechanic William Bird, who served with No.229 Squadron at Hornchurch in April 1944. *(W. Bird)*

*Top*: Men of No.207 Flight, No.55 Maintenance Repair Unit are photographed in front of one of their lorries with Flight badge. They did much repair work during the V1 campaign from June 1944 onwards.

*(H. Bullock)*

*Middle*: The RAF Hornchurch Voluntary Band, August 1950.   *(D. McNaught)*

*Right*: Wellington aircraft MA903 seen on show during the 'At Home' display in September 1950.

*Top left:* David Bendon worked for Short Brothers and Harland at Hornchurch during the early 1950s. Seen here with Towing Tractor.

*(D. Bendon)*

*Top right:* A Chipmunk aircraft of the No.17 Reserve Flying School at Hornchurch 1951.

*(D. Bendon)*

*Above:* The dedication service of St.Michael's and All Angels, the Station Church was held on 10th March 1952. The Lord Bishop of Chelmsford is seen pictured 3rd from left with Group Captain Jefferson, the Station Commander.

*Left:* John Cox joined the Royal Air Force Volunteer Reserve at RAF Hornchurch aged 17 years. He learnt to drive with them and helped out with the Motor Transport Section.

*(Author via J. Cox)*

*Top*: Men and motors of the RAF
Hornchurch Motor Transport Section 1954.
*(Author via J. Cox)*

*Above*: A De Havilland Mosquito aircraft
of the No.1 Anti-Aircraft Co-Operation
Unit in 1954.          *(Author via D. Bendon)*

*Right*: Spitfire TE-358 of the Anti-Aircraft
Co-Operation Unit at Hornchurch 1954.
*(D. Bendon)*

*Top*: The RAF Hornchurch Station Band leads a parade through the streets of the town circa 1955/56. *(Author's collection)*

*Middle left*: RAF candidates arrive to take tests at the Aircrew Selection Centre, Hornchurch, 1950s. *(MoD)*

*Middle right*: Future RAF officers? Undertaking one of the many aptitude tests at the ASC. *(MoD)*

*Left*: Men of No.289 Parachute Light Regiment, Royal Horse Artillery (TA) based at Romford, are seen being interviewed by an officer at RAF Hornchurch in 1959. *(R. Little)*

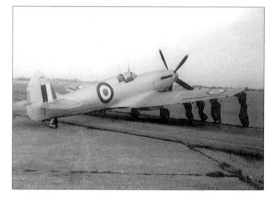

*Top*: Getting ready to take to the air! Soldiers of No.289 Parachute Regiment climb into the cage beneath the static barrage balloon, before being winched up to a height of 800 feet to jump, in 1959.

(R. Little)

*Middle left*: Lance Bombardier Roy Little of No. 289 Parachute Regiment seen here with a couple of mates and his daughter, during a break in parachute practice, 1959.

(R. Little)

*Middle right*: A Spitfire MkXV is readied for flying at the last RAF Hornchurch air display in 1960.

(R. Little)

*Right:* A Prefect single seat glider of No.614 Gliding School seen here at Hornchurch in 1960.

(R. Little)

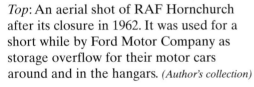

*Top*: An aerial shot of RAF Hornchurch after its closure in 1962. It was used for a short while by Ford Motor Company as storage overflow for their motor cars around and in the hangars. *(Author's collection)*

*Bottom left*: Nature begins to take hold!

The main guard room and flag staff at the entrance to RAF Hornchurch 1963.
*(Author via R. Ballard)*

*Bottom right*: An excellent view of one of the hangars after the airfield's closure.
*(Author via R. Ballard)*

*Top left*: A view across the deserted airfield from one of the dispersal pens. Today the pen is used as the Country Park car park.
*(H. LaRoche)*

*Top right*: The Main Gates of RAF Hornchurch as they stand now at Biggin Hill near the entrance to St George's Memorial Chapel. *(Author's collection)*

*Centre*: The military plot at St.Andrew's Church, Hornchurch, where three of Hornchurch's Battle of Britain pilots rest at peace, along with Flying Officer Sanders Draper and other pilots and personnel who served at the station. *(Author's collection)*

*Above*: The RAF Hornchurch Officers' Mess as it stands today, now used as a medical centre. *(Author's collection)*

*Top left*: The Mitchell's School House Points Board and Spitfire Pilot's Trophy Cup which was inaugurated into the school in 1972. *(Deere collection)*

*Top right*: Many of the roads which have now been built up on the Airfield Estate, sited on the old airfield, are named after many of the famous pilots who served at RAF Hornchurch. This one is named after Squadron Leader James Leathart who commanded No.54 Squadron in 1940. *(Author's collection)*

*Bottom*: Air Chief Marshal Sir Harry Broadhurst unveils the RAF Hornchurch Memorial Stone on 5th July 1983. *(Author via Press Association)*

*Top*: Finally laid to rest! The mortal remains of Sgt. John Gilders of No.41 Squadron who remained missing for more than 50 years, are laid to rest at the Brookwood Military Cemetery in Surrey in 1994.

*(Author's collection)*

*Bottom:* 'Honour among Airmen'. Squadron Leader E. D. Dave Glaser DFC pictured right, greets German fighter pilot Ulrich Steinhilper at the Battle of Britain exhibition held at The Purfleet Heritage Centre/Hornchurch Wing in 1998.

would operate from Tangmere airfield the next morning, starting at 6.30 am. When the next day dawned however, the weather had changed and was very unfavourable for the operation, so it was postponed until weather conditions improved. During the afternoon, aircraft of No.239 were again sent off to do a shipping reconnaissance. The only sighting was of 60 fishing vessels, two miles off Le Touquet and 30 similar vessels off Le Treport. By 4.00 pm, the weather had changed enough for operations over France to continue.

The Wing, now led by Wing Commander Crawford-Compton, took off from Tangmere, to act as second escort to a large force of Flying Fortress B17s on a raid to Evreux and Couches ammunition dumps. The raid was a diversion for a much larger force which bombed targets in the Villacoublay area. The Hornchurch squadrons landed back at base at 7.30 pm.

George Mason recalls some of the marvellous personalities he had the privilege to know during his time flying from Hornchurch with the Wing:

> Bill Crawford-Compton was a really tough, aggressive and popular squadron and wing leader. As No.64 Squadron's commander, he used to chase us all out for cross-country runs and the like. An example of how he looked after his chaps took place early one morning, when I landed heavily at Manston airfield knocking off a wheel complete with oleo leg, which bounced into my numbers 2, 3 and 4 doing minor damage to them all. Bill rushed out and grabbed my escape knife from my boot top and slashed the tyre of the wheel to ribbons and said, 'You landed with a burst tyre, no wonder the thing came apart.' I thought he was mad, but he explained that Group Headquarters were having a blitz on flying accidents and if I was held to blame, I would probably lose my flight and be posted to some non-operational job. I have always remembered that particularly when acting as president of boards of enquiry into flying accidents. I can't recall ever having found a pilot to blame.
>
> Then there was Don Kingaby, we called him Kingo. Always laughing, always smoking, but essentially a sympathetic kindly man, except to the enemy! Quick as a flash in the air and a wonderful shot, but he always looked after his chaps. I remember him most for his cry of 'Climb boys, climb' over the R/T whenever the enemy was sighted. His flight or squadron always seemed to be about a thousand feet above everyone else, except when diving to attack, when he was a thousand feet lower.
>
> Michael Donnet, the Belgian, was a really super chap. He kept his almost schoolboy enthusiasm going throughout the war. He kept the Stampe biplane in which he and his comrade Leon Divoy had escaped from Belgium; it was still at Hornchurch and I was privileged to fly it more than most. J7777 was its registration number. I flew it to Hendon in September '43, when he finally had to surrender it to the

Belgian authorities. Clive Mellersh was our Intelligence Officer, and highly respected in 64 Squadron. He had a way of debriefing pilots after an operation, when they really just wanted to unwind, without being obstructive. Fighter squadrons were far less formal than bombers over debriefing.

On 31st August, the Wing was airborne at 6.41 am, to act as 'high cover' to a force of 36 Marauders who were to bomb targets at Lille and Veuderville. Led by Squadron Leader Gonay, the Wing escorted the bombers until they reached the target area. The bombers were then attacked by 10 to 12 FW190s. The Wing dived down and claimed the following:

| | | |
|---|---|---|
| Flight Lieutenant Mason, No.129 Squadron | 1 FW190 | Destroyed |
| Flying Officer Rushwaldy DFM, No.129 | 1 FW190 | Destroyed |
| Pilot Officer Bradshaw, No.129 | 1 FW190 | Destroyed |
| Flight Lieutenant Tripe, No.222 Squadron | 1 FW190 | Probable |
| Flight Lieutenant Watson, No.129 | 1 FW190 | Damaged |
| Flight Lieutenant Mason, No.129 | 1 FW190 | Damaged |
| Pilot Officer Young, No.129 | 1 FW190 | Damaged |

A red letter day for No.129 Squadron. It was Pilot Officer Mervyn Young's first claim and Pilot Officer Bradshaw's first destroyed. In addition No.122 Squadron claimed one enemy aircraft destroyed. Unfortunately there were casualties; Sergeant Roggenkamp of 129 was slightly injured as a result of crash-landing near Dover and was recovering in Dover Hospital. There was also no news of Flight Sergeant Thompson of 222 Squadron, who was last heard of over Lille.

A big show was laid on for 6th September. At 11.16 am, the Hornchurch Wing was airborne to take part in Ramrod S35. But the route was changed at the last moment and they met up with a large force of B17 Flying Fortresses on the bombers' return trip, south of Amiens. The Wing escorted them well out to sea and then turned around to look for stragglers. Enemy fighters were sighted and engaged. During the following combat, five of No.129 Squadron's pilots fired their guns, but only Pilot Officer Bradshaw and Pilot Officer Wood each claimed a Focke-Wulf 190 damaged.

The Wing then crossed out back across the Channel, six miles north-east of Dieppe. While crossing back, four to five Fortress bombers were seen ditched in the sea with three dinghies nearby. The Wing orbited these until they were sighted by air-sea-rescue launches. It was later learnt during the afternoon back at Hornchurch that 101 men had been picked up out of the sea.

B17s were landing all over the south of England owing to lack of fuel. One landed at Hornchurch and another at Fairlop. The one which landed at Hornchurch had been damaged, but not badly. The pilot, Lieutenant Butler, stated that his B17 No.25852 of the 384th Bombardment Group, 103 Combat Wing based at Grafton Wood, had bombed Stuttgart and remained over the target for 50 minutes. His aircraft landed at Hornchurch at 12.57 pm. He said he had only enough petrol to make one circuit of the airfield before coming in and was lucky to get in on his first approach.

The American crew were full of genuine praise for the work of the Spitfire escorts, again saying how much they preferred them to the P47 Thunderbolt fighters for escort work. They maintained that they owed their safety to the Spitfires which 'brushed off' at least two direct attacks from Focke-Wulf 190s.

On 8th September, an operation code-named 'Starkey' was put into effect. This deception operation against the Germans was put together by the Allied Joint Planning Staff. After many months of careful planning, Lieutenant-General Sir Frederick Morgan, who was Chief of Staff to the Supreme Allied Commander, Dwight Eisenhower, was then directed to carry out the deception plan. His task, to convince the German High Command that any intended Allied invasion back into Europe, would take place in the Calais area. This would be done by increasing the amount of bombing operations and fighter sweeps in that area. In the south-east of Britain, vast decoy army camps were built, as well as a build up of shipping and barges in various ports to deceive German air reconnaissance.

The Royal Navy was also heavily involved, making more sweeps up and down the Channel, within the range of the German coastal batteries. The deception was to continue well into 1944, when finally the Allies would be ready to launch the invasion of Europe. The Hornchurch Wing would be heavily involved with escorting the bombers during these raids and also attacking targets of opportunity like trains, marshalling yards, canal barges etc.

At 8.45 pm, Fairlop's station commander, squadron and flight commanders came over to Hornchurch to be briefed for Operation Starkey. Also present were Hornchurch's commanders, operations officer and personnel due to be on duty during the operation. The conference was called by the station commander who gave the general outline of the operation. Earlier during that day, news of Italy's surrender caused much celebration when it was relayed over the Tannoy system around the aerodrome and also by R/T to the boys in the air, who were on a sweep. The news was passed to the Fairlop Wing by the Polish controller, and produced a similar reaction.

On 15th September, a commemoration service was held at the station church conducted by the Padre Connop Price, in honour of the fallen in the Battle of Britain. It was the third anniversary of Fighter Command's momentous victory.

On 24th September, No.129 Squadron was again given the job of bomber escort, this time to Amiens. George Mason remembers the operation with good reason:

> We were just coasting out on the way home from the target, when Ricki [Hornchurch Sector control] warned us of Huns behind us. We turned sharply about and as I was attacking one FW190, I saw another diving at me from the stardboard beam. I thought he could not possibly hit me from there so I carried on with my attack.
>
> Silly me. One shell hit the engine a foot or so in front of me and another the radio, which was a foot behind me; there was

smoke everywhere. I thought I might make it back, at least far enough out to sea to be picked up by our side. The smoke turned to flames and I had to leave the aircraft. I baled out and became a prisoner-of-war.

I was sent to Dulagluft, then to Stalag Luft 3 in Sagan. I was moved from there to Balaria before the 'Great Escape'. Towards the end of the war, we were marched out of Balaria to avoid the Russian advance and finished up at a Stalag about 30 miles from Berlin. We were liberated by the Russian Army who frightened me more than the Germans. I escaped from them and eventually joined up with Patton's 3rd US Army at Halle.

Mervyn Young also flew with 129 Squadron and recalls:

We had three commanding officers while at Hornchurch. The first was a chap called Gonay, who didn't always see the difference between an American P47 Thunderbolt and a Focke-Wulf 190. He had a couple of close shaves, but managed to get away with it. He was a very nice person with a great sense of humour.

Then we had a guy named Tripe, then finally Charlton 'Wag' Haw. 'Wag' had flown during the Battle of Britain and then had been posted over to north Russia, flying Hurricane fighters against the Germans, near Murmansk. For this he had been awarded the Order of Lenin; I think there were only four people in the British forces who had received this award.

While I was at Hornchurch, one of the other squadrons was 222. They had a New Zealander called Ray Hesselyn, who they nicknamed 'Hess'. He had the most fantastic eyesight and had great success flying in Malta, claiming 12 victories before coming to Hornchurch. Our wing commander used to fly mainly with No.222, basically because he thought Hesselyn's eyesight was that good; it was very important to catch sight of the enemy, before they caught sight of you. During a patrol the wing commander would ask over the R/T, 'Hess, what do you see?' I don't know what the Germans thought about this.

On 3rd October, at 4.35 pm, the Wing was again airborne, led by Wing Commander Crawford-Compton, to act as 'high cover' for 72 B26 Martin Marauders of the 9th United States Army Air Force, on their way to the target, the Beauvais aerodrome. Just after leaving the target, the formation was bounced by 30-plus 109s and FW190s. Crawford-Compton led 222 Squadron down after them and at low level Flight Lieutenant Ray Hesselyn destroyed a 109 which he caught climbing up. Hesselyn himself was hit by a FW190 and his aircraft was set on fire. He managed to bale out, but suffered wounds to his legs. He became a prisoner of war.

Presentation of Spitfire (Uruguay XVI) by the Uruguayan Chargé d'Affaires took place at 11 am on 6th October. Air Vice-Marshal Roderic

Hill, Air Vice-Marshal Saunders, and Admiral Harwood were all in attendance; also Captain Harold Balfour, the Under Secretary of State for Air.

Weather was bad on the 14th; Ramrod 269 was laid on, but due to fog the Wing was unable to take off. Nearby an American P47 Thunderbolt fighter aircraft from Metford in Suffolk crashed at Herongate, near Brentwood, killing the pilot. Later in the day, a B17 Flying Fortress from Snetterton Heath landed at Hornchurch while returning from a raid on Schweinfurt in Germany. A large part of the aircraft's tail was shot away, and one member of the crew was wounded. The crew claimed seven enemy aircraft destroyed. They remained at Hornchurch with their aircraft overnight before being transported back to their base.

During the night of 17th/18th October, a German Messerschmitt Me410 twin-engine aircraft was shot down near Hornchurch by a pilot of No.85 Squadron. This crashed in a field close to Hornchurch's dummy airfield 'Q' site at Bulphan. The aircraft with a full bomb load disintegrated to such an extent when it crashed that only small pieces gave evidence that it was a Me410. All the crew were killed.

The Wing was detailed on Ramrod 263 to sweep Lille and Vitry on 20th October at 9 pm. In the Ostend area, Blue Section of No.485 NZ Squadron was attacked by four FW190s. Flight Sergeant Transom was hit in the oil tank; he was able to reach North Foreland, but he had to bale out west of Margate. Neither Blue 2, Flying Officer Baker, nor Blue 4, Flying Officer Thomson, returned and it was thought they had been shot down. The rest of the squadron continued with the sweep, which was uneventful over the Lille area.

On 25th October 1943, Acting Wing Commander David Scott-Malden, DSO, DFC, was posted from Headquarters Fighter Command, to Hornchurch as Station Commander. His Royal Highness the Duke of Gloucester visited on the 26th, to present No.164 British Argentine Squadron with their new badge. The aircraft of this squadron had flown in from Fairlop and were placed in a semi-circle around the presentation point. The presentation of the badge was made by His Royal Highness to Squadron Leader H.A. Russell, the commanding officer of 164 Squadron. Also present was Air Vice-Marshal Roderic Hill, CB, MC, AFC, the prospective Air Officer Commander in Chief of Fighter Command, and Air Vice-Marshal H.W.L. Saunders, CB, CBE, MC, DFC, MM, the Air Officer Commanding No.11 Group.

Representatives of Argentine interests in this country were also present and included the Right Honourable, the Viscount Davidson, GCVO, CH, CB, Mr Norman Leslie, Secretary of the Argentine Club, Robert Graham Esquire, Secretary of the River Plate House and Mr Ronald Leslie, President of the Anglo-Argentine Chamber of Commerce.

His Royal Highness was also shown the new and secret type of Hurricane fighter aircraft that was on view and in which he showed great interest. Afterwards, the party was taken to the Officers' Mess for cocktails and after a brief stay, the Duke left to represent the King at the funeral of Admiral of the Fleet Sir Dudley Pound.

Two representatives of the New Zealand Associated Press, Mr A.H.

Mitchell and Mr H. Warburton, also visited the station that day to interview and photograph personnel of No.485 (NZ) Squadron. It was also this day that RAF Fighter Command changed its name briefly to the Air Defence of Great Britain. Every fighter airfield would become a numbered unit. Hornchurch was designated as No.135 and Fairlop as No.136. Fortunately the name Fighter Command was reinstated on 15th October 1944. Visits were arranged for pilots on 1st November, as the rain continued to stop operations. One party of pilots went to the Ford Works at Dagenham, one to the Ind Coop and Allsops Brewery at Romford and the third party went to the Watneys Brewery near Victoria in London.

On 3rd November, squadrons of the Hornchurch Wing met up over Bradwell at 3 pm led by Squadron Leader Tripe of No.129 Squadron; their task was to provide cover to B26 Marauders attacking Schiphol Aerodrome. The bombers attacked in three box formations; the Wing covered each in turn over the target and then flew out to the coast. Bombing was excellent on the three main aerodrome dispersals, but intense flak was encountered and one Marauder, receiving a direct hit, went down in a mass of flames.

While the last formation was leaving, three 109s were seen below. Flying Officer Bradshaw (Blue 1) of 129 Squadron led his section down and destroyed one of the Me109s himself, seeing the pilot bale out. Half way home, the Wing was ordered to land at Manston, where they stayed overnight.

At 10.00 am on the 6th, seven Thunderbolt pilots from the United States Army Air Force Station Mitfield arrived and were given a talk on RAF defensive procedure. Later at 11.00 am, Station Commander Wing Commander David Scott-Malden gave the Wing a lecture on the policy of the air forces of the Allied Nations.

On 8th November, Squadron Leader K.T. Lofts led No.66 Squadron into Hornchurch, where they replaced their MkVI Spitfires with Spitfire LF IXBs, while New Zealand Squadron No.485 left for RAF Drem.

Many distinguised visitors were shown around the station during the month of November. The Regent of Iraq, His Royal Highness Emir Abdullah Illah, arrived on 15th November; his visit was part of his tour of this country's war effort. He was accompanied by Lieutenant General Ismail Ibrahim, Chief of General Staff, Brigadier Harry Chapman-Sinderson, physician to the Regent, Mr John Chaplin, Secretary of Intelligence at the Air Ministry and Wing Commander Growdon, the Foreign Office Liaison Officer.

On 21st November, the weather was very foggy and cold. The pilots of No.129 Squadron spent the day relaxing in anticipation of the squadron party. This took place in the station cinema and was attended by all the members of the station and by a large number of guests from '222' and station personnel. There was dancing and refreshments were provided in liberal measure. The gathering was honoured by the presence of Captain S.T. Binstead, the Trade Commisioner for Mysore and representative in London for His Highness the Maharajah of Mysore, who was interested to hear a report of the general activities of the squadron in recent months. The party was a complete success, being the first given by a squadron whilst at Hornchurch and remained another memorable occasion.

The day also marked another milestone in the history of the squadron. Squadron Leader P.V.K. Tripe, who in the few short months as commanding officer had gained the esteem of the whole of the squadron, was posted to Air Defence of Great Britain.

The Arabian Princes Emir Feisal and Emir Khalid visited on the 22nd. They were dressed in their national costume and looked quite stunning. Their Highnesses paid great attention to the aircraft and newsreel film was taken with them inspecting one.

No.129 Squadron received a new commanding officer on the 23rd, when Squadron Leader Charlton 'Wag' Haw DFM and Order of Lenin, took over.

On the 25th, His Excellency Senor Don Guillermo de Blanck, the Cuban Ambassador, presented two Spitfires on behalf of Cuba and representatives of the British community in Cuba, to No.222 Squadron. Also present was Lord Sherwood, who helped the Cuban Minister inspect one of the Spitfire cockpits; the aircraft was named 'Cuba Libre', and the other Spitfire was named 'Spirit of Marti'. Official confirmation was received that day that Flight Lieutenant George Mason of 129 and Flight Lieutenant Ray Hesselyn of 222 Squadron were prisoners of war.

On 18th December 1943, Peter James Simpson was appointed Wing Leader at RAF Hornchurch; he was the last Wing Leader that the station would have before the fighter squadrons were moved from Hornchurch down to advanced airfields in the south-east of England, to prepare for the D-Day invasion.

On 30th December, No.350 Belgian Squadron returned for their third tour at Hornchurch, and it was there that they changed to Spitfire IXBs, but they were to have a few problems. Sergeant fitter Alf Allsopp explains:

> The aircraft arrived whilst I was on leave. On my return from leave I found the squadron was grounded with engine trouble – surging (engine speed varying without any control from the pilot). When I arrived at 'B' Flight dispersal, I saw the flight sergeant standing watching the squadron engineer officer working on the carburettor of a Spitfire's flow meter-depth gauge etc. My reaction was, 'What's he think he's doing, I'm the sergeant fitter!'
>
> The flight sergeant had brought me up from being a corporal to being his second in command and we were the best of friends. He explained that no one had been able to diagnose or cure the trouble.
>
> As I explained to Chiefy my ideas, saying 'I can cure that in 20 minutes,' the Station Engineer Officer arrived and overheard my rash statement. Chiefy said to me, 'OK, big head, carry on.' I had serviced my first Spitfire in May 1939 with No.72 Squadron and had been working on nothing else since. The Station Engineer Officer then asked me what tools I required. I answered, screwdriver, pair of pliers, an oil can and a pilot. Off I went, did the necessary, up went the Spitfire with Flying Officer Venesoen in the cockpit. He landed 30 minutes later quite satisfied. Our own engineer officer came

up to me to find out the big secret. It was standard servicing procedure. Remove the triangular cover on the boost relay piston housing and insert oil to specification 34A/43B(anti-freeze)3.5cc(one teaspoonful). The engineer officer went into hospital shortly after this incident and I was promoted to consultant engineer until he returned, which was fun as soon after the Spitfires started to leak oil and a few spots of oil on a Spitfire's windscreen makes a landing difficult. I have seen them land with hoods open, side door open and the pilot leaning out to see where they're going.

With 1943 at a close, Hornchurch had played its part in the build up of Fighter Command's offensive preparations against the German 'Iron Coast'. In 1944 this would culminate in the Normandy invasion, but what would the future hold for RAF Hornchurch?

# CHAPTER 5

# ADVANCE INTO EUROPE
## 1944

The beginning of 1944 saw the emphasis of the Allies' fight against the Germans continue with diversionary raids, to keep the enemy guessing where their main objective for launching a second front into mainland Europe would be. Many months of planning by the staff of Allied Supreme Headquarters had taken place and with it, the hope that by June, they would be ready to undertake such a large and formidable venture without considerable losses to the invasion forces.

For RAF Hornchurch, the coming year would see a considerable change in the aerodrome's operational standing and the duties it would undertake. The 1st January 1944 saw dull weather and no offensive operations. Flight Lieutenant (Acting Wing Commander) Peter J. Simpson DFC was posted from Hornchurch to No.20 Fighter Wing as Wing Commander Flying. Various VIPs visited Hornchurch's satellite airfield at Fairlop on 2nd January. Major Bigland of No.115 Heavy Anti-Aircraft Regiment, Royal Artillery, arrived to discuss matters arising from an exercise in which No.164 Squadron was to co-operate with the army. Other visitors were Captain E.C. Axe and Lieutenant W.C. Jenkins of the 52nd Battery Essex Home Guard, who made a routine visit to the station commander regarding airfield defence.

A large bombing operation was laid on for the morning of 6th January, which would have included the Hornchurch Wing, but this was cancelled later owing to unfavourable weather. However, six Ranger operations were planned of which four actually took place. Two by No.350 (Belgian) Squadron, one by No.129, and the other by No.66 Squadron.

The first operation of the day 'Ranger 3' was undertaken by 350 Squadron. Four of their aircraft took off at 12.25 pm and crossed the Belgian coast near Nieuport, then to Renaux and Courtrai. Near Weveleghem, one Spitfire was attacked by a FW190, which was lost in cloud. This Spitfire returned home alone crossing out at Ostend, but the remaining three Spitfires carried on and sighted 25 German 'E' (motor torpedo) boats heading to Dunkirk from the Nieuport direction.

Before the Spitfires were able to initiate an attack on the boats, they were suddenly attacked by two FW190s, which did such tight turns that the Spitfires were unable to get on their tails. The FW190s disappeared into cloud, and the Spitfires, now low on fuel, headed for home. After refuelling at Manston they landed back at Hornchurch. Ranger 4 was also undertaken by 350 Squadron at 1.35 pm but was uneventful, and they landed at 3.45 pm.

At 2.30 pm, Squadron Leader K.T. Lofts led a section of four aircraft of No.66 Squadron on the next Ranger. The French coast was crossed at Dieppe/Le Treport, the weather was very clear so the section penetrated as far as Londinieres, searching for motor transport targets. One large motor transport vehicle was seen, attacked and damaged. The section then crossed out south of Le Treport and landed at Hornchurch at 4.05 pm.

Flight Lieutenant Hancock led the last section on the final Ranger mission of the day. Four aircraft of No.129 took off and crossed the French coast, east of St Valery-en-Caux. A tugboat was seen towing three large covered barges, which they attacked diving from 3,000 feet down to 100 feet, observing many hits. Ten miles south, the section sighted two army service vehicles and they too were attacked. Strikes were again noted and the second enemy vehicle stopped and burst into flames. On their way out to the coast the Spitfires attacked further barges along the waterways. Thus ended quite an interesting, reasonable and profitable day.

On 11th January, the Wing led by Wing Commander Simpson was airborne at 10.35 am, when they flew up to Coltishall in Lincolnshire. There, they refuelled and acted as 'withdrawal cover' to 576 B17 Flying Fortresses and 165 Liberator aircraft, which were bombing targets in Germany. However, the weather was too bad to enable the Wing to take off. Later when it was possible to take off, the 'Return Group' insisted on the Wing remaining at Coltishall.

The Hornchurch Station Commander, Wing Commander David Scott-Malden, DSO, DFC, was also flying with the Wing that day. He remembers his time at Hornchurch during this period:

> When I went back to Hornchurch as Station Commander, most of my job was administrative, but I did do a little flying on the more exciting sorties, if Peter Simpson, my CO Flying, would allow.
>
> I do remember that because Hornchurch was so close to London and very accessible, we were a target for a lot of foreign visitors of all kinds, and this was really one of the things that took up a lot of my time. There were all sorts of Arab princes who had given money for the war effort and they wanted to see the Spitfires named after them and so on. Fortunately at the time I had a Squadron Leader Administration named Watts Jones, who in peace time had been the manager of Fenwicks, the fur garment store in Bond Street, London. He masterminded the whole reception of these visitors, and the program, which he produced. We followed it for every visitor who was inspecting an aircraft, and then had a flypast and a ceremonial lunch. So all I had to do was meet the distinguished guests and hand them over to Watts Jones, who treated them as if they were coming in to buy an expensive fur coat from his store. This took a great deal of weight off my mind.

During the early hours of 22nd January at 5.00 am, an enemy raid took place in the vicinity of the airfield and lasted for about an hour. When it was light, it was learnt that four unexploded bombs of about 50 kilograms were lying in the south-east corner of the airfield; one being extracted was seen to be minus a fuse and had a cracked casing. The bomb disposal section officer considered that this bomb had failed due to sabotage. There were in addition two larger bombs, which exploded on impact causing a large area to be covered with phosphorus.

Two senior officers of the Brazilian Air Force, Colonel Fabio Sa Earp and Lieutenant Colonel Reynaldo Joaquim de Carvalho arrived on the station on 24th January, to gain information for the Brazilian Air Staff about the organisation and life of an RAF fighter station. The two officers stayed here for three days and were accompanied by an interpreter from 11 Group. During the afternoon, the Station Commander, Wing Commander Scott-Malden gave a talk on the organisation of the station and its place in the chain of command from Air Defence of Great Britain.

Owing to the recent bombing, Air Training Cadets camp was cancelled at Hornchurch, on 29th January, but several cadets were given air experience during that Saturday afternoon. During the evening at 8.30 pm, an air-raid warning was given and at 8.50 pm, a number of incendiary bombs were dropped around the flying control building and the bulk petrol installation area. The station fire crew, under the direction of the Duty Fire Chief Officer, quickly dealt with two bombs which were burning on top of the petrol installation. The remaining bombs did not ignite and no damage was caused to any property in the area. The fire crew remained standing by throughout the night.

On the 30th, Squadron Leader Allcott, the No.11 Group Press Relations Officer, visited the station. It was learnt from him that the Hornchurch Sector total for enemy aircraft shot down was to date recorded as 905 destroyed. During the month of January, it was recorded that 24 officers of our American allies belonging to the 8th United States Army Air Force passed through the station for training liaison duties.

At the beginning of February, Hornchurch played host to members of the National Fire Service, when they gave a demonstration on 3rd February, on the method of combating fires and rescuing personnel from crashed aircraft. The party of firemen came from the fire station at Ilford.

Wing Commander David Scott-Malden, DSO, DFC, was posted away on 6th February, to No.84 Group, Mobile Control Unit for operations. He recalls:

> It was at Hornchurch that No.84 Group, Mobile Control Centre was formed ready for the Allied invasion of Europe.
>
> At the beginning of 1944, one of the mobile radar units, which were to be used for the proposed invasion of Europe, was formed on the airfield. We being the host station provided the entire administration etc, while all the rest of these people got all their lorries organised of the various sorts they were going to need. Their commanding officer was a chap named Group Captain Gerry Edge, who came to live at Hornchurch. He had to get all the mobile radar and the complete tented

camp organised and ready to move. I thought at the time, this would be a far more interesting job than being left behind at Hornchurch once the invasion had begun.

So I suggested to him that he might need some wing commanders when he finally went across the Channel; he agreed to take me on, along with Alan Deere and Miles Duke-Woolley. So when all of this material of men and machines was ready to move and could be packed up and put on the road, it was sent down south to of all places, the Goodwood race course.

The day started bright on the 13th. The Wing led by Wing Commander Simpson left Hornchurch at 1.00 pm, to act as close escort to 36 B26 Martin Marauders bombing construction targets in the Neufchatel area. No enemy fighters were intercepted.

Another air-raid alert was sounded at Hornchurch at 8.20 pm and lasted about 80 minutes. Gunfire was intense all around the local district and one enemy bomber, later identified as a Junkers Ju88, crashed in a meadow behind Havering Court swimming pool. There were only three in the crew, of whom two were killed and the other baled out and suffered a broken arm. He was taken for treatment to Oldchurch Hospital in Romford. Next day, he was interrogated, but he was very security-minded. Nevertheless the contents of the German's pockets were emptied and found to be very interesting. He had been carrying a valuable list of call signs and a lecture book of data.

On Friday, 18th February, at 7.35 pm, the final order for the closure of the Hornchurch Sector Control Room was received. Wing Commander Ronald Adam, who had previously been Operations Room controller at Hornchurch, sent this from Headquarters Fighter Command at Uxbridge. The final order on Ops 'A' Line to Hornchurch Sector read:

> Hornchurch Sector Operations Room, which has controlled Malan, Gray, Bader, Berry, Lock, Scott, Mungo-Park, Tuck, Kingcome, Wells, Gillam, Broadhurst, Freeborn, Stapleton, Denholm, Kingaby, Hugo, Esmonde, Stephen, Duncan-Smith, Scott-Malden, Hesselyn, Beaumont, Walsh, Deere, Finucane, Gilroy, Compton, Stevens, Gribble and many others who have contributed to the total of 906 enemy aircraft confirmed destroyed since the outbreak of war, will now cease to operate.
>
> Despite 7 major daylight bombing attacks during the Battle of Britain and innumerable night bombings, Hornchurch Sector never allowed itself to become non-operational by reason of attack. Hornchurch Operations Room will now stand down and its personnel are released to their duties elsewhere. What of the future? Though the Sector no longer exists its unique spirit of comradeship lives on.
> Per Ardua ad Astra

Not long after, the Operations Room at the Masonic Hall was stood down, and a farewell party was laid on for the personnel. Joy Caldwell was invited back as a guest. She remembers:

> A large crowd of Hornchurch Ops, WAAFs and other Ops personnel attended. During the middle of the evening, the side doors opened and in stepped 'Boy' Bouchier, 'Broady' Broadhurst and Ronnie Adams. They had all had a real 'skin full' previously in the Mess; we clapped like mad when they appeared. Drinks and food were consumed in great quantities, then much to my embarrassment 'Boy' Bouchier came over to me and gave me a great big hug saying, 'There's one of my Battle of Britain girls.' He wanted to know how I was, and where I was being posted to etc. I couldn't believe he could remember me after three years, then I guess the Battle of Britain was a special time at Hornchurch. It's hard to imagine now how closely we worked in Ops, during the summer of 1940. Rules, regulations and rank didn't stand for much. When I worked at Biggin Hill Ops, it was never the same for me.

On 19th February, Squadron Leader R. Watt-Jones, who had been the Station Administrative Officer for nearly a year, took over command of the station. During the early morning of that day, an air-raid alert had been sounded at 12.30 am, when an estimated 90 enemy aircraft flew over and a large number got through to the London area causing quite a lot of damage.

The very next day the Hornchurch Wing carried out two successful escort missions. Taking off early down to Manston airfield, they landed and refuelled before taking off again at 10.00 am to act as 'high cover' to 72 B26 Marauders bombing Gilze Rijen. The sortie was uneventful and they landed back at Hornchurch at 11.30 pm. At 2.25, they took off again, this time to provide withdrawal support to a large force of Liberators and Fortresses returning from a raid deep into Germany. The bombers were met south-east of Brussels and escorted back to this country without incident. One of the B17s, which had been to Leipzig, landed at Hornchurch in a somewhat battered condition. Fortunately all the crew was safe and it was accommodated on the base.

On 22nd February, the Wing carried out one of the longest shows ever undertaken. Airborne at 9.45 am, they provided close escort to 72 Marauders on a raid to Soesterberg, near Utrecht. The distance exceeded 440 miles and the estimated duration was two hours. They all arrived back at 11.30.

An impressive ceremony took place in front of the Watch Office during the morning of the 23rd, when Monsieur Pierlot, the Belgian Prime Minister, arrived to decorate six Belgian pilots, to commemorate their 100th enemy aircraft victory. Among those present were Air Marshal R. Hill, Air Vice-Marshal Saunders, Air Commodore McEvoy of No.84 Group and Monsieur Gutt, the Belgian Finance Minister.

Another raid had taken place on London and surrounding districts during the early hours. About 150 enemy aircraft made landfall of which 80 reached London. At the start of the raid the barrage was intense and only slackened off shortly before the 'All clear' had been sounded. It had easily been the heaviest attack in the district for some time. A stick of three bombs had been dropped on the south-east corner of the airfield and eight Spitfires of No.504 Squadron were completely destroyed.

The windows in the new Watch Office were all blown in and three dispersal huts were damaged. Three airmen were injured, two seriously. It was estimated that the enemy aircraft had been flying at approximately 8,000 to10,000 feet and had made a deliberate attack. The National Fire Service had responded quickly to the request for help at Hornchurch and by 2.00 am all the fires had been extinguished. By 4.00 pm, several new aircraft had arrived to replace those that had been written off.

Robert Ballard remembers:

> D-Day was looming and it was noticeable that not so many Spitfires were around: that they had all moved to forward advanced landing grounds on the south coast in April 1944, was not generally known. They were just not such a familiar sight, there was of course plenty of general air activity, but not directly related to stuff flying into and out of Hornchurch, but with one exception. Miles Martinet and Vultee Vengeance target towing aircraft were now a regular sight intermingled with the odd Spitfire.
>
> By now I was a member of the local Air Training Corps, 106 Orsett Hundred Squadron, as we were known.

On 5th March, North Weald assumed control of the Hornchurch Sector. A visit was made to Flying Control and Intelligence Section and the squadrons visited by the following officers; Flying Officer H.J. Crooks, Pilot Officer R. Mirams, Staff Officer B. Kenyon and Staff Officer J. Arthur.

No.349 Belgian Squadron flew into Hornchurch from Friston on 11th March for a brief stay, and while here undertook several operations before being moved down to Selsey on the south coast of Sussex on the 11th April.

At 12.50 am on 22nd March, most of the station personnel were kept awake by the heavy local gunfire as another German raid came over. Flares were dropped north-east of the aerodrome and two incendiary bombs dropped near the Sergeants' Mess, but were quickly dealt with. Another raid over the night of 24th/25th March between 11.45 pm and 1.00 am near Fairlop aerodrome, saw two enemy Junkers Ju88s shot down. One crashed in Redbridge Lane, Ilford, the other at Chigwell Row, Essex. The tail unit of one fell on the runway at Fairlop. Three of the German crew were reported to be at large somewhere in the area, but they were eventually captured and taken into custody at Barkingside Police Station. The five other crewmen had all perished, and arrangements for their funerals were made between RAF Fairlop and Hornchurch.

The defences at RAF Hornchurch were again tested during exercise 'Paradrop' on 14th April. The defence exercise started at dusk and continued until 11.59 pm the following night. Troops involved included No.2718 Squadron, RAF Regiment and the station's anti-aircraft flight and support flight, while the enemy troop's role was played by the men of the 20th Battalion, Essex Home Guard and Sector School personnel.

Another two new squadrons arrived to operate from Hornchurch on 24th April 1944. These were No.229 Squadron who had returned from Sicily, led by Squadron Leader N.F. Harrison and No.274 commanded by Squadron Leader J.F. Edwards. William Bird was a flight mechanic with No.229 Squadron when they were sent to Hornchurch, and recalls:

> I had previously visited RAF Hornchurch in 1940 as an air cadet with No.106 Orsett, One Hundred Squadron. My second contact was as a LAC flight mechanic.
>
> We had spent a two-week sea journey from Naples and arrived at Gourock, Scotland before being transferred to a troop-train to travel down to Hornchurch, with only one short stop at Preston. We arrived late in the evening at Hornchurch and were given a satisfying hot meal. The WAAFs had made our beds, the little angels, and were told that morning parade would be at 11.00 pm. These little girls in blue made us feel very important, as did everybody else on the station.
>
> The next morning we sung and hummed our squadron song as we serviced our Spitfires.
>
> (Sung to Lili Marlene)

> We are the fighting 229
> When we're not saluting, we're on the blessed line,
> We fight your battles anywhere,
> from Malta to Trafalgar Square.
> We are the 229, the fighting 229.
> We are the 229, the fighting 229.

> Our Spitfires were clipped wing Mark IXs, which we rode on to assist the pilot when taxying. One of the pilots did manage to put his aircraft's nose down into the allotments at Sutton's Lane, adjacent to the airfield. Contrary to expectations, it happened in the best of squadrons; 'prangs' were not that uncommon. Most certainly against the rules and regulations, was the occasion when one of our pilots flew over Hornchurch's hangars with flaps down. How foolhardy can one get? Although I have to admit at the time, we enjoyed this dangerous spectacle.

Another station defence exercise also took place on 29th April, code-named 'Solus'. A taxying accident occurred at 1.50 pm on 10th May, when an Avro Oxford which was about to take off for Lasham hit the windows of the Watch Office with its starboard wing tip. The aircraft's aileron was damaged, but no one was hurt.

No.274 Squadron fitted one of its Spitfire aircraft with bomb-racks on 15th May, and the pilots proceeded to try their hand at some bombing practice on the Rainham and Purfleet Ranges with four small smoke bombs.

No.80 Squadron flew into Hornchurch on 17th May, for refitting and re-organisation, before proceeding to Detling airfield for operational duties before passage to the Italian Front.

On 21st May, the station received four armoured Morris Reconnaissance Cars to add to the Station Defence Armoured Flight and given an operational role. No.274 Squadron carried out more practice bombing on the Purfleet Firing Ranges until around midday. A practice formation take-off was also tried out, and all twelve aircraft were airborne within 30 seconds.

During the early evening a fighter sweep was carried out by the squadron along with No.229, led by Wing Commander E.P. Wells. This was in support of a bombing operation by 24 Boston aircraft on the Douai marshalling yards. The weather was fine with no clouds, but the enemy was not tempted up to interfere with the raid.

As the build up to the D-Day operation continued, the south-east of England was now looking like one giant army camp. At Hornchurch it was no exception. John Cox recalls:

> Where I was living at the time, near Upminster Bridge, every road seemed to have army lorries or tanks parked on one side. They seemed to stretch for miles, obviously they were going to be sent to Tilbury or other ports, to be taken over to France. One of the roads near the aerodrome, Station Lane, also had vehicles lined up ready for the invasion. I remember doing the odd errand for the American soldiers who were in the area at the time; one in particular would get me to pass messages onto his girlfriend, for this he would give me chewing gum.

The Station Commander made a special announcement during the morning of 6th June 1944. His message over the Tannoy system relayed the news to station personnel that the invasion of Europe, D-Day had started, 'Operation Overlord' had begun. The Allies now had a foothold into Europe. The hope of all the people of the free nations was that very soon they would be able to undo the tyranny and unshackle the chains of Nazi Germany from the countries in Europe that had been overrun in 1939/40.

The German response a few weeks later to the invasion of the Allies at Normandy heralded a new and threatening age of weaponry. The new German wonder weapon was named Vergeltungswaffe or V1. The weapon was an unmanned flying bomb, which carried a high explosive warhead of 850 kilogrammes. Launched from long firing ramps, the rockets were guided by a pre-set directional compass and a gyroscopic unit, which sent signals to the elevator and rudder controls in flight. On the night of 12th/13th June 1944, the first reports of an unidentified object with flames pouring from the tail were received. The flying bomb continued its flight over Gravesend and once its jet pulse engine stopped, it crashed to earth and exploded on open ground at Swanscombe. There were no casualties.

For the next nine months, a total of 9,251 of Hitler's new vengeance weapon would rain down on the civilians of London and the south-east of Britain. The people of Britain who had endured so much hardship and pain during the blitz in 1940/41, were again to suffer considerably from the 'Doodlebug' menace, as it was now to become known. Over 5,500 civilians would perish.

An air-raid alert was sounded on the station during the early hours of the morning that the first hostile unidentified flying bomb was heard and seen. They were afterwards identified as pilotless flying bombs. During the evening of the 23rd June, an ENSA show was interrupted briefly by a flying bomb that exploded a few hundred yards from Hornchurch aerodrome. A few windows were broken in the Station Cinema and other buildings on the Sutton's side of the drome. At 7.07 am, a V1 flying bomb exploded on the flightpath of the aerodrome leaving a rather large crater, which had to be filled in later in the day. One V1 also exploded in Elm Park causing many casualties.

On 27th June, no less than 59 V1 flying bombs had been logged on record by Hornchurch Flying Control on that day. The Station Commander received a letter of appreciation on 12th July 1944 from the residents of Hacton Lane, Hornchurch. Hacton Lane was the scene of a flying bomb incident on 23rd June. RAF Hornchurch organised rescue squads and first-aid parties to help at the scene. A cheque for £7 15 shillings was donated by the residents for the RAF Benevolent Fund.

A conference was held at Hornchurch's Station Headquarters on 10th July, to discuss the formation of No.55 Maintenance Repair Unit at Hornchurch. Officers present during the meeting were: Group Captain Moore, Air Defence of Great Britain, Group Captain H.W. Evans, Officer Commanding No.55 Repair Unit, Squadron Leader Harkness, also of No.55 RU and Group Captain Lowe of Headquarters No.11 Group.

A full Station Church Parade was held on 16th July, led by the massed bands of the Air Training Corps (Hornchurch Wing) who also played in the church for hymn singing. A short musical interlude was also introduced at the cinema. This was very well received, the film being Jane Eyre.

On 20th July, the old cookhouse, which had been used as a gymnasium for some time, was re-opened as a dining hall. No.2 Mess Hall was now completely taken over by No.55 Repair Unit detachments, which had been arriving at Hornchurch for the last couple of days.

A summary of V1 flying bomb activity in the local vicinity for July recorded that 215 were seen by Flying Control, 55 were heard, but not seen, while 19 crashed into the London barrage balloons. Two crashed approximately 100 yards outside south-west of the 'drome, four were seen to crash 300 to 400 yards outside the aerodrome. No operational squadrons were now located at Hornchurch or at Fairlop, which had been reduced to a Care and Maintenance basis.

During August, there was no change of policy laid down for RAF Hornchurch; the station continued to be used as a Holding Establishment and as a Forward Station in the North Weald Sector. No.55 Repair Unit was located here. The function of the unit was to repair the property in London, that had been damaged by enemy flying bombs. The areas to be covered by the unit from Hornchurch would be Deptford under the command of Warrant Officer Kelly, Hackney (under Warrant Officer Watson), Lewisham (under Warrant Officer Horner), Leyton (under Warrant Officer Castle),

Walthamstow (under Warrant Officer Caley) and Wanstead and Woodford (under the command of Warrant Officer Bailey).

Harry Bullock served with No.207 Flight, Maintenance Unit, No.55 Repair Unit, and recalls:

> We were an all volunteer unit formed with people with building trade experience and were formed at RAF Hornchurch. I was then with No.25 Squadron at RAF Coltishall, where they operated Mosquito night-fighters. I was a very fed-up young airman at the time, for all of my friends had gone to Normandy. They would not let me go because of my dental problems, so I volunteered for the London job.
>
> I was a joinery apprentice, so was, I suppose acceptable. I would think we were over 1000 strong. We were then formed into flights, mine being No.207. Each flight was issued with a Bedford QL troop carrier and a truck something like a pick-up. The Ministry of Works supplied tools and materials. Hornchurch airfield resembled a large builder's yard.
>
> Every morning we left Hornchurch at about 7.00 am, and it was quite a sight to see all these vehicles leaving the camp. Our destination for the first few weeks was Wandsworth, which was quite a run from Hornchurch. Although we were up to a point under the Ministry of Works, we were still very much in the RAF and subject to RAF discipline. Because of the hazardous nature of the job, we were given a 48-hour leave pass every four weeks. And hazardous it certainly was. We did a 12-hour day and there was very little sleep at night with the V1 flying bombs coming over most of the time. Narrow escapes were many and we did suffer casualties.
>
> The worst of these I seem to remember was at a lunchtime when some of our chaps were in a Woolworth's store in New Cross. A flying bomb hit the store and casualties were high. It was very upsetting having to dig people out of piles of rubble, many dead and badly injured, men, women and children. The unit stayed at Hornchurch until around the middle of December, we were then moved to Kew in London.

It was noted that there was a lack of adequate bathing facilities for the personnel of No.55 Repair Unit, who were employed in some of the worst slum areas in London, and this was causing some concern. It was therefore decided to install communal showers in the laundry of the Sutton's Institute, situated near the station. This was approved by Headquarters, Air Defence of Great Britain, and was put into effect immediately.

At 3.30 am on the morning of 6th August, a flying bomb cut its engine over the aerodrome and glided over the Officers' Mess crashing onto houses next to the railway line at Elm Park. Considerable damage was done. The commanding officer immediately despatched the station ambulance to assist in the evacuation of any casualties. No warning of flying bomb activity had been passed from the Operations Room B at North

Weald and the civilian alert had been late in sounding.

During the last four days in August, the following movements of units to and from Hornchurch took place.

On the 26th, No.5516 (Works Flight) moved from Lashing to Hornchurch for employment at Fairlop to repair the living quarters that had been damaged by flying bombs. An advance party of 200 personnel of No.24 Balloon Centre arrived on the 28th, and then departed for Fairlop, where a Balloon Centre was to be located concerned with the deployment of the Anti-Diver Balloon Barrage to counter the threat of the flying bombs. The main party of this unit would arrive on 3rd September. On the 29th, No.93 Embarkation Unit left the station for Fairlop.

A heavy explosion was heard at 8.20 am south-west of the aerodrome on 12th September 1944. Dagenham police reported that the Heathway Special School had been struck, and that Mr Ingliss of estate agents Messrs Kelsey and Hayes had witnessed the object that struck the school. He described the weapon as being cigar-shaped with a burning light glowing from one end, falling vertically. This was the start of the V2 rocket campaign.

The V2 rocket was the next giant step up from the V1 flying bomb. Designed by German rocket engineer Dr Werner von Braun, it was 46 feet in length and had the power to climb to an altitude of 50 miles, where no Allied aircraft could intercept as they could with the V1. The rocket travelled at up to 3,600 miles per hour and carried one ton of explosive in its warhead. Because of its incredible speed, there was no warning and no defence against this super weapon; it took just over five minutes from taking off to reach its target in London. In reality, this was the first intercontinental ballistic rocket. Between September 1944 and March 1945, 1,115 V2 rockets were launched against Britain, with some 2,824 civilians killed.

After the war, Werner von Braun was taken to the United States of America and during the 1950s and 1960s he was heavily involved with America's rocket development, which finally led to the space programme and the landing of a man on the moon on 20th July 1969.

RAF Southend ceased to be a satellite of Hornchurch on 27th September and was transferred to Balloon Command on occupation of No.951 and 958 Squadrons. On 6th October 1944, Hornchurch's dummy airfield 'Q' site ceased to operate and was permanently withdrawn.

At 7.30 pm on 10th October, an Avro Anson endeavoured to land and attempts were made to home it in on searchlights. Unfortunately on landing the aircraft ploughed into No.3 hangar. The pilot was very seriously injured and two of his passengers suffered shock and minor abrasions.

The alert was sounded over the aerodrome at 1.42 pm on 15th October, when a Doodlebug flying bomb passed over travelling west-south-west, pursued by one of our fighter aircraft which was firing at it. It finally crashed four to five miles away.

At 12.40 am on 5th November, a V2 rocket fell approximately 100 yards off the south-east corner of the aerodrome. The explosive stores were damaged by the blast, some of the walls being badly wrecked and the steel doors blown in or blown open. The explosives were re-located to other storage buildings. 'A' Flight of No.278 Squadron, arrived at Hornchurch on 7th November. The squadron was here to carry out Air-Sea-Rescue duties.

On 14th November, a detachment of No.765 Squadron, Naval Co-Operation, Fleet Air Arm, led by Lieutenant D.H. Coates arrived on the aerodrome with its Vickers Wellington aircraft, to liaise with No.567 Squadron to record the efficiency of radar installations, calibration, target towing and gun-laying.

At 4.25 pm on the 15th, a Vickers-Armstrong Warwick aircraft of No.278 Squadron crashed at Toothill near North Weald, ten minutes after taking off. The port engine had caught fire because of a defective petrol pipe. The pilots, Flight Lieutenant Garden and Flight Sergeant Evans, were seriously injured; the remainder of the crew suffered from shock and bruises. The aircraft completely burnt out.

The station was visited by one of its old commanders on the 19th, when Air Commodore Cecil Bouchier CBE, DFC, arrived to spend a few happy hours talking to various personnel on the base. At 11.00 am on 23rd November, a Hawker Hurricane LF577 of No.567 Squadron (No.70 Group) crashed at Detling, and the pilot Flight Sergeant Daniel, was killed.

A very heavy explosion was heard at 11.02 am, west of the aerodrome on 26th November. A rocket had exploded near Cherry Tree Lane, near Rainham. A few windows and very slight damage was done by the blast to the aerodrome buildings.

An important conference had been held at the Air Ministry on 24th November, which Hornchurch's station commander and administration officer both attended. It was held to decide action to be taken to transfer the major part of No.55 Maintenance Repair Unit to Regent's Park and to form the 'Marshalling Area' at Hornchurch. It would consist of a Concentration Area, at present at Old Sarum, Wiltshire. The Marshalling Area would be known as 'S4', operations to start from 14th December 1944. It would be used to accommodate a large number of vehicles, ready to transport the large amount of incoming service personnel and equipment coming back from Europe.

On 27th November, two further conferences were simultaneously held on the station. The first conference included representatives from the Air Ministry Department of Organisation and Works, Headquarters Fighter Command, No.11 Group and the Superintendent Engineer of the General Post Office. The chief points of the conference were as follows:

> *Accommodation:* In view of the stipulation by the Air Ministry that accommodation must be based on a 32-square-feet basis as a minimum, it became apparent at Hornchurch that the eight Army huts located in Sutton's Lane would have to be brought into use. Once this accommodation was available, it would be possible to house 900 senior NCOs and men in the Sutton's Institute, and leave sufficient accommodation to house the transit personnel in the remainder of the institute.
>
> The static staff of the Marshalling Area section would be accommodated in the main camp. It was agreed that senior NCOs and officers in transit should not use the station messes.

*Motor Transport:* It was agreed that a Marshalling Area should hold up to 400 vehicles and that they would be set up in the side roads of Maybank Avenue, near the main station entrance. In this connection, it would be necessary to provide suitable roadside latrines.

*Catering:* It was agreed that No.2 Mess should be set aside for the transit personnel and the repair unit detachment.

*Entertainment and Welfare:* It was agreed that the entertainment and welfare of transit personnel was of paramount importance, and to this end, the Entertainment's Officer provided on the establishment of Old Sarum airfield was to be transferred to Hornchurch. A 24-hour service would be required in the NAAFI allocated to the use of transit personnel.

The second conference, at which the same representatives as the first attended, prepared a new station establishment, to meet the additional commitments.

A signal was received at Hornchurch on the 28th, that the whole of No.55 RU would be transferred from Hornchurch, thereby leaving sufficient accommodation for the Marshalling Area within Sutton's Institute without taking over the army huts.

On 1st December 1944 at 12.15 pm, Biggin Hill Control reported that a pilot of No.567 Squadron was in trouble. Unable to contact him over the R/T, it was later learnt that the aircraft, Hurricane LF584, had crashed and that Flight Sergeant M.L. Williams had been killed. It was also on this day that Group Captain R.J. Clare-Hunt was posted from Headquarters No.10 Group to command RAF Hornchurch.

A Miles Martinet of No.567 Squadron force-landed on the 6th December at Linford, Kent. Fortunately the two-man crew of Flight Sergeant Brees and Sergeant Lawes escaped uninjured. At 4.50 am on the 9th, an enemy rocket landed in the centre of the north/south flightpath, but by 5.30 pm that evening the damage had been repaired. Group Captain R.J. Clare-Hunt assumed command of the station from Squadron Leader R.S. Davies on the 11th December.

The Marshalling Area duly commenced the transit of service personnel to and from Europe on the 14th. Between 14th and 31st December 1944, 1,532 personnel were passed outwards through the base and 270 inward. Two ENSA Shows and one Gang Show were held during the month. Henry Hall broadcast from the Station Cinema at lunchtime in a 'Break for Music' programme on 24th December. There was a special all ranks invitation dance on Christmas Day and a programme of varying entertainments was arranged to the end of the year, culminating in a New Year's Eve Dance.

# CHAPTER 6

# VICTORY AND PEACE
## 1945 – 1946

The opening of the New Year was well and truly celebrated at RAF Hornchurch, where the New Year's Eve dance held at Sutton's Institute building finished at 1.00 am on 1st January. However everyone was brought back to earth at 1.53 am, when the first enemy rocket explosion of 1945 was heard nearby. The weather on 1st January was fine with some sunshine, although visibility was restricted. The station football team continued to play matches. On 6th January the team played Tilbury Fort and won by six goals to one.

A signal was received on the 16th that 27 Naval officers and 38 ordinary ratings had arrived at Tilbury Docks, the survivors of Craft No.436, which had been torpedoed in the Channel. On arrival at Hornchurch they all attended sick quarters and were given an issue of rum. There were no serious injuries amongst the men, but three were admitted to hospital overnight.

The weather on the 17th was foggy and visibility was down to 500 yards when a Lancaster bomber aircraft made a hurried but successful landing at Hornchurch. Robert Ballard recalls the event:

> A Bomber Command Lancaster made a speedy landing. It made its approach from across the Sutton's end of the aerodrome, seemingly to just miss the chimneystack of St George's Hospital, such a familiar landmark at that time because it was then much taller than that seen today. The Lancaster touched down safely, and taxied up to the Watch Office area. Out stepped a Group Captain; the Lanc then without delay turned and taxied hurriedly back from where it touched down and hastily took off again, the whole venture lasting no more than a few minutes. I remember thinking at the time, how skilfully the Lancaster had been flown.
>
> It was also around this period when we were seeing Warwick aircraft of the Air-Sea-Rescue at the airfield. They had a lifeboat slung beneath the fuselage. They were dispersed mainly over at the south-east corner of the airfield. I remember they took a longish run across the field before becoming airborne.

On the same day, Squadron Leader L.V. Fisher, Flight Lieutenant E.P.

Loader and five other pilots arrived from the Aeroplane and Armament Experimental Establishment at Boscombe Down, for experimental trials of 500lb MC bombs with anti-ricochet parachute attachments and spikes, which were to be tried out against railway targets at Shoeburyness.

On 28th January, the weather had turned cold and there was a slight snowfall. The entire WAAF section moved from their sleeping quarters in the Married Quarters to Wellington Block owing to the severe freeze. The Central Signals Workshop was transferred from its temporary location in the High Frequency Transmitting Station to a permanent location in the Main Signals Block. This move contributed to a large degree to increasing the efficiency in the servicing of aircraft equipment. The Station Signals strength stood at:

|         |     |
|---------|-----|
| RAF     | 14  |
| WAAF    | 40  |
| Civilian | 3  |
| Total   | 57  |

The number of messages handled by Signals in January was: In 1,743/Out 677.

The month of January was chiefly memorable for the extremely cold weather which continued right up to the end of the month, when a complete thaw set in. The night temperatures were the lowest for some years. Fuel supplies were somewhat limited, but the electric power on the aerodrome never failed.

The Marshalling Area (S9) continued to function normally despite the weather, although there were a certain number of cancellations both inward and outward. In some cases personnel were 'shut out' at the Port of Embarkation, and had to return to Hornchurch.

The statistics of transit up to the 31st January 1945 were as follows:

| | |
|---|---|
| Number of personnel in transit (including reverse parties) | 8,902 |
| Number of units in transit | 306 |
| Number of vehicles in transit | 2,767 |
| Number of vehicles repaired by MTRS | 462 |

Number of meals served:

| | |
|---|---|
| Breakfast | 12,251 |
| Lunch | 13,641 |
| Tea | 9,524 |
| Supper | 6,471 |
| Total | 41,887 |

Haversack Rations      6,667

| | |
|---|---|
| Amount of Sterling exchanged | £31,655.13s.d. |
| Number of Belgian francs issued | 3,806,355 |
| Number of French francs | 93,500 |
| Number of Dutch guilders | 5,913.50 |
| Approximate cash takings of NAAFI | £3,000 |

A number of vehicles of the troop carrier type, together with a number of load carriers of various types, were allotted to Hornchurch and taken on strength to cope with the new commitment of ferrying men and kit to the docks. They would also collect bulk petrol from storage and convey the fuel to the vehicle marshalling area. It soon became evident however, that the existing motor transport facilities were quite inadequate to cope with the expansion of the station, running transport, convoy servicing and refuelling commitments.

At the beginning of January, the original Motor Transport Yard was turned over completely to the Motor Transport Repair Service and became the central repair depot for all transport running on the station, in addition to undertaking repairs and servicing for No.6221 Bomb Disposal Flight. Up to the end of January 1945, some 460 vehicles from various convoys had been brought in for work of all kinds, necessitated to make them serviceable, and in all 2,630 vehicles had passed through the transit camp.

The weather at the start of February remained dull with slight drizzle and no flying took place. On 7th February, nearly 700 personnel arrived which brought the numbers into the camp up to 900. This was the largest figure up to date for any one day.

At 11.20 am on 9th February, a Tiger Moth of No.567 Squadron landed in a field at Rohenfield, Tunbridge Wells. The pilot of the aircraft, Flight Sergeant Powell, tried to take off again and crashed; the plane caught fire and Powell leapt clear although he sustained injuries to his left leg and burns to his face. He was taken to Tunbridge Wells Hospital.

The aerodrome was reported as U/S, when bad weather including a gale swept the area on 12th February. On the 14th, an Auster Mk1 aircraft, serial No.LB337 with a Cirrus Minor engine was flown in to Hornchurch for the use of the Station Commander. A visit of inspection was paid by Squadron Officer G. Wilson of Headquarters No.70 Group on the 22nd, to WAAF personnel of No.567 Squadron. She reported that the airwomen appeared to be happy and contented. The WAAF officer took a personal interest in their welfare.

On 26th February, a Vultee Vengeance aircraft of No.567, flown by Flying Officer Gibbon, was seen to be on fire while coming into land on the west extension flightpath. The station crash-tender was soon on the scene and extinguished the flames; no one was hurt. Approximately 200 personnel and three vehicles of No.616 Squadron arrived from Tilbury on 28th; the unit departed from Hornchurch a few days later, but for some reason was not allowed to disembark. The personnel were all fed, currency was exchanged and they were sent off to St. Andrews Field.

Local police at Romford informed Hornchurch on 5th March 1945, that they should be on the look-out for two escaped German prisoners of war, one a fighter pilot, the other a soldier. However the following day news arrived that they had been recaptured at Warmington Airfield.

On 8th March, 25 Italian co-operators (POWs) were posted to RAF Hornchurch from Hednesford. Sergeant Brown was the officer in charge. After arriving they were accommodated on the main camp. The Station Commander would act as Camp Commandant with the Station Intelligence Officer in charge. The Italians started work at Sutton's camp (S9), sweeping roads and generally tidying up around the outside and insides of buildings like living quarters, canteens and mess rooms etc. Their working hours were 8.30 am till 5.15 pm with an hour for lunch, here they were under the orders of Flight Lieutenant Bernard and supervised by Sergeant Waterfield. On the whole the POWs behaved well, but to get the best out of them it required more supervision than could be given, considering the size and dispersion of buildings in which they worked and which were a mile from the camp.

At 12.15 am on 12th March, a V2 rocket exploded on the aerodrome. The NAAFI buildings were almost destroyed, while the airmen's cookhouse and rest room and the Sergeants' Mess was badly damaged. Other buildings had to be brought into use or doubled up to carry on with normal functions which were already stretched by the coming and going of transients.

One of the main features of March 1945 was the wonderful summery weather. On some days during the third and fourth weeks, it was very hot. On the 17th, the temperature in London was recorded at 82 degrees and 24th March was recorded as the hottest March day in fifty years; the number of flying hours put in by the squadrons was above average. Although ground mist hampered flying to a certain extent, sixty aircraft arrived during the month for re-fuelling or daily inspections.

Robert Ballard remembers his visit to RAF Hornchurch on 24th March 1945:

> My opportunity came when a party of our Air Training Cadets was selected to go to Hornchurch for weekend camp. It was the sort of adventure encouraged at the time so as to give us young budding would-be RAF types, an experience of an active RAF station. Having first assembled at Grays railway station at the first light of dawn, we travelled by train and then on the District Line, and alighted at Elm Park station, where upon our small party formed ranks for the march to the RAF station. After all, we cadets were to arrive in due smart order befitting the ATC and in accordance with discipline, indeed the very sharp discipline; always very much in evidence at Hornchurch.
>
> Breakfast in the airmen's mess was followed by a visit to the astro-dome trainer situated behind the Good Intent pub. The astro-building was a domed massive thick concrete structure, equipped with a special projector reflecting film onto the ceiling of aircraft flying with realistic sound. The idea was gunnery training utilising an imitation type machine gun like a Lewis, with which we took sight and aim, and squeezed the trigger when our sights lined up on a cine film aircraft. It was all realistic and good fun. The only trouble was the contraption that recorded the hits revealed that the cadets were scoring more hits than rounds being fired.
>
> The more serious real bullet rifle shooting on the station's rifle range was situated at the north-eastern corner of the airfield perimeter, near to Sutton's. Here we were initiated to

the art of 0.303 calibre rifle shooting, and it turned out our marksmanship left much to be desired.

The afternoon treat of a flight was what we had all eagerly been waiting for. An Airspeed Oxford, with camouflaged upper and yellow undersides, serial No. P8919, was available for the purpose, taking half a dozen of us up at a time for an approximate 40-minute flight. The route for each trip was out across Rainham, Purfleet, Grays and down the Thames to Southend Pier; upon reaching that point, the pilot did a couple of turns over the pier before flying back via Rochford and across Bulphan fens. The three camouflaged hangars at Hornchurch came into view upon where the pilot made a gentle landing and taxied back to the watch office by the main central hangar from where we had started. After the flight, those of us that had been up, lingered by the T Square near the watch office, watching the remaining cadets go off and later return. An unforgettable experience.

On the 26th, the aerodrome escaped another near miss, when a V1 exploded west of the aerodrome at Ravenscourt Drive in Hornchurch. The blast caused minor damage to Sutton's sick quarters' roof.

During the month of March 1945, 59,006 meals had been served to personnel in transit. Over 50,000 haversack rations consisting of two rolls, one meat, one cheese and a bun had been packed since 1st December 1944. All the contents of these packs had being made on the station. Because times of transit departure were now being spread considerably, the messes were now serving meals for 21 hours of each day. On 3rd April, transit vehicles carrying explosives were allocated special selected hard standings while on the aerodrome. This was done in agreement with the Station Commander and the Bomb Disposal Officer in charge.

An interesting wartime incident was reported to Flying Control at Hornchurch on 15th April 1945. No.11 Group Intelligence warned them that a private, who had escaped detention in the Paris area, had stolen a Piper Cub aeroplane and had landed at Rochester in Kent, posing as a Sergeant Coombs. From there he took off again and headed for the American airfield at Earls Colne in Essex. It was later reported that he eventually landed at Raydon in Suffolk, where he was apprehended and placed into custody.

The next day, Flight Sergeant Downing of No.567 Squadron distinguished himself by landing his damaged Vultee Vengeance aeroplane at Hornchurch. His aircraft's elevators had become jammed while towing a target drogue during an anti-aircraft exercise. The drogue towing cable had been severed by anti-aircraft fire and had coiled itself around the elevators. He managed to land the aircraft without serious damage and was praised by fellow officers.

Robert Ballard, now a regular visitor to the aerodrome with the ATC, recalls:

The target towing operating types of aircraft were still in

residence. The Vultee Vengeance was a very large aircraft for a single engine machine with an unusual cranked type wing shape. Occasionally the odd American C47 Dakota or P51 Mustang would be parked on the airfield, no doubt making use of the convenient airfield location to London. I also remember the sight of some 30 or more black Avro Oxford aircraft, all parked over the eastern side of the perimeter, near to the wartime-built Control Tower. Our weekends spent at the station saw us cadets either billeted in one of the airmen's building blocks on the station or another time across at the Sutton's Institute.

The 19th April saw the arrival at the station of 47 dog handlers with 46 police dogs. The dogs were chained to upright posts opposite the administrative offices in Anson block. As there appeared to be no ships available to transport the animals over to Europe, the dogs were moved away and allocated to huts behind Defiant block. The dogs should have been fed condemned meat, but the Royal Army Service Corps could not obtain supplies, so horse flesh was obtained.

On 24th April 1945, Warrant Officer Dandridge of B Flight No.567 Squadron, in a Vengeance aircraft, was over the Thames estuary when his engine cut out at 1,000 feet. He then proceeded to do a 180-degree turn and landed on a sandbank about 10 miles north of Herne Bay, which was covered at high water. The pilot only received very slight head injuries and was rescued along with crew-member Flight Sergeant Baldwin who was unhurt. The aircraft was not salvaged.

The month of May opened with the high hopes of a speedy end to the hostilities in Europe. On the evening of the 1st May at 11.45 pm, the BBC Empire News broadcast the report of Adolf Hitler's death, although this was still officially unconfirmed. At Hornchurch on the 2nd, the advance parties of No.287 Squadron attached to No.80 Group and 116 Squadron of No.11 Group arrived for Army co-operation, calibration etc, and in the case of No.116, eventual disbandment.

The Director of the WAAF, Lady Welsh, accompanied by Group Officer Balfour and Wing Officer Pearson, visited the station on the 4th. The party visited all sections of the Station Headquarters and also Sutton's Institute and No.567 Squadron.

The hopes of victory were fully realised on the morning of 7th May 1945. Almost five years after the German invasion of France and the Low Countries, General Jodl on the orders of Admiral Dönitz, now head of the German government, signed the instrument of Germany's unconditional surrender to the Allies. The actual ceasefire took place as from 10.01 pm GMT. Hostilities however did not formally cease till midnight the following day, owing to Soviet disagreement.

The next day, 8th May, became Victory in Europe Day. This was made a public holiday, including for all personnel at RAF Hornchurch. A special Thanksgiving Service was held in the station church, but celebrations were the order of the day. At night the searchlight display over London could be clearly seen, as well as the glow of bonfires and fireworks. The Flying

Control staff, not to be outdone put up quite a good show. Throughout the evening parties were held in the various messes and much beer was consumed. A couple of days later the excitement of the victory in Europe was coupled with the premonition of changes and partings to take place in the near future. The station gradually began to assume a peacetime atmosphere.

On 11th May, a German naval officer prisoner of war, Lieutenant Noebauer, arrived under the escort of Lieutenant Commander McFadden, Royal Navy. He was taken aboard a Mitchell bomber aircraft that had landed at Hornchurch. The pilot, Flight Sergeant Wallace, and navigator, Warrant Officer Cross, flew it out of England and proceeded to Camp B3 near Bremen in Germany.

Another service of thanksgiving was held on 13th May. The whole station including the squadrons paraded and marched to No.2 hangar, where Padre Baker conducted the service accompanied by the station band.

An aircraft rarely seen at Hornchurch arrived at 4.35 pm on the 16th. A Flying Officer of No.287 Squadron flying a Hawker Tempest aircraft was unable to lower his undercarriage, but he managed to make a successful belly-landing.

A mini version of the Great Escape took place at RAF Hornchurch on 10th June 1945. Two airmen who were being kept under close arrest in the main guardroom, escaped by picking the lock and making their getaway over the high wall of the exercise yard. A few days later, they were spotted by a corporal who was in charge of the Italian co-operators at S9; they were trying to mix in with the transit units, presumably with the idea of getting over to Europe. They were immediately arrested and put under lock and key.

A Chinese journalist, Mr Nei-Chang Li gave a lecture on the Far East on 12th June. He was half an hour late in arriving, so records were relayed over the loudspeaker system to while the time away. On 15th June 1945, the station was transferred from Fighter Command to No.28 Technical Training Command with effect. This resulted in the closing of the Flying Control and the departure of the squadrons and aircraft to everyone's regret. Hornchurch also lost its three anti-aircraft co-operation squadrons on this day. No.287 Squadron flew out to Bradwell Bay, No.567 went to Hawkinge and No.116 disbanded. Also leaving Hornchurch for the last time was the Fleet Air Arm Squadron No.765 which flew down to RAF Manston before eventually returning to the Royal Navy Station at Lee-on-Solent.

Officers from Hornchurch attended a Royal Observer Corps Rally held at North Weald on 24th June. A flypast by numerous aircraft, including two German machines, was brilliantly displayed. Six of the new Meteor jets flew in formation and a helicopter gave a demonstration. About 1,800 personnel of the Royal Observer Corps marched past afterwards and Sir Norman Battersley on behalf of the Royal Air Force presented a cup to Wing Commander Crerar, representing the Royal Observer Corps.

A Coastal Command pilot had to make an emergency landing at the aerodrome on 9th July 1945. Avro Anson coded JM-G serial No.529 from 1693 Flight had taken off from Copenhagen with Lady Bowhill aboard as a passenger. The pilot, Flying Officer Gamlin, made the emergency landing at 8.05 am coming in on one engine and unserviceable brakes. The undercarriage sheared off as the aircraft swung to starboard when it overshot the flightpath; fortunately there were no casualties. The aeroplane was transferred to a hangar for preliminary examination of the starboard engine to figure the cause of failure.

The 19th July 1945 saw the formation of No.33 Personnel Despatch Centre at Hornchurch. An airman of No.6221 Bomb Disposal Unit Flight was rushed and admitted to the Rush Green Hospital near Romford on 24th July, after suffering from the effects of di-nitro benzene poisoning after having been engaged in steaming out the contents of an enemy bomb.

It was at midnight on the 14th August that a news broadcast relayed that the Japanese had accepted the surrender terms. The 15th and 16th August were declared public holidays for Victory over Japan celebrations and once again much celebrating took place at Hornchurch. His Majesty the King asked that Sunday 19th August be observed as a National Day of Prayer and Thanksgiving for victory and peace.

The station was visited by Air Commodore A. MacGregor, CBE, DFC, Air Officer Commanding No.28 Group on 28th August. After inspecting several sections of the station and talking with personnel he was taken for lunch at the Officers' Mess. The strength of station personnel at RAF Hornchurch up to 31st August 1945 was as follows:

| | |
|---|---|
| RAF officers | 49 |
| WAAF officers | 5 |
| WAAF | 59 |
| Airmen | 230 |
| Total | <u>343</u> |

The total number of ex-overseas personnel dealt with during the period from 10th to 31st August 1945 was 1,907. On average they were cleared from Hornchurch for leave within 48 hours.

On 3rd September, one of Hornchurch's old fighter squadrons, No.222, returned to the airfield's transit camp. One officer and 39 other ranks departed the next day for Western Zoyland. The aerodrome remained serviceable for emergency landings only, during the whole of that month.

On 1st October 1945, two teams were chosen from the station personnel for a Field Firing Competition, which consisted of two flying officers and 20 other ranks. The competition was held at Hornchurch and the Rainham firing ranges.

No.6221 Bomb Disposal Flight was still hard at work with enemy munitions. Prior to D-Day, the flight had been carrying out experimental work on all kinds of enemy munitions, which had been sent here from occupied and enemy countries for rendering safe. The information obtained from this was sent to the Air Ministry then to various disarmament commissions at present working in these countries. Lorries were bringing into Hornchurch an average of about six tons per month of munitions. They were also supplying various museums which had started in this country, such as the Armament School at Mawby, the Bomb Disposal School at Doncaster, the Historical Museum, RAF Farnborough and the Royal Arsenal, Woolwich.

October witnessed an impartial and interesting change in the work of the station armoury. On 2nd October, No.9 PDC Armoury, Regent's Park Unit moved to Hornchurch and the staff combined to become No.33 PDC Armoury. The workshop was re-arranged and fitted to facilitate a speedy and easy system to re-arm ceremonial units for parades dealing with 100 to 150 men. Stocks of rifles, Sten guns and revolvers had risen beyond all previous levels. Disposals were still going ahead for the remainder of the operational ammunition as used when the station was still an aerodrome of No.11 Group, Fighter Command.

During that month, No.2 RAF Gang Show was resident on the station for about a fortnight. They gave two shows while they were here, and then disbanded. No.1 Gang Show arrived on the station, was reformed and began rehearsing for a new show.

By the end of November, figures of transit personnel passing through Hornchurch had reached 67,423 since its inception. Two aircraft made emergency landings that month, a Mustang and a Percival Proctor due to fuel shortage.

The strength of RAF Hornchurch personnel at the end of December 1945 stood at: RAF officers 31; WAAF officers 2; WAAFs 210; other ranks 524. By the end of 1945, RAF Hornchurch had come to the end of its wartime service. The station had served valiantly through the dark days of 1939/40 to keep the Germans from invading this country. It then brought the fight to the enemy in 1941 and carried on until victory was achieved. Many pilots had lost their lives in the service of their country while flying from Hornchurch and their names are listed in a roll of honour at the back of this book. We must never forget the sacrifice.

## 1946

During January 1946, the No.6221 Bomb Disposal Flight at Hornchurch still continued to render safe enemy munitions and to carry out experiments on the new types of munitions found in the post-occupied countries. They performed their precarious work near Gerpins Lane, Rainham. Approximately 18 tons of explosives were dealt with since 1st November 1945. The transit camp was now designated as No.3 Personnel Disposal Centre and was handling around 500 airman a day.

The airfield was serviceable throughout the month. There was no emergency or crash-landings. The local Air Training Corps used the airfield for flying training on three days during January. The station sick-quarters held a display of venereal disease photographs in the station gym, during the last week of January, and over 50% of the station personnel attended.

The station's personnel strength at this time was:

| Officers | RAF | | WAAF |
|---|---|---|---|
| | 59 | | 5 |
| Other ranks | 613 | | 209 |
| Total | | 886 | |

During February, the transit of service personnel to and from Europe continued; on the 17th, four French WAAFs arrived for repatriation, departing on the following day. On the 28th, Hornchurch personnel completed the ferrying of captured German radar equipment from Tilbury to RAF Farnborough. Over the period of 6th, 7th and 8th March, 1,500 Belgian servicemen passed through the camp in parties of approximately 500.

No.6221 Bomb Disposal Flight still continued to render safe enemy munitions. During March, they dealt with the following: three HS.293 German glider radio controlled bombs, two German flying bomb warheads, one Italian circling torpedo, 18 German incendiary bombs and six anti-personnel bombs, a total weight of seven tons. The strength of personnel at RAF Hornchurch at 31st March stood at 839.

On 16th April, the mobile ENSA cinema, which had given so much pleasure, was withdrawn after having shown approximately 600 performances since its inception at RAF Hornchurch.

The bomb disposal squad of No.6221 carried out a reconnaissance at North Weald, to try to detect a 1,000kg bomb, which had been dropped in 1940. Although they covered over 2,000 square yards, they did not find it. By 31st May, figures showed that the number of service personnel who had passed through the transit camp since its inception, had now reached 82,544, and the total of vehicles passing through 14,051.

During May, the personnel of 6221 BD Flight were busy preparing a new 'boiling out' site at the Upminster gravel pits. Specimens of German radio-controlled glider bombs were made ready to be despatched from the airfield to No.94 Maintenance Unit and abroad to the Royal Australian Air Force. One nose of a flying bomb was patched and riveted by a local blacksmith. The unit also did extensive experiments with Polish mine detectors adapted for short-range bomb location.

On the sports front, Hornchurch continued to do well, both in football and cricket. The station football team played Purfleet Camp on 8th May, and came out winners 3-2, while the cricket team, playing against Tunnel Cement in Grays, won by 2 wickets.

Hornchurch received another new Station Commander on 14th July 1946, when Wing Commander G.W. Day took over from Group Captain Clare-Hunt. Airman LAC Avenell was involved in an accident at the aerodrome on 21st July 1946. He was admitted in critical condition to the Horton Military Hospital and then Queen Victoria Hospital at East Grinstead on the 26th. The station held its first ever Arts and Crafts exhibition during 23rd-28th September. Many works were entered by various ranks, and some by the wives living in married quarters.

Air Marshal Sir Ralph Sorley, KCB, OBE, DSO, DFC, the Air Officer Commander in Chief of Technical Training Command arrived to inspect the station on 18th November. After less than six months as Station Commander, Wing Commander Day was posted and his position was taken by Wing Commander S.H. Page.

On 9th December, the station was visited by Air Officer Commanding No.28 Group, Air Commodore C.P. Ledger CBE, who was accompanied by Major General A. Richardson DSO of the RAF Regiment. They had arrived to inspect a draft of 45 RAF Regiment officer recruits. At the end of the year the aerodrome fell silent as another Christmas approached. The hard work of transporting and helping service personnel at the transit camp had finally come to an end.

CHAPTER 7

# NEW RESPONSIBILITIES
## 1947 – 1950

The general duties and running of the station remained much the same; but in early 1947, owing to a major fuel crisis that hit the country and a severe winter that was spreading across Great Britain, the Aviation Candidate Selection Board, which had first opened its doors at Hornchurch in January was closed on 26th February. This was brought into effect because of the need to economise on main essential services. Since January, the Selection Board had dealt with some 800 applicants. By spring, RAF Hornchurch was up and running again, and on 28th June, the station received a new commanding officer when Air Commodore D. McFadyen CBE arrived to take up his position. Hornchurch at this time was also chosen as the site for the new Officers' Advanced Training School. This would remain at Hornchurch until August 1948. In October 1947, the Hornchurch Urban District Council announced that it had officially adopted RAF Hornchurch.*

### 1948

On 5th January 1948, the officer commanding along with the main party of the Recruits Advanced Drill Unit arrived at Hornchurch. A photographer and reporter of the *Air Force Review* also visited in order to obtain the necessary material to write an article. The unit was formed to provide the Royal Air Force with a ceremonial unit, which could be on hand to cover Royal or State occasions, military parades or funerals etc.

The 17th February saw Hornchurch supply an officer and 20 airmen, for a memorial service at St. Margaret's Church, Westminster for Air Marshal Sir Arthur Coningham, KCB, KBE, DSO, DFC, AFC. Coningham had been commander of the 2nd Tactical Air Force in North Africa during the war. Seven officers and 140 airmen formed part of an RAF contingent, on 26th April, as a route lining party on the occasion of the 25th anniversary of King George VI and Queen Elizabeth's marriage.

The formation of the No.86 Reserve Centre at Hornchurch in May 1948 saw regular flying return once again to the aerodrome. On opening, its establishment consisted of a squadron leader and two officers plus 12 airman. Their job was to keep up the standard of flying and navigation

---

*Author's note: RAF Hornchurch Operations Book for 1947 was unavailable at the Public Record Office at Kew, either having been destroyed or stolen.

competence for the many ex-RAF service types, who had now re-enlisted into the Royal Air Force Volunteer Reserve.

On 25th May, Flight Lieutenant L.T. Turner of the Recruits' Advanced Drill Unit at Hornchurch commanded the Guard of Honour at Northolt aerodrome for the arrival into England of the famous American Army Air Force General Carl Spaatz. Geoffrey De Freitas, the Under Secretary of State visited Hornchurch on the 8th June, but the highlight of the following day, the 9th, was when men of the Recruits' Advanced Drill Unit provided the lining route party for the King and Queen's cavalcade drive through Hornchurch Town centre, as part of their anniversary celebrations.

Squadron Leader J.S. Sallows visited RAF Uxbridge on 29th June, in connection with a Guard of Honour for the Secretary of State for Air and the handing over of the RAF Depot to the Olympic Committee of Great Britain.

On 1st July 1948, No.17 Reserve Flying School was formed. It was operated by the Shorts Aircraft Company, which was based at Rochester in Kent. The Reserve Flying Schools were seen as a suitable way of providing ex-pilots and navigators with the chance of renewing their flying skills, while learning more up to date methods and information. The pilots would use Tiger Moth and Chipmunk aircraft, while the navigators would learn on the Avro Anson and Airspeed Oxford twin engine aeroplanes.

One applicant who arrived during this period to pass through the Selection Centre for testing was Norman Tebbit. He passed through with flying colours and became a pilot officer. His first posting was to North Weald, where he joined No.604 'County of Middlesex' Squadron who were flying the Meteor jet aircraft at that time. He would later come to prominence as a Conservative politician and under the government led by Prime Minister Margaret Thatcher would become a Minister of State in the cabinet. He is now Lord Tebbit.

A Guard of Honour consisting of two officers and 50 airman under the command of Flight Lieutenant J. Nee, paraded for Air Vice-Marshal Ivelaw-Chapman who attended Hornchurch for the purpose of the Passing Out Parade of the Officers' Advanced Training School Course. During the month of July, the RAF Central Depository at Hornchurch experienced more releases of clerks' general duties. The Bomb Disposal Flight carried out more constructional work at the Upminster bomb cemetery and a 24-hour guard was now maintained. A German V1 flying bomb exhibit was lent to the recruiting centre at Romford, for display purposes at Chingford.

Ralph Reader who had been the originator of the wartime Gang Shows, visited the station on the 2nd September to organise the programme for that year's Festival of Remembrance, held at the Royal Albert Hall. A contingent of 150 airmen led by Squadron Leader J.S. Sallows participated in the event. A service held at the Romford parish church was attended by 40 airmen from Hornchurch on 19th September, commanded by Flight Lieutenant C.E. Turner. From there, they took part in the Battle of Britain Parade and service held at St Andrew's Church, Hornchurch.

On 11th October 1948, an advance party of the RAF Combined Selection Centre from North Weald, which was about to move to RAF Hornchurch, arrived under the command of Wing Commander R.S.

Derbyshire to prepare accommodation for receiving the CSC. The Combined Selection Centre opened its doors to candidates at RAF Hornchurch on 25th October 1948. Here candidates were put through various tests to assess their potential as future pilots and aircrew. These included medical, aptitude and intelligence exams.

By November 1949, RAF Hornchurch had been in existence for over 30 years and thus qualified itself for the honour of a station badge, which is given to squadrons and airfields within the Royal Air Force after 25-year service. Mr J.D. Heaton-Armstrong, the Chester Herald at the College of Arms, was contacted and told of the station's wishes and also the design that was to be put forward for the badge. This design would incorporate a bull's head to signify the town of Hornchurch and with it a portcullis, which would encompass the role which RAF Hornchurch and Sutton's Farm had earlier played in the defence of London and Great Britain.

A summary of work completed by the CSC during the period of 1st November up to 30th November 1948 detailed:

| *Direct Entry Volunteers* | | *NSA Special Pilot Entry Scheme* | |
|---|---|---|---|
| Total arrived | 387 | Total arrived | 30 |
| Recommended aircrew | 149 | Accepted | 10 |
| Commissioning | 26 | Rejected by medical | 1 |
| Rejected by CSC | 173 | Rejected by CSC | 19 |
| Rejected by medical | 32 | | |
| Withdrawn at request | 7 | | |

| *Serving Airmen* | | *Glider Pilots* | |
|---|---|---|---|
| Total arrived | 51 | Total arrived | 14 |
| Recommended aircrew | 24 | Rejected by CSC | 5 |
| Commissioning | 3 | Rejected by medical | 2 |
| Rejected by medical | 4 | | |
| Rejected by CSC | 20 | | |

| *Ex-released aircrew for re-enlistment* | |
|---|---|
| Total arrived | 135 |
| Recommended aircrew | 83 |
| Rejected by medical | 8 |
| Rejected by CSC | 35 |
| Withdrawn at request | 9 |

The station badge, which had been submitted to the College of Arms in November, was accepted after being sent to King George VI for his final approval. The King signed the commissioned artwork along with Mr Heaton-Armstrong. Royal Air Force Station Hornchurch would now be the proud recipient of a station badge. The motto at the base of the badge read 'First Things First'. With Christmas approaching, station personnel started to disperse for the holiday period on 23rd December until 28th December. Essential services on the aerodrome were maintained.

**1949**

The 8th January 1949 saw a public sale at the aerodrome of unwanted and unclaimed personal effects received by the RAF Central Depository. The sale raised £1,040 for the benefit of the RAF Benevolent Fund. On 31st January, Air Vice-Marshal R.V. Goddard KCB, CBE, visited the Combined Selection Centre for the purpose of seeing how it worked and also talking with future RAF airmen. The West Essex Wing Headquarters of the ATC was opened at Hornchurch on 22nd March, with a permanent officer and adjutant.

On 12th April, a visit was made by Flight Lieutenant F.G. Tipping and Flight Lieutenant H.G. Christmas to No.146 Gliding School, who were using the aerodrome.

On the same day, Mr E.N. Barrow, Mr C. Wigmore and Miss B. Sinclair, all of the Public Relations Bureau, Whitehall, visited for the purpose of taking official photographs of the RAF's new pattern uniform.

Demolition of some of Hornchurch's wartime blister hangars was approved by the Air Ministry on the 19th April. The buildings were now unwanted and becoming derelict.

With much unrest in the British workforce during 1949, the London docks were hit by a number of strikes, which brought the Port of London to a standstill. It was during this period that RAF Hornchurch was involved, for the accommodation of service personnel and transport units to keep the docks running.

On 6th July 1949, Operation 'Thames' ('Homeland') was put into action. The station received the orders by telephone that day, putting the operation into effect. A signal was received from the Air Ministry on the 7th, and during the day advance parties started to move into Hornchurch consisting of emergency transport units and emergency labour units. The extra men were accommodated in hangars and in a self contained tented camp on the western extension of the airfield. The signal for operational readiness was given on 22nd July, at 7 am. A force of 1,310 personnel was on hand to go to work on that day, out of an effective strength of 1,960 men.

Nos 3, 4 and 7 Emergency Labour Units were commanded by Wing Commander J.M. Southwell DFC, and known as 'A' Force. Nos 1, 2, 8 and 9 Emergency Labour Units were led by Wing Commander C.E. Draper, and known as 'B' Force, while Wing Commander A.K. Gatwood, DSO, DFC was in charge of the emergency transport units.

There had been a slow increase of personnel employed in the docks to tackle the strike, from 671 on the 15th, to 3,030 on the 23rd. Personnel ceased work at mid-day on the 23rd, when the strike was declared over. Dispersal of service personnel started on the evening of 26th July. The bulk of the force had left the station by 3 pm on the 27th. The station was back functioning normally by 8th August. Throughout the operation, the normal functions of the aerodrome had continued without serious interference. This proved that the basic plan of 'Homeland' was sound and workable.

Because of Hornchurch's lack of a concrete runway, jet aircraft were a very scarce item on the aerodrome. However, on 29th August, a Provost Jet flown by Squadron Leader Gillen visited the station. After he took off there were visible scorch marks along the grass flightpath.

The RAF Central Depository records for that month show that they were now dealing with fewer and fewer wartime personal effects:

| | |
|---|---|
| Casualty effects received | 85 |
| Casualty effects despatched | 41 |
| Unclaimed baggage received | 9 |
| Unclaimed baggage despatched | 19 |

No civilian clothing became available during this month for forwarding to the Air Movement Section at Oakington, for the RAF German refugee scheme.

RAF Hornchurch's commemoration of the 9th Anniversary of the Battle of Britain took place with the 'At Home' display on Saturday 17th September 1949 between 2 pm and 6 pm and admission was free, although the programme was one shilling. During the afternoon there was an aerobatics display by Meteor jet aircraft of No.500 Squadron, a flypast by a USAF B50 Superfortress and a Short 'Solent' flying boat as well as a Lincoln bomber. On the ground, the RAF Regiment Bofors anti-aircraft gun team gave demonstrations. Paratroops of the No.285 Q Battery Airborne Regiment Royal Artillery (TA) made jumps from a captive balloon. There were also trade exhibition stands, which displayed all types of aero-engines, weapons and equipment. In all, over 20,000 people attended. Special trips by air were also available. One could fly from Hornchurch to Rochester and return for the sum of £1 per person. The flying programme ended with a marvellous display by a Spitfire doing solo aerobatics.

On 25th September, Hornchurch provided a large escort and firing party for the funeral cortege of Flight Lieutenant Leonard Alfred Smith DFM, who had been killed when his Spitfire exploded at a Battle of Britain display at Leuchers, Fife. He had become an ace while flying with No.152 Squadron in Europe and in Burma against the Japanese. He was credited with 5 and 1 shared enemy aircraft destroyed and 2 damaged.

The funeral was held at the Romford Cemetery, off Crow Lane; the procession had moved off from the home of his sister, Mrs J. Rouse of 86 Norwood Avenue, Romford, led by the Central RAF Band from Uxbridge. As it approached the gates the band broke into two files, allowing the procession to pass through the cemetery, where a short service was conducted in the chapel by the Reverend F.A. Stroud, rector of St Andrew's, Romford. Many sympathetic neighbours gathered at the graveside to hear the salute fired and the Last Post and Reveille sounded. Among the mourners was his fiancée, Miss Mary Inglis, who had travelled with the body, when it came under escort from Scotland.

An Air Ministry signal P.3989, dated 11th October, was received at Hornchurch at 5.18 pm to order the start of the two-day Mobilisation Exercises 'Hawker' and 'Jamaica' which were carried off without any problems arising. Hornchurch was again brought to readiness for RAF assistance during the power station strike in December 1949. The first signal was received on 12th December, and stated that service personnel were required to provide labour to maintain electrical power stations in the

London area. RAF personnel started to arrive at Hornchurch during the night, to move into Littlebrook power station. By the following morning, other personnel had arrived to move to Barking power station. Group Captain Sturgis, the Station Commander, reported that no serious administration or operational difficulties arose, although it occurred during one of the peak accommodation periods for the Central Selection Centre. It was possible to accommodate up to 100 men in the station gym. In all some 165 service personnel were available.

One officer, two sergeants, four corporals and 27 airmen were dispatched to Barking, while one officer, two corporals and eight airmen with one 3-ton vehicle went to Littlebrook. On 17th December, the Air Ministry sent a signal to Hornchurch, which was confirmed by Squadron Leader Stephen, to stand down and put into operation the dispersal plan. The police provided escort through the picket lines, as there was still some civilian staff at the power stations. There were also some 80 Royal Navy personnel at Barking. All RAF personnel had arrived back at Hornchurch by 12.15 am.

The Station Dramatic Society was formed on 12th December 1949. There were 25 members, including officers, NCOs, airmen and wives, together with civilian girls employed on the station. The first play to be presented, *The Good Young Man* by the comedian Kenneth Horne, was to be performed by February 1950. By the end of 1949, the aerodrome's strength of personnel stood at 61 officers, 494 airmen, and 110 candidates. There were no WAAF officers and only 12 airwomen.

## 1950

A Families Club was officially opened at Hornchurch on Tuesday 17th January 1950. The object of the club was to improve the social and welfare facilities for the families of RAF personnel at the aerodrome. The new club started with 36 members.

Another dock strike hit the Port of London in late April 1950, and once again RAF Hornchurch was called upon. On 24th April, Operation 'Springtide' (Homeland) was put into effect. During that day, 250 men and 50 officers arrived on camp, 1,500 more arrived by the end of the next. Most were accommodated in tents once again, but in order to make more room, the WAAF personnel of Hornchurch were despatched to Uxbridge, until 5th May, when the strike was abandoned.

The RAF Hornchurch Sports Rifle Club continued its success in May. On the 15th, in a contest between the Metro Gas Company, Hornchurch won by 253 points to 239, out of 300. Within their ranks were also three outstanding WAAF shootists.

The station was again brought to state of readiness on 26th June, when a signal was received that a strike relating to Food and Cold Storage depots was to take place. Emergency Units from the RAF would again supply men and vehicles to keep the facilities running. The operation was titled 'Oxhide'. No.15 Emergency Transport Headquarters ordered Nos.10, 11, 12 and 13 ETUs to travel down and form at Hornchurch the following day. Bed and mattresses for 450 personnel were provided for and put into No.2 Hangar, the Dance Hall and Gym.

On the 28th, some vehicles and personnel moved to the Royal Artillery

Barracks at Woolwich. Seventy-seven vehicles departed to Smithfield's and various cold storage depots, and the force operated at nearly maximum effort up until Saturday 1st July. It was stood down on Wednesday 12th July at 1.45 pm, when orders to disperse were given and the units started to depart from Hornchurch.

On 14th July 1950, the new RAF Hornchurch Station Badge was presented to the station by Air Vice-Marshal B.V. Reynolds, who commanded No.22 Group, Technical Training Command. During the ceremonial parade, the badge was proudly accepted by Group Captain F.C. Sturgis. Don McNaught was posted to RAF Hornchurch in August 1950, and remembers his time there:

> I arrived after doing my square-bashing at Bridgenorth. Later after full trade qualification (training was done in the former briefing room) I became Clerk GD Personnel Assessor as SAC, Acting Corporal Paid. I was with another chap, Corporal Tom Meldon, in the upstairs NCOs room in Typhoon Block. Here we had home comforts such as a radio and a good supply of coal in the winter. The block was used to house aircrew candidates, who usually brought their own supervising NCOs with them. Corporal Meldon and myself worked in the Aptitude Testing Section of the Combined Selection Centre. There were also a sergeant and two pilot officers who also had an office in the block and who supervised.
>
> Our main job was administering the battery of aptitude tests and marking and checking the aircrew candidates' completed test papers. You were given details of the types of candidates and aircrew categories from your research literature. Most working days, we would be testing and marking all day. There were the usual digressions like kit inspections and a monthly bull-session when all hands had to clean and polish both floors of the AT Block.
>
> Soon after my arrival at Hornchurch I joined the Hornchurch Voluntary Band. Before call-up I had been playing trumpet in a small New Orleans-style jazz band, so I had a lot to learn as regards reading all the sheet music and the whole ethos of the 'oompah' world. Voluntary bandsmen had a most valuable paper chit confirming their status, which enabled us to avoid a lot of rather unpleasant duties, especially when senior NCOs required 'volunteers'. To balance this, we always had to be on parade and playing when any visiting VIP arrived. The band was always inspected, at varying speeds and degrees of intensity, but most of such officers had a word with several players. Once a month, we would be on parade for the commanding officer's general parade of station personnel. I remember it had been raining and while playing on the march, lots of water would shoot up your trouser leg, especially if you marched through a puddle. Learning to avoid letting the water upset your playing was a good exercise in self-discipline.

Later I also joined the Station Dance Band, and played in that for most of the rest of my service. Dances were held at the station monthly in part of one of the hangars. We had four very talented musicians in the dance band – Gerry Butler (piano), Len Beadle (trombone), Gerry Silverman (drums) and Ken Quint (sax).

It was during this period at RAF Hornchurch that one of Britain's finest comedians was posted, whilst doing his National Service. Ronnie Corbett remembers with affection:

I did two years there in 1950/51 and it was a nice station to be on. The work was interesting, under the command of Squadron Leader Smythe on personnel selection.

It was also near Elm Park station, so we were able to get the District Line up to the West End on our weekends off.

It was here at RAF Hornchurch that I met a life-long friend and someone who was to have a great influence on my life – the actor Edward Hardwicke. I would spend weekends with him and his mother in St John's Wood. It was largely due to her help and encouragement that I was given the confidence to go for a career as an entertainer. Edward and I would do cabaret turns to amuse our colleagues on the base. In later years, we would come back to where it all started, RAF Hornchurch, and do shows for the 'The Troops.'

Hornchurch's 'At Home' display on Saturday, 16th September, was another success, with over 23,000 visitors filing through the gates. Attending the show were many aircraft, which were visiting the airfield for the first time. These included a Vickers Wellington and De Havilland Mosquito, which were included in the static ground display. On the flying programme, a Sunderland flying boat, a Lincoln bomber and Vampire jets all added to create interesting talking points for those on the ground. The RAF Trades exhibition consisted of many interesting items including a German Doodlebug V1 flying bomb, armament and bombs.

The 7th November 1950 was a sad day for the station. The last WAAF personnel left and the offices closed down. During RAF Hornchurch's long history; starting in 1917, women had played a great role in the aerodrome's 'behind the scene' operations. During the First World War, as general duty telephonists, motor drivers and despatch riders; then, during the Second War, as plotters, signallers, teleprinter operators working in the Operations Room, packing parachutes, working in storage, plus many other duties. I expect that many an airman, who was feeling down and fed up, was at sometime perked up by the sight of a smile or quick chat from a friendly WAAF.

# CHAPTER 8

# THE TWILIGHT YEARS
## 1951 – 1959

Two De Havilland Tiger Moth aircraft of the No.17 Reserve Flying School took off for a routine flight on 27th January 1951. While over South Ockendon, Essex, the two aircraft collided and both crashed, but fortunately both pilots survived. Corporal Don McNaught was the NCO in charge of the crash-guard, and remembers the incident:

> What had happened was that the prop of one of the Tiger Moths had sawed the tail unit off the aircraft in front. The result was that No.1 came down very steeply and buried itself in a farm field up to the bulkhead behind the forward cockpit. So it was as well that the pilot was operating from the back cockpit; he was lucky to survive that. The second Tiger came down, crash-landing in the next field, slowing its progress by ploughing through a hedge. I believe this aircraft was repaired and did fly again. I had some Erks with me to help and we guarded the aircraft overnight, using a barn nearby as our base. I remember it was a very cold night with a hard frost; we were all glad and relieved the next morning, though I seem to remember we did have some hot drinks.

The two Tiger Moth aircraft involved in the collision were N6706 and N6987. On 2nd April, Group Captain Sturgis relinquished command of the station to Group Captain H.L. Parker.

Air Marshal Sir John Whitworth, KCB, CBE, the Air Officer Commanding Technical Training Command, inspected the station on 12th April. Air Vice-Marshal B.V. Reynolds CBE, Air Officer Commanding No.22 Group, accompanied him. During April, a detachment of No.49 Maintenance Unit arrived with one large trailer loaded with transportation equipment plus six empty trailers. One Vampire jet aircraft was also brought in and then despatched to its final destination.

No.86 and 17 Reserve Flying School amassed a very large amount of flying training hours, both day and night.

|  |  | *Aircraft Hours Flown* |
|---|---|---|
| *Day* | Tiger Moth | 1267 hrs |
|  | Avro Anson | 113 hrs |
| *Night* | Tiger Moth | 60 hrs |
|  | Avro Anson | 22 hrs |

Thirty Cadets of the West Essex Wing were invited to Hornchurch for flying experience during April. Twelve of them received instruction on gliding. John Cox was just sixteen, when he got a job on the aerodrome working for Short Brothers who ran the flying school. He remembers:

> The first job in the morning was to go into the hangar; there a couple of us would pick up a Tiger Moth by the tailplane and wheel it out and line it up with the rest of the aircraft. I would then have to check the oil. The Tiger Moths had quite a few oil dipsticks and you had to check every one, then make sure there was plenty of fuel. The pilots would then come out once everything was ready and you would then swing the prop for them. Once they had gone off the rest of the time was your own.
>
> One day in particular, a nice sunny day, we had got rid of all the Tiger Moths and three Airspeed Oxfords had taken off. We were relaxing on the grass when we heard the noise of engines; suddenly the three Oxfords appeared over the station at just above hangar height, just as their commanding officer was taking off in a Beaufighter.
>
> They seemed to be headed on a collision course, but they suddenly broke in all directions. That nobody collided was pure luck.

A Court of Inquiry was held at the station on 16th May, in regards to an aircraft crash. A Tiger Moth had crashed on 11th May, after hitting a tree, near a low flying area. The aircraft was severely damaged and the pupil killed. No.49 MU again returned to Hornchurch during the month, this time loaded with three Vampire aircraft and six crates of aircraft mainplanes. They were brought in and shipped out within a couple of days.

Hornchurch's entertainment was broadened, when on 20th June, a jazz club was officially opened on the station. A committee was formed by a unanimous vote and it was decided that all tastes in jazz would be catered for. A meeting of the club was held in the Education Section, where an illustrated talk was given to interested airmen and women on the origins of the music.

During September, the airmen who also had a touch of the sea in their veins and belonged to RAF Hornchurch's Sailing Club finished what had been a very successful season. The club emerged as joint winner of the Thurrock Yacht Club Points Race. In a serious of five races, the club 12-square-metre international yacht gained two firsts and one second positions.

Howard LaRoche recalls his childhood days living near the aerodrome:

> My fascination with Hornchurch aerodrome began along with some of my earliest memories as a child growing up in the 1950s. As a toddler, living in a side-road off Sutton's Avenue, I remember looking up at the various shapes and noises in the sky that attracted my attention – most were monoplanes, but

there were definitely some biplanes.

As my strength and stamina increased, occasional weekend walks down Sutton's Lane would be undertaken, to finish at the double gates at the end of the northern extension, opposite St George's hospital, or on a really good day, those at the very bottom of the lane, marking the original northern boundary of the airfield.

Once, having made an illegal entry through a gap in the fence, I was confronted by an RAF policeman whilst learning to ride my first bicycle in one of the blast pens that lay alongside this lane. He was a kind man though, and allowed me to finish my exercise before shepherding me back through my point of entry.

During October, Major W.S. Winneshiek, United States Air Force and the Air Attaché at the American Embassy, visited the station. The Festival of Britain Shoot, a rifle-shooting contest organised by RAF Hornchurch and by 'D' Company 14th Essex Home Guard, took place in October. The prize, the Battle of Britain Trophy, a shield presented by the PSI Hornchurch was placed fourth in the event with 349 points; the winning team scored 363.

In December, a visiting lecturer, Werner Burmeister Esquire BA, gave a talk on the situation between Soviet Russia and the United States of America; what would be known later as the Cold War between the two super powers. A formal visit was made by two of His Majesty's Inspectors, Mr Greenaway and Mr Marchant, accompanied by Wing Commander Beveridge. The object of the visit was to enquire information about education in the Royal Air Force.

On 17th December, with Christmas approaching, a children's Christmas party was held for all the families. A station variety show was staged during the evening.

## 1952

David Bendon had just finished his time at school, when soon after he managed to get a job working on the aerodrome:

I had left Sutton's School in December 1951, and started at Hornchurch at the beginning of 1952. In retrospect it was one of the happiest times of my life.

Short Brothers and Harland had the contract for a Reserve Flying School and there was also the No.1 Civilian Anti-Aircraft Co-Operation Unit, which used to operate Beaufighter, Oxford, Anson and a couple of Spitfire aircraft. The Beaufighters were used for target tug practice, while the Airspeed Oxfords etc were used for communications. The No.17 Reserve Flying School comprised Chipmunks, Ansons and a few vintage Tiger Moths.

At this time I can remember they had the RAF Combined Selection Board over there, testing the aptitude of young men just out of school or university to see if they were suitable for pilots or navigators. Early morning they would get into a truck and travel to the other side of the airfield, where the wartime control tower was, and there they would undertake various exercises. They would all be dressed in overalls with numbers painted on their backs.

The actor Kenneth More visited the aerodrome around this time; he was filming *Reach for the Sky* at the time. He came over to Hornchurch to do some publicity shots for the film. We had to wheel out the Spitfire onto the apron and I can remember him having to be helped with putting a parachute on, he then climbed into the Spitfire, then they photographed him sitting in the cockpit. It was all quite interesting for me as a young lad.

Of the Spitfires that were sent to the Anti-Aircraft Co-Operation Unit, one was Spitfire LF MkXVIE serial No.SL542; the other Spitfire LF MkXVIE serial No.TE476. SL542 had arrived at the aerodrome on 7th December 1950, after being transferred from No.695 Squadron. It remained at Hornchurch only until 11th June 1951, when it was sent to storage at No.29 MU High Ercall, where it was mothballed. Spitfire TE476 had been built at Castle Bromwich in June 1945 and was then stored until 1949. It was not until 19th October 1949, that the aircraft was transferred to No.33 Maintenance Unit at Lyneham. Here it stayed until 4th July 1951, before being sent to a flying unit at Hornchurch, where it served using the code letter 'D'.

With the completion of the new Station church, named St Michael and All Angels, inside the aerodrome, a service of dedication was held on Monday, 10th March 1952. This was conducted by the Lord Bishop of Chelmsford, the Right Reverend Faulkner Allison, along with the Chaplain-in-Chief of the Royal Air Force, the Reverend Canon Leslie Knight CBE, and the Reverend Canon R.A. Courthope, the Vicar of Hornchurch. Also attending were the Reverend J.A. Busley and the officiating chaplain, the Reverend M.W. Wall.

The RAF Combined Selection Centre at Hornchurch received a change in title, and from 1st April 1952 became known as the Aircrew Selection Centre. This was due to the wider entry of applicants and a broader range of positions available for example, navigators, engineers, and operation controllers and of course pilots. The centre was visited by the Right Honourable George Ward, the Under Secretary of State for Air on 2nd May, accompanied by the Air Officer Commanding No.54 Group, Air Commodore Bett. During his visit they were shown around the various examination rooms and talked to candidates who were being tested. It was during this year that John Cox, aged 17, joined the RAF Volunteer Reserve and served in the Motor Transport Unit at Hornchurch. He remembers this period:

I went to Hornchurch and learnt to drive by being taken around the airfield's perimeter track in an old truck. I was paid a shilling an hour, while learning to drive. The commanding

officer of the unit was Flying Officer Mayle. My older brother
Harry was a corporal and already a driver with the unit, and
would help me with any problems that arose. We used to take
the Air Training Corps over to the Rainham firing ranges for
rifle shooting during the weekends. Harry would also drive the
coach that was involved in picking up the candidates from the
local railway stations to the Aircrew Selection Centre. He also
was a very good boxer and fought in lightweight bouts
representing the station.

On 15th June, a detachment from the Royal West Essex Territorial Army
Unit consisting of three officers, three senior NCOs, 50 gunners complete
with guns, searchlights and motor transport vehicles visited Hornchurch.
The purpose of this visit was to carry out an anti-aircraft exercise with the
aircraft of No.17 Reserve Flying School; arrangements for the provision of
aircraft were made with the officer commanding the flying school.

Royal Air Force Hornchurch was selected and given the honour of
hosting the farewell lunch given to Air Marshal Sir Hugh Walmsley, KCIE,
CB, CBE, MC, DFC, on 22nd July 1952. Officers representing all units in 54
Group were present including Air Commodore Bett, AOC 54 Group, who
was the president. David Bendon also recalls:

> I remember while I was there that two jet aircraft flew into
> Hornchurch. A Vampire and a Meteor came in for testing the
> runway. I can remember that when they took off the heat from
> the engines just burnt all the grass, only a big brown mark was
> left. They'd come in to see if the runway was long enough for
> emergency landings if there were any engine failures; this
> lasted for a week or two. We always made sure that we had
> plenty of fire extinguishers at hand, but they had their own
> RAF personnel come and look after the machine while they
> were there on test.

Robert Ballard also remembers this period:

> Still living with my folks in Grays, we moved to Upminster in
> September of 1952 and in so doing, I was enabled to view
> events at the aerodrome rather more closely. A cycle ride
> across from the Hacton side of the airfield and along by the
> River Ingrebourne and I was there.
>
> Up on a slope, this would bring me to a good vantage point
> near the disused rifle range by one of the north-east dispersal
> pens. Chipmunk and some Tiger Moth aircraft of a Reserve
> Flying School probably linked to the Aircrew Selection Centre
> were still seen on the airfield, but soon after the Selection
> Centre departed. This left a couple of Spitfire and Mosquito
> aircraft operated by the Civilian Anti-Aircraft Co-operation
> Unit.
>
> One Sunday afternoon sortie in autumn, I remember, was

typical of the flying at Hornchurch. At 2.00 pm, the two Mosquito aircraft took off from the Albyns Farm end, one following the other a short distance behind. Once airborne, banking to port over Elm Park as the landing gear retracted, they then did 180 degrees, which brought them back over the airfield, climbing out towards the east. The sound of the Rolls-Royce Merlins echoing out again must have renewed many wartime memories for local residents. After a couple of hours they were back and landed apart from one of the Mosquitos which turned up some time later, by which time the autumn mist was beginning to creep across the airfield. The aircraft made a couple of unsuccessful approaches coming over Albyns Farm, only to open up the throttles and go around again. Eventually the pilot must have pleaded with the Control Tower to 'light my path'. Suddenly a RAF lorry appeared coming across from the hangars. Out of the lorry popped some RAF chaps who proceeded to position flares on the airfield. The Mosquito successfully landed on its third attempt, no doubt much to the relief of the pilot.

Preparations were well in hand for that year's Battle of Britain Display, which was to be held on 20th September. Two conferences had been held and the following officers were dealing with the programme of events for the display under four main headings:

Flying display and aircraft parking – Wing Commander J.E. Haile
Ground display – Squadron Leader C.M. Owen DFC
Catering, car park, cinema and general administration –
  Squadron Leader H. Chambers
Programme and publicity – Squadron Leader H.T. Sutton OBE, DFC

The Air Officer Commanding in Chief, Flying Training Command, Air Marshal L.F. Pendred, CB, MBE, DFC, visited the station on 25th August, arriving by air at 9.15 am. He was met by the commanding officer and a Guard of Honour with the station band being in attendance. He later visited the Aircrew Selection Centre and other parts of the aerodrome. A formal luncheon was given in the Officers' Mess.

The Battle of Britain 'At Home' Display which took place on 20th September was considered a great success, and over 40,000 members of the public attended. David Bendon remembers this period:

Eventually Short Brothers lost the contract for the Reserve Flying School, then the company 'Aerowork' took over part of the contract for the No.1 Civilian Anti-Aircraft Co-Operation Unit. The aircraft would fly out to Sandwich and Folkestone for the naval gunnery practice, towing the target drogues behind them. The drogues would be released about quarter of a mile behind the aircraft for gunnery practice, then they would fly back to Hornchurch and fly low over the airfield, release the drogue and we would go out onto the field and retrieve it. Finally two Mosquito aeroplanes replaced the Beaufighters, but they still retained the two Spitfires for communication use.

I remember the occasion when the Avro Oxfords went over to Redhill in Surrey one day for some thing or another. Like a brave young lad I asked if I could come on the trip and they said 'yes', so off I went. While we were up, one of the pilots asked if I would like a go on the controls, the Oxford was dual-control. The controls were so sensitive you hardly had to touch them to turn left or right. Once we came back to Hornchurch we had to refuel and carry out maintenance on the aircraft.

The three hangars contained the various units, the main middle hangar was for the Reserve Flying School, the left hangar nearest the Southend Road was used by the Glider and ATC units, the right hangar for the Anti-Aircraft Co-Operation Unit.

## 1953

As the year began, the weather was extremely cold and gales from across the North Sea were steadily increasing during January. Over the night of 31st January and 1st February, this reached a peak when a combination of severe gales and high spring tide caused massive flooding along the east coast of England from Yorkshire down to the Thames estuary as far as Purfleet, near London. One of the worst areas hit was Canvey Island in Essex, where 58 people were drowned. The area at Canvey was totally underwater with all buildings being completely uninhabitable. A massive civilian relief operation was put into action, which was co-ordinated between the three armed services and the Chief Civil Engineer of Essex. Not only would they have to deal with the civilian relief, but also the work of trying to stem the flooding by working on the sea defences that had been breached.

RAF Hornchurch was heavily involved with the operation which was titled 'King Canute'. Hornchurch would provide medical assistance as well as participating in help with accommodation of civilians and work on local sea defences. The RAF Headquarters was set up at Tilbury in the World's End public house. Squadron Leader D. Acres of RAF Hornchurch recorded:

> I was resident in South Benfleet and news was brought to me at 10.30 p.m. that the evacuation of Canvey Island was under way. I reported to South Benfleet Police Station with my car, where it was suggested that I go on to the island to help with the evacuation of sick and injured. This I did during the morning, bringing off a number of chronic sick in my car.
>
> In the afternoon I stationed myself at Benfleet Primary School which had become Emergency Headquarters and Reception Centre. A first-aid post was set up and manned by members of the St John's Ambulance Brigade. All the flood

victims evacuated passed through this centre and about 250 were dealt with by the first-aid post. In the evening I contacted my unit, RAF Hornchurch, where Squadron Leader Troup, in the absence of Wing Commander Clarke-Taylor, gave permission for me to remain at South Benfleet.

During the morning of 2nd February, RAF Hornchurch provided an ambulance unit, which was engaged in transporting patients from flooded houses in Tilbury to various rest centres, and from the centres to hospitals.

The hospital bed situation became very strained by the morning and Flying Officer Altham, the Station Medical Officer, was asked to set up a medical reception centre at the Day Nursery Centre, No.3 Whitehall Lane in Grays. Patients to be admitted were those who required medical attention, but who were not ill enough to be admitted to hospital. The staff at the nursery were placed at the disposal of Flying Officer Altham, to help in any way they could. However it was found that there was a shortage of adult size furniture, and a request was therefore sent to the equipment officer at Hornchurch to supply 35 beds and mattresses. The items arrived on a three-ton lorry, belonging to RAF Chigwell, with six airmen and one medical orderly from Hornchurch. Once the beds had been erected the six men were attached to the nearby rest centre and were employed until the early hours of the morning in bringing refugees out of Tilbury. When all the patients had been settled comfortably, the medical officer was then sent to Chadwell Heath Rest Centre, and was employed during the evening in evacuating patients on stretchers from houses in Tilbury.

Owing to the excessive depth of the floodwater in some places it was necessary on some trips to leave the ambulance at the water's edge and transfer the stretchers with patient to army lorries, which had greater ground clearance. On one such trip the lorry caught fire and patients and equipment were hurriedly transferred to another passing lorry. Squadron Leader Acres remembers:

> I was still working hard at South Benfleet, when Flying Officer E. Sherville of RAF North Pickenham (281 Maintenance Unit) reported. He told me that he had been given permission by his senior medical officer to proceed to Canvey on either general or medical duties. He had been engaged on supervising the filling of sandbags. I detailed him to a first-aid post at the fire station on Canvey Island, where he assisted with the casualties amongst civilian and RAF personnel.

By Tuesday 3rd February, owing to the difficulty in obtaining medical equipment and supplies, RAF Hornchurch was again asked to help, supplying penicillin and insulin. During the afternoon a call for help came from a nearby clothing distribution centre, where difficulties had arisen when trying to control an unruly crowd. The medical officer and three nursing attendants went to the scene, cleaned the building and organised an orderly queue outside. The main complaint had been the slowness in dealing with the crowd's needs. Thereafter, a policeman was brought in to duty at the centre. Squadron Leader Acres:

> During the afternoon of the 3rd, Her Majesty the Queen Mother and Her Royal Highness, the Princess Margaret, visited us. Several of the workers at the Reception Centre had the honour to be presented to Her Majesty, including Dr Tyndall and myself. I saw seven cases of pneumonia during the day.

On 4th February, in view of the feeding difficulties encountered on the previous days, T Rations were obtained from Hornchurch and formed the basis of the mid-day meal for patients and staff. Another medical officer, Flying Officer Markham, arrived at the nursery centre in Grays, and was relieved by Flying Officer Hines the following day. The centre was visited by Group Captain J.N. Jefferson CBE, Commanding Officer RAF Hornchurch, during that afternoon.

By Friday 6th February, as the pressure of work had decreased, Flying Officer Hines was transferred from Grays to Canvey Island. During the afternoon a visit to Benfleet, near Southend was made by Squadron Leader Acres to ascertain his position regarding medical supplies and personnel. It was found that he was in great need of medical equipment, another medical officer and penicillin. On 9th February, as Squadron Leader Acres recalled:

> During the morning Wing Commander Baldwin, head of control at Chelmsford, contacted me. At his suggestion I inspected proposed accommodation at Southend Airport and Eastwood church hall. These were reasonably satisfactory for a short period and I arranged supplementary latrines to be supplied from RAF Hornchurch.
>
> Heavy rainfall on the next day created problems at most rescue centres, particularly with the emergency latrines at Canvey, which were totally unprotected and became very muddy. Slatted boards supplied by Hornchurch and clinker from local sources helped ease the problem. One of the principal problems was that of providing dry clothing. Supplies were sent from RAF Hornchurch and smaller consignments from elsewhere.
>
> On 13th February, in spite of an exceptionally high tide, there was no further emergency. Snow fell throughout the day on the 14th, making travel difficult and reducing work on repairs to the sea wall. Flying Officer Stephens arrived from RAF Hullavington, via Hornchurch. This fourth medical officer enabled me to allow one of the others off duty for 24 hours at a time, the rest being much needed.
>
> Visits were made to all the outlying stations, and during the night a medical officer, ambulance and crew stood by at Cory's Wharf, Purfleet, to provide coverage for night operations. Although both tides were very high, the sea wall withstood the strain.

On 18th February, Flying Officer Altman returned to Hornchurch with a mild attack of influenza. On 20th February, we spent the morning sorting and packing equipment. In the afternoon, Wing Commander Weston paid a visit to Benfleet and witnessed the details for the winding up of the various centres. By the evening Flying Officer Markham and Flying Officer Stephens had returned to Hornchurch with the two remaining ambulances as the medical side of the operation was completed.

Two visits by RAF top brass took place in July; Air Marshal Pendred CB, MBE, DFC, arrived on the 9th, while Air Vice-Marshal A. Mckee, CB, CBE, DSO, DFC, AFC, Commanding No.21 Group, visited on the 14th.

A change in command took place at Hornchurch on 21st July 1953. Group Captain E.J. Corbally CBE assumed command of the station from Group Captain J.N. Jefferson CBE. On 31st July, the No.17 Reserve Flying School was finally disbanded at Hornchurch after giving good service for many years to those who wished to keep their flying skills up to date.

The sad news of the death of Binder, RAF Hornchurch's mascot dog was recorded in late August 1953. The mongrel dog had been present on the station during the war, and had befriended many pilots including the ace 'Paddy' Finucane who was killed in 1942. Joseph O'Rouke was a flight sergeant and head of the RAF police at the aerodrome in 1953, and had looked after Binder for a number of years up until the dog's death. He recalls:

> The dog would go to the edge of the flightpath, but never on it when an aircraft came into land. He slept in the hall of the guard's room near to my office. He would arrive at 11.00 pm every evening and sleep through to 6.00 am. He would then get up and head for the airmen's kitchen, then the sergeants' mess. He would then go and sit outside and look over the parade ground. He had an uncanny ability to know when the National Servicemen were due to arrive on base.
>
> Binder would walk up to them and escort them through the station gates up to the Aircrew Selection Centre buildings, once the men were safely through the doors he would wander off. Now a very old dog, he had to be finally put down after falling down a flight of steps.

When Binder came to be buried Mr E. Morris, general manager of the local Romford stonemasons Haines and Warwick Ltd, insisted that the dog's resting-place should not go unmarked. He had a RAF crest carved on a headstone and had one of his employees, Albert Bishop, engrave the lettering. They both used their spare time to work on the headstone, which was styled similar to the ones supplied by the War Graves Commission.

The company presented the memorial headstone to RAF Hornchurch on 15th September 1953, Battle of Britain Day. Mr Morris and Mr Glyn Richards, the editor of the *Romford Recorder* presented the stone to Flight

Lieutenant O'Rourke. Binder's memorial stone was placed on his grave, which was just inside the main gates opposite the guardroom.

When the aerodrome closed in 1962, the memorial stone was salvaged from the rubbish tip; it had been damaged and was found broken into three pieces. Clare Kelsall, the sister of 'Paddy' Finucane, was notified of this and she employed experts to restore it. In 1990, Clare presented the stone to the Battle of Britain Museum at Hawkinge, where it remains at present. Binder's dog collar can be seen at The Hornchurch Wing collection at the Purfleet Heritage and Military Centre, Purfleet.

David Bendon was now working for Aerowork Limited who occupied one of the hangars at Hornchurch:

> Every day we started work we would go through the main gate, and get our pass chits signed by the station adjutant. We would then go into the hangars to get the Chipmunks ready for that day. The Chipmunks used to have a Coffman starter, like a little gun cartridge, which would help start the engine; we would have to go over to the armoury every few weeks to get these cartridges. Once a fortnight they used to have night flying and we had to make sure we had the gooseneck lights ready for the flightpath. They always had the three emergency vehicles on stand-by, the ambulance, fire-tender and a jeep. There were several crashes while I was there, either through the pilots forgetting to lower their undercarriages or coming in on one wheel. I remember a Spitfire coming in, forgetting to put his undercarriage down and just plopping down onto the field. The airscrew was just all bent back and I remember the aircraft was stuck up in the air.

Hornchurch held its Royal Air Force 'At Home' Battle of Britain Air Display on Saturday 19th September 1953. As the public flocked into the station, they were to be entertained with a wide selection of ground displays as well as a full flying programme.

The RAF Hornchurch Station Band played at various parts of the camp throughout the afternoon. There was also a photographic competition held behind the central hangar by members of the Station Camera Club, members were asked to judge the photographs and pick the winner. Some of the highlights of the flying programme were a demonstration by four Canberra jet aircraft, which had only just come into service recently. The Royal Navy's new strike aircraft, the Wyvern, did a flypast as did the RAF's new bomber, the Vulcan. Nine Meteor aircraft from Nos.601 and 604 Auxiliary Squadrons based at North Weald put in an appearance, led by Group Captain Alan Deere, ex-Hornchurch 54 Squadron.

Flight Lieutenant Anderson of No.614 Gliding School gave a demonstration of gliding aerobatics. An exercise in air support for infantry was also on display to the public. This was enacted by troops of the Essex Regiment, who carried out an attack on an enemy-held strongpoint on the far side of the airfield. Meteor jets flew in to neutralise the enemy position while the troops advanced and captured the target. 1,000 balloons were released in the afternoon. They were on sale for sixpence each and the monies raised went to charities. Howard LaRoche remembers:

> I suppose the die was really cast when, in 1953, my father took me to an air display commemorating the Battle of Britain. For various reasons I have quite distinct memories of certain parts of this visit. Firstly, in the static display, there was a four-engined bomber (a Lincoln I think) and for some time I marvelled at its size and number of gun turrets. Then there was a formation display by some Meteor fighters led, I later found out, by Alan Deere – what must his thoughts have been?
>
> The highlight of the day, though, was a 'five bob' flip in a De Havilland Dragon Rapide; my heart has been sold on flying ever since and I still have a photograph recording the event.

Approximately 80,000 people attended the At Home display, which was greatly in excess of the number attending the year before. The result was that £650 was made available for the Royal Air Force Benevolent Fund and Association.

Again in October of that year, the threat from striking labour unions put the country's fuel supply in jeopardy. A strike by fuel tanker drivers in the London area brought a preliminary warning, which was received at Hornchurch on 22nd/23rd October 1953, for the implementation of Operation 'Tanker'.

The commanding officer held a conference and operation order No.1 was issued; preparations were made to receive approximately 1,000 airmen and 40 vehicles from various units arriving from the Midlands and the South. By the 24th/25th, service personnel had been conveyed to fuel storage depots in the London area, from where they undertook the distribution of fuel.

On the 26th, news was received that civilian drivers had decided to return to work. The next day arrangements were put in hand to disperse personnel concerned with Operation 'Tanker' and by 28th October, the complete dispersal of all service personnel units at Hornchurch was at an end.

The Right Honourable the Lord De L'Isle and Dudley VC, visited on 5th November. He arrived by road and was met by a Guard of Honour at the main entrance of the station. Air Marshal L.F. Pendred, CB, MBE, DFC and the Station Commander were on hand to greet the Secretary of State for Air for his tour.

## 1954

With the new year came a change of command at RAF Hornchurch, which was initiated on 18th January 1954. Wing Commander A.J. Hicks AFC assumed command of the station, taking over from Group Captain Corbally. Another visitor to the station, this time on 5th March, was the Air Officer Commanding No.21 Group, Air Vice-Marshal G.E. Nicholetts, CB, AFC. The visit was to carry out his annual inspection of the base and his review of the Ceremonial Drill Unit. Wing Commander A.J. Hicks' short time as Station Commander came to an end on 8th March, when his place was taken by Wing Commander W.G. Devas, DFC, AFC.

On 6th May, Air Marshal Sir Dermot Boyle, KCVO, KBE, CB, AFC, the Air Officer Commander in Chief of Fighter Command, visited. Boyle had been a famous wartime commander, and had worked alongside Air Vice-Marshal Harry Broadhurst as Senior Air Staff Officer No.83 Group before and after the D-Day landings in June 1944. He arrived at Hornchurch in connection with the flypast for Saturday 15th May, in honour of the return of Her Majesty, Queen Elizabeth II. This was followed by a visit on the 7th, by Air Vice-Marshal J.R. Whitley CB, CBE, DSO, Air Officer Commanding No.1 Group, and on 13th May by Air Vice-Marshal H.A. Constantine, CB, CBE, DSO, Air Officer in Charge of Administration, Fighter Command.

Hornchurch saw another change in command on 4th December, when Wing Commander C.A.R. Crews replaced Wing Commander W.G. Devas. By the end of December 1954, the station strength was as follows:

| | |
|---|---|
| Officers | 62 |
| Warrant Officers | 5 |
| Flight Sergeants | 9 |
| Sergeants | 17 |
| Corporals | 46 |
| Airmen | 196 |
| Total | 335 |

Howard LaRoche remembers:

In 1955, the family moved to Cranham on the outskirts of Upminster, but my interest in the airfield remained strong. I now owned a larger 'bike' and I would badger less interested friends to accompany me on circular trips which involved a hike past Berwick Ponds, Albyns Farm and on to the old Southend Road, where it had been closed to accommodate the western extension flightpath.

What became apparent during this period was that the amount of 'powered' flying from the aerodrome was reducing and being replaced by the silent gliders of No.614 Air Cadet Gliding school. Some of 614's original aircraft were actually captured during the Allied advance through Germany, presumably at one time having been used to train future members of the Luftwaffe. The original instructors at the school certainly received instruction in Germany. Eventually training centred on use of the tandem Kirby Cadet MkIII and the side by side seated Slingsby Sedburgh gliders, the latter being affectionately known as the 'Barge'. More advanced training would be given in the single seat Prefect and Swallow allocated to the unit from time to time. I can also remember the Chipmunk aircraft operating with the gliding school; they were giving aero-tows to the gliders, because normally the standard method of launching the gliders was by winch. They basically had to winch up wind to the edge of the airfield and tow the things up, but occasionally they would have aircraft come in or use the station aircraft to tow them up. I can remember standing in my back garden seeing them being towed up, which happened on this day to be up over Upminster.

The commanding officer for the majority of this period was one 'Bill' Verling; during his tenure, hundreds of young men gained their first taste of solo flight, whilst many of the staff achieved noteworthy British Gliding Association certification in soaring and cross-country gliding.

Station Commander C.A.R. Crews was posted away on 9th May 1955, and his replacement was Wing Commander A.N. Jones. On 23rd May 1955, a signal was received from the Air Ministry warning the station to readiness, to put Operation 'Main Line' into effect in view of the railway strike which threatened to commence on the night of 28th/29th May. By the 26th, instructions were received giving details of how the operation was to be executed.

The base was informed that the emergency forces to be deployed would be similar to those planned under the previous operations. The requirement at Hornchurch was to provide accommodation for an Emergency Transport Wing and two augmented Emergency Transport Squadrons comprising of 199 personnel. By the evening of the 28th, the commitment had grown considerably and the accommodation requirements were such that it was not possible to handle it from the station resources, because the Aircrew Selection Centre was still operating.

Fortunately, North Weald aerodrome were able to make a party of 14 airmen available, to help in erecting beds. The total commitment was:

|  | Officers | SNCOs | Airmen | Vehicles |
|---|---|---|---|---|
| 41 & 84 Emergency Transport Squadrons | 7 | 9 | 184 | 60 |
| 31 Emergency Labour Squadron | 2 | 4 | 28 | 2 |
| 61 Embarkation/Despatch Centre | 5 | 2 | 70 | 25 |
| Record Office Detachment | 2 | 5 | 30 | 1 |
| Mobile X-Ray Unit | 1 | 2 | 7 | 3 |
| Hitch Hike Commitment |  |  | 8 | 4 |
| Transport Accommodation |  |  | 300 |  |
| De-kitting Unit Accommodation |  |  | 140 |  |
| Total Accommodation Required | 17 | 22 | 767 | 95 |

To add to any difficulties on this day, vehicles and drivers started to arrive a day early, before the headquarters controlling the operation had been set up. Personnel to man the various 'Main Line' units had arrived from all over the country and had to be handled entirely by station personnel because the Wing Headquarters was not set up until late in the evening.

Despite the disruption of the station caused by mounting Operation 'Main Line' it had been decided to continue with the annual parade review of the ceremonial and inspection by the Air Officer Commanding, Air Commodore E.J. Corbally CBE. The parade was held in perfect weather and the inspection was completely satisfactory. The Air Officer Commanding congratulated the Commanding Officer on the very high standard attained for this inspection, despite the upset on the station, and said that the parade was the best he had ever seen.

By the beginning of June, the operation had been well under way and many of the small difficulties that had arisen had been solved. Wing Commander A. Haywood from No.30 Maintenance Unit, Stoke Heath, commanded the emergency forces.

During the period from 28th May to 1st June, the number of personnel reporting to RAF Hornchurch through being unable to get to their parent stations, was in the region of 4,000. The Emergency Transport Squadrons did excellent work in transporting airmen and airwomen back to their units. The Station Flight also co-operated in this work, and the Avro Ansons did many flying hours throughout the period in question.

On 17th June, the operation came to an end, and by 20th June the personnel engaged in the emergency forces had returned to their units. A report on certain aspects of the 'Main Line' operation was drawn up and certain recommendations were made in case of future operations.

Some confusion was caused regarding the maximum accommodation potential of the station. The Air Ministry was using published figures of 1,600, whereas, because the station was still functioning, the maximum available was between 1,150 and 1,200. Two separate figures were drawn up showing that 1,600 could be accommodated if the Aircrew Selection Centre was closed and only 1,000, if the Centre continued to function.

On 3rd December 1955, the last Spitfire ever to fly from RAF Hornchurch flew out for the last time. Spitfire TE358 of the Civil Anti-Aircraft Co-Operation Unit piloted by Squadron Leader P.F. Hart, was taken to the Maintenance Unit at RAF Kemble in Gloucestershire.

## 1956

During January 1956, the aerodrome continued much the same, but its duties were steadily being cut back as was its personnel staff. Ten officers were enrolled for an instructional course, to be given by the station education officer and civilian part-time teachers as candidates for the Staff College Qualifying Examination, which was to be taken in the August of that year. On 27th January, the station was visited by Air Marshal R.L.R. Atcherley CB, CBE, AFC.

In April, numerous officers and airmen were posted into Hornchurch on 16th, to form the nucleus of No.160 Wing, which was to be formed here. The Station Sports Day was held on Wednesday the 16th May. The station divided on a competitive basis into two wings, the Aircrew Selection Centre versus Station HQ.

The final result was ASC 204 points, Station HQ 141 points. The outstanding contestant in the individual events was Corporal Lanning, who threw the javelin a distance of 178 feet.

In July 1956, Hornchurch became the examination centre for the General Certificate of Education, which was sat by 36 candidates, 18 from

Hornchurch. The exams were from the 9th July until the 20th, and during this period all teaching activities at RAF Hornchurch were suspended. The station was visited in August by Mr H.P. Davis of No.614 Gliding School and by L.H. Harrison of the Air Ministry Bomb Disposal Section.

Tragedy was to strike nearby at the old Upminster bomb site at Gerpins Lane on 27th November 1956, when an unexploded 2 kilogramme German Butterfly bomb which had been discovered locally, exploded while being examined. The device was being dealt with by Flight Lieutenant Herbert Donnington of No.6221 Flight, Bomb Disposal Unit when it exploded. He was immediately rushed to Oldchurch Hospital at Romford, but died of severe injuries the same day. Many bombs had been dealt with during and after the war at the Upminster site, so it was with sadness that the aerodrome learnt of this fatal accident.

By December 1956, the strength of RAF personnel at RAF Hornchurch stood at:

| | |
|---|---:|
| Officers | 57 |
| Warrant Officers | 5 |
| Flight Sergeants | 10 |
| Sergeants | 19 |
| Corporals | 45 |
| Airmen | 198 |
| Total | 334 |

## 1957

January 1957 saw visits to RAF Hornchurch from the following: Mr H. Bennett from the Air Ministry as Inspector of Explosives, Wing Commander L.F. Jennings to visit West Essex ATC Wing Headquarters and Flying Officer K.D. Patten of No.71 Maintenance Unit from Bicester who came to assess the Mosquito aircraft of the Anti-Aircraft Co-Operation Unit.

On 13th March, a station swimming gala was held at the Hornchurch swimming baths. The gala was organised by Flight Lieutenant I.S. Balderstone, with 450 spectators attending. Thursday, 21st March, an Air Officer Commander's Inspection was carried out. A detailed model of the aerodrome had been made and installed in the station's information room.

During May, four cases of Rubella (German measles) were reported on the base and measures were taken to isolate further contacts. Educational visits were arranged for personnel to the County of Essex Court and the Houses of Parliament with 23 people attending. In October, an educational visit to Ford Motor Company at Dagenham was made. On 30th October, Wing Commander H.D.U. Denison took over command of Hornchurch from Wing Commander A.N. Jones. The strength of the station on 31st December 1957 stood at 20 officers and 173 airmen.

## 1958

Life on the aerodrome continued much the same into 1958. The only major occurrence to upset the normal coming and goings of everyday life was to be noted in the Station Operation's Book in July, when a plague of mosquitos on the marshes near the aerodrome became quite unbearable. The aerodrome was sprayed with oil, DDT and kerosene under the supervision of the medical staff. The Airmen's Mess, Whirlwind block and other major buildings were sprayed until the insect pest had been reduced.

The annual Battle of Britain church parade took place on 21st September. A contingent of officers and airmen from the station attended at churches in Romford and Hornchurch. On Remembrance Sunday, 9th November, the station sent contingents of officers and airmen to services at Westminster Cathedral, Romford and Hornchurch.

The Commander in Chief, Flying Training Command, Wing Commander W.H. Jones arrived at Hornchurch on Friday 28th November to present the Flying Training Command Motor Transport Efficiency Cup (Junior Section) to the Station Motor Transport Section.

The station was used by the Rover Scout Association for a conference over the weekend of 29th/30th November, when scout leaders congregated from all over the country. By December 1958, the personnel strength had dropped to 13 officers and 124 airmen.

## 1959

The year of 1959 brought some new arrivals on the aerodrome. A detachment from the RAF Balloon Unit, whose base was at Cardington in Bedfordshire, arrived at Hornchurch on 18th February 1959, with all the required equipment to start and set up static balloon jumping training for the Special Air Service (TA). Together with one Mark IX barrage balloon and jump cage came a winch lorry. However the weather conditions on that day prevented any parachute jumps.

Roy Little was a Lance Bombardier with No.289 Parachute Light Regiment, Royal Horse Artillery (Territorial Army), which was based at Romford. He remembers his time over at Hornchurch:

> Once we got over to the airfield, we were given our parachutes; these were all contained in a sealed box. You didn't do your own parachute packing in those days; you put your trust in the WAAFs. The amount of men allowed to go up into the cage was five if you weren't carrying any heavy equipment; if you were, then only four were allowed to jump out, plus the dispatcher. I think the minimum of weight you could carry was 45 lbs and the most a hundred-weight, otherwise the balloon would be too heavy to go up. The standard height for jumping from the balloon was 800 feet. Once we were all packed in, it would take about 3 minutes to get to jump height. I spent many hours over there practising parachuting techniques.
>
> One amusing thing I remember was that some of our guys had landed and were standing chatting with an officer, when all of a sudden, a top set of false teeth suddenly landed right next to the officer. The teeth belonged to the dispatcher, who had been shouting orders to jump, when his top plate of teeth suddenly dropped out.

The Secretary of State for Air, the Right Honourable George Ward MP, visited on 6th March, and a visit by the new Commander in Chief, Flying Training Command, Air Marshal Sir Hugh Constantine, KBE, CB, DSO took place on 12th March. The annual inspection of RAF Hornchurch was carried out on 10th July by none other than Air Commodore Donald Finlay CBE, who had led No.41 Squadron back in 1940. A visit by the Under Secretary of State for Air, Mr W.G. Taylor CBE and his private secretary, Mr R.G.S. Johnston took place on Tuesday 3rd November.

On the 27th, at 11.45 am, Air Commodore H. Ford, CB, CBE, AFC, with Wing Commander D. Penny from Headquarters Flying Training Command arrived to present the Junior Motor Transport Efficiency Cup again to RAF Hornchurch. This was the third year in succession that the trophy had been won by Hornchurch. To commemorate the achievement a shield was presented to the Motor Transport Section for its permanent retention.

Remembrance Sunday was commemorated on 8th November. Air Commodore D. Finlay CBE led a contingent of airmen to Romford, and Wing Commander B.L. Duckenfield AFC, who had served pre-war with No.74 Squadron, led a party of airmen to St Andrew's in Hornchurch. Wing Commander H.D.U. Dennison, the Station Commander, attended the Jewish Synagogue at Romford and Squadron Leader G. Gaskin-Thompson, MBE, DFM, led a service and parade at Rayleigh in Essex. By the end of 1959 the station strength stood at 15 officers and 116 airmen.

# CHAPTER 9

# THE FINAL COUNTDOWN
## 1960 – 1962

By the beginning of 1960, Hornchurch was beginning to see a drop in the number of aircrew candidates attending the Aircrew Selection Centre. The days of National Service were also coming to an end. The strength of station personnel had now dwindled down to just 125 airmen and civilian staff.

It was a very quiet year and one of the few highlights took place on 3rd September 1960, when the very last air display took place. The event was organised by the Joint League of Friends of Romford, Hornchurch and Dagenham Hospitals' Air Display Committee under the Chairmanship of Mr G. Welham. Their prime objective was to raise money for the local surrounding area, to provide support and amenities that were beyond the scope of the National Health Service at this time. Other distinguished people who supported the event and were there on the day included wartime Duty Controller Ronald Adam and veteran pilots Robert Stanford Tuck, Norman Ryder, Colin Gray and Ronald Berry.

At 12 noon, the main gates were opened to the public, who flocked into the aerodrome in their thousands. There were many ground-based attractions for them to view including the RAF Police dog team demonstration and the RAF Ceremonial Drill team, who gave an exhibition of continuity drill without the individual word of any command from their officer. The rest of the day's programme was as follows:

3.00   Formation and circuit over the airfield by members of the Tiger Club Turbulent and Tiger Moth aircraft
     Flying demonstration of the Arrow Active, piloted by Mr C. Nepean Bishop
     Display by Turbulent aircraft
     Balloon bursting competition by four Tiger Moth aircraft
     Demonstration by Garland Linnet aircraft
     Formation flying by three Tiger Moths tied together
4.00   Air Race Round 1
     RAF Ceremonial Drill team
     Formation acrobatic display by three RAF Chipmunks
5.00   Spitfire flying display
     Flour bombing contest by three Tiger Moths
     Demonstration of Jackaroo aircraft
     Solo aerobatics in Tiger Moth

Flying demonstration of the Jodell-French two-seater aircraft

Tiger Moth formation flying

Parachutists take off for the delayed parachute jumps

Air Race Round 2

Parachutists spot land

Parachute descents made from static balloon by the 10th Parachute Battalion

7.00 Gliding demonstration by the 614 Gliding School of ATC based at Hornchurch

Crowds of over 20,000 were reported. It was all great fun for the spectators particularly when three Tiger Moths made a low-level attack on a moving vehicle, dropping bags of flour on it as bombs. Unfortunately the only black mark of the day was the postponement of the Spitfire display. The Spitfire, a clipped-wing Mk14 with a five-bladed propeller, was loaned from the Vickers-Armstrong Aircraft Company. However, grouped around the aircraft during the day were some of the 'Few'.

A BBC film unit had arrived and was undertaking interviews conducted by Wing Commander Ronald Adam, by then an actor and playwright. He interviewed Norman Ryder ex-41 Squadron, Colin Gray ex-54, 'Raz' Berry ex-603 and Norman Duckenfield of No.74 Squadron. They were there to film a prologue to use in a television play written by Ronald Adam about the Battle of Britain titled *An English Summer*. The actor, Joseph O'Conner, would play the part of Duty Controller Armstrong, based on Adam's own experiences at Hornchurch in 1940. The interviews were conducted beside the station's Spitfire gate guardian RM694, a MkXIV variant. The programme was broadcast on Sunday, 18th September 1960.

Life continued much the same during 1961, but news that a new purpose-built centre at Biggin Hill was being constructed for aircrew selection signalled that Hornchurch's days were now numbered as an RAF station. Howard LaRoche recalls:

> In 1961, having reached the minimum permissible age of 13½, I joined No.452 (Hornchurch) Squadron of the Air Training Corps. By this time I think most of us realised that the old days were numbered. However, in that final year several visits to the station were made, mainly to use the indoor small-bore firing range, which was situated just inside the station, past the main guard-room. We also went there for the annual West Essex Wing Parade.

Hornchurch was to feature once more in the newspaper headlines before its final closure, when an alarming incident at the aerodrome took place. For 60 seconds on Sunday, 13th May 1961, four men gambled with death 800 feet above the airfield. The men, all belonging to a Territorial Army parachute regiment, had been taken aloft to make jumps in a fixed barrage balloon. As the balloon reached 800 feet and the first man prepared to jump, it suddenly burst and sent the cage hurtling downwards. It was only the quick thinking of the instructor, Company Sergeant-Major Albert Small, that prevented any fatalities. With seconds to spare before the cage swung onto its side, he pushed two of the men out, and they floated down to safety, but he was trapped inside the cage with Lance Corporal Reginald Watts. Ex-Arnhem veteran Sergeant-Major 'Rocky' Small coolly instructed Lance Corporal Watts to prepare himself for impact, by hanging onto the straps and lifting his feet off the ground. The cage then hit the ground.

Both of the men were then rushed to Oldchurch Hospital, but only Watts was detained with a cut face and bruises. Later Sergeant-Major Small telephoned his wife at Finchley saying, 'I've just fallen 800 feet, but don't worry, darling, I'm all right.' He told the *Romford Times*: I first knew there was something wrong when I felt an almighty lurch. I then saw a piece of the balloon fabric flapping about. I just screamed 'the balloon has gone' and I pushed two men out.

Four hours after the accident a RAF inquiry was opened at Hornchurch. If it had not been for the quick thinking and cool nerve of the Sergeant Major, they could have lost their lives.

On 9th April 1962, after 14 years of testing candidates for the RAF, the Aircrew Selection Centre finally left to take up its new site at Biggin Hill. Hornchurch was now maintained by a small RAF holding party, which maintained the buildings as best they could until 1st July 1962, when the aerodrome was officially closed after 47 glorious years. Senior Aircraftman David Phillips, who was one of the holding party, was given the official last role by the Royal Air Force of handing the keys of the stations buildings over to Mr Ronald Thornton, a representative of estate agent Messrs Hilbrey and Chaplin. There were reporters and photographers from several newspapers who were on hand to record the final act of RAF Hornchurch's history.

The Air Ministry officially put up RAF Hornchurch for sale by auction on 27th February 1963. This covered all the flightpaths, blockhouse buildings and hangars on the eastern side of the aerodrome site of Southend Road. The auction was conducted on behalf of the Air Ministry, by the estate agent, Kemsley, Whitely and Ferris of Romford. At 2.00 pm on Friday, 13th March 1963, the sale of RAF Hornchurch commenced. The auction was held in the confined space of the Sergeants' Mess building and bidding was brisk. Robert Ballard attended the final act that afternoon and recalls:

> I was an unofficial, uninvited member of the public who managed to be on the station that afternoon, curious to be around, though wanting no part of the auction. I'd glimpsed momentarily into the crowded room of excitement, afterwards wandering over to the huge deserted hangars.
>
> Inside the main central one, I noticed debris covering the normally clean floor, and then my eyes were drawn to an unusual sight of former years. Lying there was a square piece of white cardboard. I bent down to pick this up and on the reverse side was a mounted black and white photograph of a 74 Squadron Meteor jet in flight. I kept this find as mine. The airfield was deserted and empty; even Fords of Dagenham,

who for some weeks had stored new cars off the production lines on the airfield and inside the hangars, had gone. Only the bidders cars were parked on the Parade Square. And then what I feel certain was the very last aeroplane to land and take off from Hornchurch, caught my attention.

It was a Cessna 310, arriving in haste, which taxied up to the side of No.2 hangar, out of which emerged two smartly dressed gentlemen, who all but ran to the auction for fear of missing out on one last remaining bid.

The main area which consisted of the flightpath was leased to the Hoveringham Gravel Company, who would use it to excavate for gravel. Fortunately the Officers' Mess and adjoining Married Quarters blocks were saved from demolition. The Mess was used as a private company office, while the old Married Quarters were retained by the Air Ministry for personnel and their families, working for them or other RAF departments in central London. The main gates at RAF Hornchurch were removed, and they now stand at Biggin Hill, just along from the St George's Memorial Chapel, which is still maintained by the Royal Air Force. The final act of the demolition of the main 'C' Type hangar was finally completed during the winter of 1965. By 1966, the bulldozers and demolition contractors had finished their work, and there was very little to remind anyone that a famous RAF fighter station had been situated here.

### Events post-closure

Out of the darkness, however shone a light in remembrance of RAF Hornchurch, when it was decided that a new primary school would be built on the site of the old parade ground. The name put forward for the new school would be Mitchell, named after the famous aircraft designer Reginald Joseph Mitchell CBE (1895-1937), who designed the Supermarine Spitfire. The school began to take pupils on 6th September 1967, but was not officially opened until 2nd December 1968. At the official ceremony, Air Vice-Marshal R.I. Jones, CB, AFC, who commanded No.11 Group Fighter Command, presented the school with a replica of the station badge. Mr Alan Thake, the headmaster, received this on behalf of the school. Also attending that day was ex-54 Squadron pilot Air Commodore Alan Deere DSO, OBE, DFC, together with the Mayor of Havering, W.A. Sibley JP, Mrs Lydia Hutton of the Education Commitee, Mr David Wilkinson, the Chief Education Officer, Mr T.S. Jarron, the Chairman of the School Managers, and Mr John Symons, the Town Clerk.

The school's uniform would also incorporate the theme of aviation by having the school blazer and tie badge depicting a light blue Spitfire and a white 'M' for Mitchell against a maroon background. This was designed by Alan Thake. In 1971, Alan Thake was succeeded by Mr R.A. French as headmaster, who decided to introduced a new school house system that would again continue the theme of RAF Hornchurch.

In a letter to the late Air Commodore Alan Deere DSO, OBE, DFC, dated 21st March 1972, Mr French wrote:

Dear Air Commodore Deere

At this school named after R.J. Mitchell the designer of the 'Spitfire', which stands on the site of the now demolished RAF Station Hornchurch, I feel it would be most fitting, as we are beginning a House system at the school, to name the Houses after four famous Spitfire pilots who served in squadrons which were based at this Station during the war.I am sure this would be more significant to children of Junior School age, if the names chosen were those of persons still living, and the children and I would regard it a great honour if you would consent to the use of your name as a title for one of the houses along with those of Wing Commander H.M. Stephen, DSO, DFC, Wing Commander R.R.S. Tuck, DSO, DFC, and Air Chief Marshal Sir Harry Broadhurst KCB, KBE, DSO, DFC, AFC.

The choice of names follows a little research I have pursued, aided by Squadron Leader Martin at the Ministry of Defence. They commemorate, in addition to their deeds and squadrons, various other attributes not only of themselves, but of others who served at Hornchurch.

Thus yourself, as a New Zealander, represents the aid given by Commonwealth countries in the war effort. Sir Harry Broadhurst was Commanding Officer at the Station, Wing Commander Stephen, a Scot, reminds us that the United Kingdom comprises other races beside the English. Sir Harry Broadhurst and yourself remained in the Air Force after the war and rose to even greater eminence in the Service, whilst Wing Commanders Stephen and Tuck returned to the civilian life for which they had fought so valiantly.

You will know that we already have links between the school and the RAF, as I understand you visited the school on the occasion of the presentation of the badge of RAF Hornchurch. This badge is mounted in our school hall, as are the crests of the four surviving Battle of Britain Squadrons Nos.19, 54, 92 and 111.

Wing Commander Collins, present Commanding Officer of No.111 Squadron, presented the four crests earlier this year.

Our school tie, badge and scarf bear RAF colours and about one-third of our 180 children, aged between 7 and 11 come from RAF families living in the married quarters which used to serve RAF Hornchurch Station, but now accommodate members of the Ministry of Defence. The badges of the four squadrons previously mentioned are used as trophies for House competitions and a scale model of a Spitfire is used as an overall trophy for the Champion House.

Finally, in the hope that it might be possible to arrange a date on which all four personalities might visit the school together.

Yours Sincerely
R.A. French

Thus in June 1972, Air Commodore Deere and Wing Commanders Tuck and Stephen visited Mitchell's School to see the inauguration of the new House system, where they were treated to the school recorder band's rendition of the Royal Air Force march. The new House Trophy, a silver cup engraved with 'Spitfire Pilots' Trophy' was presented by the veteran pilots. Also presented to the school were four copy sketches of each of the pilots, which had been drawn by wartime artist Cuthbert Orde; these were mounted on wooden plaques and still hang today in the school hall either side of the station's badge.

Another tribute to the airmen of Hornchurch was the decision to name the roads on and around the new airfield housing estate after some of the most notable pilots that had served there. The Council of Havering chose the names along with representatives of Bairstow Eves after undertaking research on various pilots' histories. This was finally completed during the early 1970s, and since then other names have been added as new roads have been built. (For a full list of roads, see Appendix G.)

Throughout the 1970s the school was visited regularly by RAF dignitaries, including Wing Commander R. Horsfield who commanded No.111 Squadron until 1974. Alan Deere visited on annual Sports Days, as did Wing Commander Robert Stanford-Tuck who served on the School Board.

By 1979, the gravel extraction on the site of the old flightpath by Hoveringham Gravel Limited had been completed. The excavations that were left on the site were then used as a rubbish tip and filled, then levelled over with earth, raising the height of the original site by at least 30 feet. It was at this time that the London Borough of Havering Council acquired 218 acres from the Department of the Environment. The council decided that 58 acres of this land would be allocated for future housing development, while 160 acres would become a new country park. There were still some landmarks left however, which showed that an aerodrome had once stood here. Part of the eastern perimeter track, which followed the edge of the River Ingrebourne, still remained; there was also the E-Type Blenheim dispersal pen and a few pill boxes and gun emplacements.

The creation of the country park in 1980 incorporated the last dispersal pen, which became the visitor car park. The perimeter track that ran along the Ingrebourne River has also become the main walkway around the park, used by casual walkers and keep-fit joggers alike. Since then, there has been a large scale planting of trees, which has enhanced the area, and seen a return of nature taking its course. This has provided a reserve for wildlife to prosper. The country park is also visited every weekend by anglers and bird-watchers as well as the ordinary family out for a pleasant walk. The park is maintained by a team of professional rangers who also organise special walks throughout the year. They also provide the public with an insight into RAF Hornchurch's illustrious past.

In 1979, an exhibition was held at the Mitchell's School, put together by local caretaker Mr Ted Exall. The display of photographs showing the history of RAF Hornchurch and related memorabilia was a great success. With growing interest in the aerodrome's history, Ted Exall along with the help of Mr Edward 'Ted' Harrison as secretary and Mr Graham Howgego as treasurer, embarked upon the task of raising money to establish a permanent memorial stone commemorating RAF Hornchurch.

The campaign to raise money was titled 'The RAF Hornchurch Memorial Fund'. After three years of hard work, the £3,500 needed to pay for the construction of the memorial stone was raised, thanks to the marvellous response from the local public, ex-pilots and personnel and a grant from the London Borough of Havering. A donation was also made by the local Tesco supermarket, which stands today where the main hangar once stood. Money was also raised by The Good Intent public house, whose landlady at that time did a sponsored parachute jump to raise funds for the stone. The memorial stone was to be erected in the grounds of Mitchell's School, just along from where the main gates of the station once stood.

On Tuesday, 5th July 1983, the memorial was finally unveiled. Several hundred people including children from the school attended the ceremony. Many pilots, ground crews and WAAFs who had been stationed at the aerodrome during the war also attended as guests. Air Chief Marshal Sir Harry Broadhurst was the main VIP; he was there to unveil the stone, which was draped in the Royal Air Force Ensign. He arrived with Air Vice-Marshal Kenneth Hayr, Air Officer Commanding No.11 Group, along with the Mayor of Havering, Mrs Winnie Whittingham and Dr Gordon Mitchell, son of R.J. Mitchell, after attending a lunch reception at the Romford Town Hall with other selected guests. The Air Training Cadets of No.452 Hornchurch and No.1838 Elm Park Squadrons provided a Guard of Honour.

After prayers and readings conducted by Canon Peter Peatfield of St Andrew's Church, Hornchurch, Air Chief Marshal Broadhurst made a speech and unveiled the memorial stone. After the ceremony was completed the VIPs and guests were taken to the Good Intent public house for refreshments. Many acquaintances were renewed and stories of the past retold among the pilots and groundcrews. Among the pilots who attended were Squadron Leader Peter Morfill DFM and Squadron Leader Ronald Stillwell, DFM, DFC, both ex-65 Squadron. Flight Lieutenant Ludwik Martel, KW, VM, ex-603 Squadron, Squadron Leader Henryk Szczesny, KW, VM, DFC, ex-74 Squadron and Flight Lieutenant Gerald Robinson MBE, ex-264 Squadron. Representing the WAAFs were Joy Caldwell and Joan Bowell, who had served at the station in 1940. Another marvellous and historical event in the history of RAF Hornchurch had taken place.

In September of that year, Mr Ted Exall and colleagues decided to set up the RAF Hornchurch Association. This was in response to the public, who wished to find out more about the airfield or help with the annual Battle of Britain exhibition that was held at the No.1838 Air Training Cadet Centre in Wood Lane, Hornchurch. The group over the years pursued the local council to provide a suitable building to house a museum dedicated to RAF Hornchurch, but this came to nothing owing to a lack of foresight by the council about preserving the borough's heritage. They continued to keep the history of the airfield in the public eye, by organising several exhibitions over the years, including the display of an original Spitfire aircraft at the Dolphin Centre in Romford, during the Borough of Havering's Heritage fortnight in 1987.

Again in 1990, when this country commemorated the 50th Anniversary of the Battle of Britain, they managed to provide a static Spitfire with the help of the RAF Careers Department for the Havering Show held that September. They were given their own marquee to display RAF Hornchurch memorabilia. It was at this show that I became fascinated in the history of my local airfield. The association still continues to carry out exhibitions each year at Mitchell's School and other local venues.

At present, the only permanent comprehensive display on the history of RAF Hornchurch on view to the public, is The Hornchurch Wing collection, which is housed at the Purfleet Heritage and Military Centre in Purfleet, Essex. It opened in 1995, set up by Alan Gosling, Tony Philpott and myself and other interested members. The centre, just four miles from Hornchurch, now displays many of RAF Hornchurch's most famous pilots' uniforms, flying kit and memorabilia, along with many aircraft artefacts from Spitfires that flew from Hornchurch during the Battle of Britain. There is also a selection of Sutton's Farm Royal Flying Corps memorabilia on view. There are over 500 photographs and an audio-visual display telling the story of Sutton's Farm and RAF Hornchurch. They also hold annually a Battle of Britain Anniversary exhibition, which runs for one month and is attended by veterans of the battle, who attend the opening weekend. There is usually a Spitfire flypast, which is also well received by the public, which brings a tear to many an eye and lump in the throat. The Centre is well worth a visit. Over the last two years The Hornchurch Wing has displayed at the Havering Show. On 28th August 2000, during the 60th Anniversary year of the Battle of Britain, they arranged with the Battle of Britain Memorial Flight for the flypast of a Spitfire over the showground. The sight and sound of the low-flying Spitfire turned thousands of heads skyward and brought much applause.

So now we come to the end of the book. It has been an honour and privilege for me to research the history of Sutton's Farm and RAF Hornchurch and meet some of the people who served there. I also hope that you the reader have enjoyed travelling the road of history with the two volumes that make up this fitting tribute to what was undoubtedly one of this country's outstanding Royal Air Force fighter stations. I hope future generations will be equally interested in the part that this famous fighter airfield played in Britain's heritage. For the pilots and ground personnel who gave their all, I take this quote used by my good friend Squadron Leader Peter Brown AFC, who today continues to lecture to our younger generations and helps to keep the memory of Churchill's 'Few' alive.

### 'We shall not see their like again'

# APPENDIX A

## RAF Hornchurch Station Commanders
## 1941-1960

| | |
|---|---|
| Group Captain Harry Broadhurst DSO, DFC, AFC | 23.12.1940 – 14.05.1942 |
| Group Captain C.G. Lott DSO, DFC | 14.05.1942 – 05.01.1943 |
| Group Captain A.G. Adnams | 05.01.1943 – 20.07.1943 |
| Group Captain H.L. Maxwell, DSO | 20.07.1943 – 28.10.1943 |
| Wing Commander F.D.S. Scott-Malden DSO, DFC | 28.10.1943 – 06.02.1944 |
| Squadron Leader R. Watt-Jones | 06.02.1944 – 20.04.1944 |
| Squadron Leader R.S. Davies | 20.04.1944 – 01.12.1944 |
| Group Captain R.J. Clare-Hunt | 01.12.1944 – 14.07.1946 |
| Wing Commander G.W. Day | 14.07.1946 – 03.12.1946 |
| Wing Commander S.H. Page | 03.12.1946 – 28.06.1947 |
| Air Commodore D. McFadyen CBE | 28.06.1947 – 17.12.1947 |
| Air Commodore A. McKee CBE, DSO, DFC, AFC | 17.12.1947 – 12.10.1948 |
| Group Captain F.C. Sturgis OBE | 12.10.1948 – 02.04.1951 |
| Group Captain H.L.Parker | 02.04.1951 – 02.07.1951 |
| Group Captain J.N. Jefferson CBE | 02.07.1951 – 21.07.1953 |
| Air Commodore E.J. Corbally CBE | 21.07.1953 – 18.01.1954 |
| Wing Commander A.J. Hicks | 18.01.1954 – 08.03.1954 |
| Wing Commander W.G.Devas | 08.03.1954 – 04.12.1954 |
| Wing Commander C.A.R Crews | 04.12.1954 – 09.05.1955 |
| Wing Commander A.N. Jones | 09.05.1955 – 30.10.1957 |
| Wing Commander H.D.U. Denison | 30.10.1957 – 09.04.1962 |

# APPENDIX B

## Squadrons operational from RAF Hornchurch
## 1st January 1941 – 8th May 1945

| Squadron | Dates | Sqdn Code | Aircraft |
|---|---|---|---|
| No.41 | 29th August 1940 – 23rd February 1941 | EB | Spitfire MkII |
| No.54 | 23rd February 1941 – 31st March 1941 | KL | Spitfire MkII |
| | 20th May 1941 – 4th August 1941 | | |
| | 25th August 1941 – 17th November 1941 | | |
| No.64 | 10th November 1940 – 27th January 1941 | SH | Spitfire MkII |
| | 19th November 1941 – 9th December 1942 | | Spitfire V/IX |
| | 2nd January 1943 – 28th March 1943 | | |
| No.66 | 1st November 1943 – 3rd March 1944 | LZ | Spitfire MkIX |
| No.81 | 14th May 1942 – 1st September 1942 | FL | SpitfireMkV |
| No.122 | 2nd April 1942 – 8th June 1942 | MT | Spitfire MkV |
| | 18th July 1942 – 18th May 1943 | | Spitfire MkIX |
| No.129 | 28th June 1943 – 17th January 1944 | DV | Spitfire MkIX |
| No.132 | 2nd October 1942 – 10th October 1942 | FF | Spitfire MkII |
| No.154 | 8th June 1942 – 1st September 1942 | HT | Spitfire MkV |
| No.222 | 30th April 1943 – 1st January 1944 | ZD | Spitfire MkIX |
| No.229 | 24th April 1944 – 19th May 1944 | 9R | Spitfire MkIX |
| No.239 | 14th August 1943 – 1st October 1943 | HB | Mustang MkI |
| No.274 | 24th April 1944 – 19th May 1944 | JJ | Spitfire MkIX |
| No.278 | 13th November 1944 – 15th February 1945 | | Walrus |
| | | | Warwick |
| | | | Spitfire |
| No.313 Czech | 15th December 1941 – 6th February 1942 | RY | Spitfire MkV |
| No.340 French | 28th July 1942 – 23rd September 1942 | GW | Spitfire MkV |
| No.349 Belgian | 11th March 1944 – 11th April 1944 | GE | Spitfire MkIX |
| No.350 Belgian | 23rd September 1942 – 1st March 1943 | MN | Spitfire MkIX |
| | 13th March 1943 – 23rd March 1943 | | |
| | 13th October 1943 – 31st October 1943 | | |
| | 30th December 1943 – 10th March 1944 | | |
| No.403 Canada | 4th August 1941 – 25th August 1941 | KH | Spitfire MkV |
| No.411 Canada | 22nd November 1941 – 6th February 1942 | DB | Spitfire MkV |
| | 22nd February 1942 – 7th March 1942 | | |
| No.453 Australia | 23rd September 1942 – 7th December 1942 | FU | Spitfire MkV |
| | 27th March 1943 – 28th June 1943 | | |
| No.485 N.Zealand | 18th October 1943 – 21st November 1943 | OU | Spitfire MkIX |
| | 15th February 1944 – 15th March 1944 | | |
| No.504 | 17th January 1944 – 18th February 1944 | TM | Spitfire MkIX |
| No.567 | 14th November 1944 – 13th June 1945 | | Barracuda |
| | | | Martinet |
| | | | Hurricane |
| | | | Oxford |
| | | | Anson |
| | | | Vengeance |

| No.603 | 16th May 1941 – 2nd June 1941 | XT | Spitfire MkV |
| | 4th June 1941 – 20th June 1941 | | |
| | 8th July 1941 – 14th December 1941 | | |
| No.611 | 14th December 1940 – 20th May 1941 | FY | Spitfire MkI |
| | 14th June 1941 – 13th November 1941 | | Spitfire MkV |
| No.765  FAA | 14th November 1944 – 15th June 1945 | | Wellington |

# APPENDIX C

## Wing Commanders Flying
## 1941-1943

Wing Commander A.D. Farquhar DFC     15th March 1941 – 2nd June 1941

Wing Commander J.R. Kayll DSO, DFC     2nd June 1941 – 25th June 1941 (PoW)

Wing Commander F.S. Stapleton DSO, DFC     27th June 1941 – 3rd December 1941

Wing Commander H.L. Dawson     4th December 1941 – 16th January 1942

Wing Commander P.R. Powell DFC     17th January 1942 – 2nd June 1942

Wing Commander B.E. Finucane DSO, DFC     27th June 1942 – 15th July 1942 (Killed)

Wing Commander F.H. Hugo DSO, DFC     18th July 1942 – 31st August 1942

Wing Commander R.H. Thomas DSO, DFC     31st August 1942 – 27th November 1942

Wing Commander A.M. Bentley     27th November 1942 – 29th March 1943

Wing Commander J.R.I. Kilmartin DFC     30th March 1943 – 30th May 1943

Wing Commander J.R. Ratten DFC     31st May 1943 – 28th July 1943

Wing Commander W.V.C-Compton DSO,DFC     30th July 1943 – 18th December 1943

Wing Commander P.J. Simpson DFC     18th December 1943 – 29th February 1944

# APPENDIX D

## Squadron Commanders
## 1941-1945

| Squadron | Commanding Officers |
|----------|---------------------|
| No.41 | Squadron Leader D.O. Finlay DFC, AFC |
| No.54 | Squadron Leader R.F. Boyd DSO, DFC |
| | Squadron Leader N. Orton DFC – Killed 17.9.41 |
| | Flight Lieutenant F.D. Scott-Malden DFC, DSO |
| No.64 | Squadron Leader A.R. MacDonell CB |
| | Flight Lieutenant B. Heath DFC |
| | Squadron Leader D. Kain |
| | Flight Lieutenant B.J. Wicks DFC – Killed 12.10.42 |
| | Squadron Leader W.G. Duncan-Smith DSO, DFC |
| | Flight Lieutenant F.A. Gaze DFC |
| | Squadron Leader W.V. Crawford-Compton DSO, DFC |
| | Squadron Leader M.G. Donnet DFC |
| No.66 | Squadron Leader K.T. Lofts DFC – Killed 20.5.51 |
| No.81 | Flight Lieutenant R. Berry DFC, DSO |
| No.122 | Squadron Leader F. Fajtl DFC |
| | Flight Lieutenant L. Prevot DFC |
| | Squadron Leader J.R.C. Kilian |
| | Wing Commander D.E. Kingaby DFM** DFC, DSO |
| | Squadron Leader P.W. Wickham DFC, DSO |
| No.129 | Squadron Leader H.A. Gonay DFC – Killed 14.6.44 |
| | Squadron Leader P.V. Tripe |
| No.132 | Flight Lieutenant J.R. Ritchie AFC |
| No.154 | Squadron Leader D. Carlson DFC |
| No.222 | Squadron Leader E.J. Harrington |
| | Squadron Leader G.J. Stonehill DFC |
| | Squadron Leader R.F. Inness |
| No.229 | Squadron Leader N.F. Harrison |
| No.234 | Squadron Leader M.G. Barnet |
| | Squadron Leader E.P.R. Bocock DFC – Killed 13.9.46 |
| No.239 | Squadron Leader P.M. Evans |
| No.274 | Squadron Leader J.F. Edwards DFM, DFC |
| No.313 | Squadron Leader K. Mrazek |
| No.340 | Squadron Leader B. Duperior DFC |
| No.349 | Squadron Leader I.G. de Bergendal DFC |
| No.350 | Squadron Leader D.A. Guillaume |
| | Squadron Leader A.L. Boussa DFC, MC |
| | Squadron Leader L.O. Prevot DFC |
| No.403 | Squadron Leader B.G. Morris |
| | Flight Lieutenant A. Lee-Knight DFC – Killed 17.9.41 |
| No.411 | Squadron Leader R.B. Pitcher |
| | Flight Lieutenant P.S. Turner DFC, DSO |
| | Squadron Leader R.B. Newton |

| No.453 | Squadron Leader F.V. Morello |
|--------|------------------------------|
|        | Squadron Leader J.R. Ratten DFC |
|        | Squadron Leader K.M. Barclay |
| No.485 | Squadron Leader M.R.D. Hume DFC |
|        | Squadron Leader J.B. Niven DFC |
| No.504 | Squadron Leader H.J.L. Hallowes |
|        | Squadron Leader A. Banning-Lover |
| No.603 | Flight Lieutenant F.M. Smith DFC |
|        | Flight Lieutenant M.J. Loudon DFC |
|        | Squadron Leader T.H. Forshaw |
| No.611 | Squadron Leader E.R. Bitmead DFC |
|        | Squadron Leader F.S. Stapleton DSO,DFC |
| No.765 | Lieutenant D.H. Coates |

# APPENDIX E

## RAF Hornchurch's Top Scoring Aces
## 1939-1944

Victories only accounted for while operating from Hornchurch Sector, and not pilots' total wartime score. In alphabetical order.

| Pilot | Victories | Squadron |
|---|---|---|
| George Bennions | 12+5 probable | No.41 |
| Ronald Berry | 10+7 probable | No.603 |
| Robert Finlay-Boyd | 5+1 probable | No.54 |
| Harry Broadhurst | 13+7 probable | CO Hornchurch Wing |
| Brian Carbury | 13+2 probable | No.603 |
| Jack Charles | 6+7 probable | No.54 |
| William Crawford-Compton | 11+2 probable | Nos.611,64,122 |
| Alan Deere | 12+3 probable | No.54 |
| Wilfred Duncan-Smith | 11+7 probable | Nos.611,603,64 |
| William Franklin | 13+3 shared | No.65 |
| John Freeborn | 8+1 probable | No.74 |
| Colin Gray | 15+7 probable | No.54 |
| George Gribble | 6+2 probable | No.54 |
| Richard Hillary | 5+2 probable | No.603 |
| Ray Hesselyn | 6+1 probable | No.222 |
| Don Kingaby | 5+2 probable | Nos.64,122 |
| James Leathart | 6+2 probable | No.54 |
| Eric Lock | 26+8 probable | Nos.41,611 |
| Tony Lovell | 5+2 probable | No.41 |
| John Mackenzie | 6+4 probable | No.41 |
| Sailor Malan | 9+1 shared | No.74 |
| Desmond McMullen | 15+5 probable | Nos.54,222 |
| Norman Ryder | 6+1 probable | No.41 |
| Ernest Scott | 5+3 probable | No.222 |
| William Skinner | 5+3 shared | No.74 |
| Thomas Smart | 5+2 probable | No.65 |
| Gerald Stapleton | 6+8 probable | No.603 |
| Harbourne Stephen | 6+1 probable | No.74 |
| Jack Stokoe | 7+1 shared | Nos.603,54 |
| Tim Vigors | 5+4 probable | No.222 |
| John Webster | 10+2 shared | No.41 |

Total: 268 destroyed, 96 probable, 10 shared.

# APPENDIX F

## RAF Hornchurch's Pilot Casualties
## 1941-1944

| Pilot | Sqdn | Killed in Action |
|---|---|---|
| Pilot Officer H.S. Sadler | No.611 | 5th February 1941 |
| Pilot Officer E.J. Coleman | No.54 | 17th February 1941 |
| Sergeant R.A. Angus | No.41 | 20th February 1941 |
| Sergeant J. McAdam | No.41 | 20th February 1941 |
| Sergeant J.S. Gilders | No.41 | 21st February 1941 |
| Pilot Officer J.G. Pippet | No.64 | 23rd February 1941 |
| Pilot Officer D.A. Stanley | No.611 | 25th February 1941 |
| Pilot Officer J.C. Lockwood | No.54 | 3rd March 1941 |
| Sergeant J.F. Cooper | No.54 | 10th March 1941 |
| Sergeant A.A. Burtenshaw | No.54 | 12th March 1941 |
| Pilot Officer C. Colebrook | No.54 | 20th March 1941 |
| Pilot Officer J.H. Rowden | No.64 | 9th April 1941 |
| Pilot Officer A.E. Penning | No.611 | 28th April 1941 |
| Sergeant J. Claxton | No.611 | 7th May 1941 |
| Pilot Officer J. L. Brown | No.64 | 12th May 1941 |
| F/Lieutenant D.G. Gribble | No.54 | 4th June 1941 |
| Pilot Officer R.J. Burleigh | No.603 | 7th June 1941 |
| Flying Officer P.S.C. Pollard | No.611 | 22nd June 1941 |
| Flying Officer K. McKelvie | No.603 | 24th June 1941 |
| Pilot Officer C.A. Newman | No.603 | 26th June 1941 |
| Sergeant L.E. Salt | No.603 | 29th June 1941 |
| Sgt McHugh | No.611 | 3rd July 1941 |
| Pilot Officer K.E. Knox | No.54 | 5th July 1941 |
| Sergeant Feely | No.611 | 8th July 1941 (missing) |
| Pilot Officer G.H. Batchelor | No.54 | 9th July 1941 (died 15.4.42) |
| Pilot Officer N.G. Baxter | No.54 | 9th July 1941 |
| P/O Johnston | No.611 | 9th July 1941 |
| Flying Officer P.G. Dexter | No.611 | 14th July 1941 |
| Sergeant Hunter | No.603 | 14th July 1941 (missing) |
| Sergeant F.M. Laing | No.54 | 17th July 1941 |
| Sgt Grainger | No.611 | 21st July 1941 (missing) |
| Pilot Officer P.J. Delorme | No.603 | 22nd July 1941 |
| Pilot Officer Cookson | No.54 | 23rd July 1941 |
| Pilot Officer H. Blackall | No.603 | 23rd July 1941 |
| Sergeant G.W. Tabor | No.603 | 23rd July 1941 |
| Pilot Officer J.R.G. Sutton | No.611 | 23rd July 1941 |
| F/Lt E.S. Lock | No.611 | 3rd August 1941 (missing) |
| Pilot Officer N.H. Keable | No.603 | 5th August 1941 |
| Pilot Officer M. Waldon | No.403 | 19th August 1941 |
| Flying Officer McKenna | No.403 | 21st August 1941 (missing) |
| Sergeant Gray | No.611 | 26th August 1941 (missing) |
| Pilot Officer E.W Swarsbrick | No.11 Group Flight | 26th August 1941 |

| | | |
|---|---|---|
| F/Lt R. Mottram | No.54 | 31st August 1941 |
| Pilot Officer M.M. Evans | No.54 | 4th September 1941 |
| Pilot Officer J.S. Harris | No.54 | 4th September 1941 |
| S/Ldr N. Orton DFC | No.54 | 17th September 1941 |
| Sergeant J.D. Draper | No.54 | 17th September 1941 |
| Sergeant R.A. Overson | No.54 | 17th September 1941 |
| Sergeant W.J. Archibald | No.603 | 27th September 1941 |
| Sergeant J.C. Ward | No.54 | 3rd October 1941 |
| Sergeant A.D. Shuckburgh | No.603 | 13th October 1941 |
| Sergeant W. McKelvie | No.603 | 21st October 1941 |
| Pilot Officer J. Roper-Bosch | No.611 | 21st October 1941 |
| Pilot Officer J.F. Reeves | No.611 | 21st October 1941 |
| Pilot Officer N.J. Smith | No.611 | 21st October 1941 |
| Pilot Officer A. Carey-Hill | No.611 | 27th October 1941 |
| Sergeant W.P. Davies | No.611 | 5th November 1941 |
| Sergeant C.L. Hopgood | No.64 | 5th December 1941 |
| Pilot Officer J.R. Coleman | No.411 | 8th December 1941 |
| Sergeant D.A. Court | No.411 | 8th December 1941 |
| Flying Officer S.G. Fawkes | No.603 | 8th December 1941 |
| Pilot Officer S. Chamberlain | No.411 | 16th December 1941 |
| Sergeant T.D. Holden | No.411 | 16th December 1941 |
| Sergeant J. Valenta | No.313 | 11th January 1942 |
| Pilot Officer B. Konvalina | No.313 | 22nd January 1942 |
| Sergeant M. Zauf | No.313 | 18th March 1942 |
| Pilot Officer V. Michalek | No.313 | 27th March 1942 |
| Pilot Officer F.A. La Conrad | No.64 | 8th April 1942 |
| Sergeant F. Pokorny | No.313 | 10th April 1942 |
| Sergeant P. Brazda | No.313 | 24th April 1942 |
| S/Ldr R. Miller | No.122 | 24th April 1942 |
| Sergeant Pavik | No.313 | 5th May 1942 (missing) |
| F/Lt B.M.G. de Hemptine | No.122 | 5th May 1942 |
| Sergeant R.A.J. Ribout | No.122 | 5th May 1942 |
| F/Sergeant S.D. Jones | No.122 | 5th May 1942 |
| Pilot Officer J.A. Baraw | No.64 | 17th May 1942 |
| Flying Officer S. Fejfar | No.313 | 17th May 1942 |
| F/Sergeant V.J. Reed | No.81 | 2nd June 1942 |
| Sergeant R. Guillermin | No.81 | 2nd June 1942 |
| Sergeant H.V. Warnock | No.64 | 8th June 1942 |
| Pilot Officer J.L. Crisp | No.122 | 8th June 1942 |
| F/Lt G.T. Hugill | No.154 | 21st June 1942 |
| F/Sergeant R.J. Goode | No.64 | 29th June 1942 |
| F/Sgt A.R. Bray | No154 | 14th July 1942 |
| Sergeant D.S. James | No.122 | 15th July 1942 |
| W/Cdr B.E. Finucane DSO, DFC | No.154  (W/Cdr Flying) | 15th July 1942 |
| Pilot Officer A.E. Shackleton | No.81 | 29th July 1942 |
| Pilot Officer P.B.L. Evans | No.81 | 29th July 1942 |
| Pilot Officer J.G. Durkin | No.122 | 30th July 1942 |
| Sergeant T. Skjeseth | No.122 | 30th July 1942 |
| Sergeant A.M. McPherson | No.122 | 30th July 1942 |
| Pilot Officer C.E. Hurt | No.154 | 30th July 1942 |
| Sergeant I.M. Dawson | No.154 | 30th July 1942 |
| Sergeant J.J. Matthews | No.122 | 9th August 1942 |
| Sergeant E.N. McQuaig | No.64 | 19th August 1942 |
| Pilot Officer J.K. Stewart | No.64 | 19th August 1942 |
| Adjutant R.G. Darbin | No.340 | 19th August 1942 |
| Pilot Officer C.P. Shaw | No.122 | 27th August 1942 |

| | | |
|---|---|---|
| Sergeant K.G. Silsand | No.122 | 27th August 1942 |
| F/Lt C. Thomas | No.64 | 5th September 1942 |
| Adjutant F.H. de Labouchere | No.340 | 5th September 1942 |
| Sergeant E.L. Dickerson | No.64 | 7th September 1942 |
| Sergeant G. Nadan | No.122 | 16th September 1942 |
| Lt E.S. Stromme | No.64 | 11th October 1942 |
| Sergeant B.T. Nossiter | No.453 | 11th October 1942 |
| Sergeant A.R. Menzies | No.453 | 11th October 1942 |
| Sergeant E.E. Regis | No.122 | 15th October 1942 |
| Sergeant J.R. Furlong | No.453 | 31st October 1942 |
| F/Sergeant G.J. Foreman | No.122 | 8th November 1942 |
| Pilot Officer R.L. King | No.122 | 2nd December 1942 |
| Pilot Officer T.L. Parker | No.122 | 6th December 1942 |
| Sergeant L.V. Flohimont | No.350 | 22nd January 1943 |
| W/Officer S. Earwaker | No.122 | 24th January 1943 |
| Sergeant G.A. McKoy | No.64 | 26th January 1943 |
| F/Lt P.C.F. Stevenson DFC | No.64 | 13th February 1943 |
| Pilot Officer D.G. Mercer | No.122 | 26th February 1943 |
| Sergeant G.F. Crowley | No.122 | 26th February 1943 |
| Flying Officer R.S. Draper | No.64 | 24th March 1943 |
| Pilot Officer V.G. Le Blanc | No.222 | 27th May 1943 |
| Sergeant J. Carmichael | No.129 | 5th September 1943 |
| Flying Officer J.D. Mackay | No.129 | 6th September 1943 |
| Flying Officer Thiriez | No.222 | 23rd September 1943 |
| Flying Officer Rosser | No.129 | 27th September 1943 |
| Flying Officer R.L. Baker | No.485 | 20th October 1943 |
| Flying Officer J.G.Thompson | No.485 | 20th October 1943 |
| Flying Officer N.H. Cain | No.129 | 22nd December 1943 |
| F/Sergeant Williams | No.567 | 1st December 1944 |

Total of casualties: 126

# APPENDIX G

## List of Pilots and Aircrew who flew operationally from RAF Hornchurch 1941-1945

### No. 41 Squadron

F/O D.A. Adams
Sgt R.A. Angus
Sgt A.C. Baker
Sgt R.A. Beardsley
P/O M.F. Briggs
F/O M.P. Brown
P/O N. McHardy Brown
Sgt L.R. Carter
F/O G.W. Cory
P/O E.V. Darling
F/O G.G.F. Draper
S/Ldr D.O. Finlay
Sgt R. Ford

Sgt J.S. Gilders
Sgt Glew
Sgt Hopkinson
Sgt T.W.R. Healy
F/O A.D.J. Lovell
F/O J.N. Mackenzie
Sgt J. McAdam
P/O D.E. Mileham
P/O Le Roux
F/Lt E.N. Ryder
Sgt G.W. Swanwick
P/O E.P. Wells
P/O A.L. Winskill

### No. 54 Squadron

Sgt Ahern
Sgt Aitkin
Sgt Allan
Sgt Ashurst
F/Lt H.N.D. Bailey
F/O G.H. Batchelor
Sgt Bax
P/O N.G. Baxter
Sgt Beresford
Sgt Birch
P/O A. Black
S/Ldr R.F. Boyd
Sgt Burnham
Sgt A.A. Burtenshaw
P/O T.M. Calderwood
P/O A.R.M. Campbell
F/O E.F.J. Charles
P/O C. Colebrook
P/O E.J. Coleman
P/O Cookson
Sgt J.F. Cooper
P/O H.A. Cordell
F/Sgt Crisp
F/O P.G. Dexter
Sgt J.D. Draper

P/O Edsall
P/O M.M. Evans
W/Cdr A.D. Farquhar
Sgt Fenton
Sgt Faulkner
F/Lt P.M. Gardiner
Sgt Gilmore
P/O Grant-Govern
F/Lt C.F. Gray
F/O D.G. Gribble
Sgt Guthrie
Sgt H.K. Hall
F/O R.M.D. Hall
P/O J.S. Harris
P/O Harrison
F/O B. Hordern
Sgt D. Ibbotson
P/O Jones
Sgt E.J. Kean
P/O J.D. Keynes
Sgt H. Knight
P/O K.E. Knox
Sgt Karasek
S/Ldr J. Kayll
Sgt B. Konvalina

**No. 54 Squadron (continued)**

Sgt F.M. Laing
P/O Lawrence
Sgt J.C. Lockwood
Sgt McDougal-Black
Sgt Mason
P/O Keynes
F/Lt J.S. Morton
F/Lt R. Mottram
Sgt Mountseer
P/O W.J. Noble
S/Ldr N. Orton
Sgt R.A. Overson
F/Lt T.G. Pace
P/O V.D. Page
Sgt J.W. Panter
F/Sgt Pavlu
Sgt Plasil
Sgt Pook
P/O Pont
P/O Powling
Sgt Preece

F/Sgt Raises
Sgt Richards
F/O S.N. Rose
Sgt Schade
S/Ldr F.D. Scott-Malden
F/O D. Secretan
P/O H.S. Sewell
F/O N.E. Shuckburgh
S/Ldr F.S. Stapleton
P/O J. Stokoe
Sgt Stratton
Sgt H. Squire
Sgt Thompson
P/O J.A. Tuckson
Sgt F.E. Tullit
S/Ldr J.D. Urie
Sgt J.C. Ward
Sgt Waite
Sgt Worrall
F/O C.P. Wilcock
Sgt Woodhouse

**No. 64 Squadron**

Sgt Allen
Sgt Anderson
F/Lt Ashton
Lt A. Austeen (Norwegian)
P/O J.A. Baraw (USA)
F/Sgt W.J. Batchelor
P/O P.H. Beake
Sgt H. Bennett
Sgt W. Bern
P/O Berriman
Sgt W. Bilstand
Sgt V. Brennan
F/Lt D.O. Brevot (Belgian)
Sgt C. Brooker
Sgt F.R. Barnard
Sgt A. Burge
P/O H.V. Calder
Sgt D.G. Campbell
P/O P.C. Campbell
Sgt D.F. Chadwick
F/Lt E. Charles
Adj M.P.C. Choron
P/O D.A.S. Colvin
P/O F.A. Conard (Belgian)
F/Lt A.H. Corkett
Sgt Cooper
F/Lt E. Cowich (USA)
W/Cdr W.V. Crawford-Compton
F/O J. Curd
Sgt J.N. Dean
Sgt E.L. Dickerson

P/O L. Divoy (Belgian)
Sgt W. Dobson-Smyth
Sgt J. Doherty
P/O A.G. Donahue (USA)
S/Ldr M.L. Donnet (Belgian)
P/O J.C. Dowler
P/O R. Sanders-Draper (USA)
S/Ldr W.Duncan-Smith
F/Lt A.F. Eckford
Sgt R. Engelsen (Norwegian)
W/Cdr A.D. Farquhar
F/Sgt C. Finney
F/Lt F.A. Gaze
F/Sgt R. Goode
S/Ldr C.F. Gray
P/O T. Gray
Sgt J. Gunn
P/O P.S. Hannan
F/O J.W. Harder
Sgt S. Harper
P/O Hawkins
F/Lt B. Heath
P/O H.C. Homes
W/Cdr P.H. Hugo (Dutch)
Sgt G. Inkster
Sgt R. Johnson
Sgt T. Johnson (Norwegian)
P/O R.L. Jones
S/Ldr D. Kain
P/O Kelly
Sgt T. Kenny

### No. 64 Squadron (continued)

F/Lt D.E. Kingaby
F/Sgt Kirkman (Australian)
S/Ldr A. Corkett
P/O D.P. Lamb
P/O J. Lawson-Brown
Sgt D. Levington
Lt Lindseth
Sgt G.D. Loftus
F/O G.A. Mason
S/Ldr A.R.D. MacDonell
F/Lt MacPhail
Sgt Marshall
Sgt Matthews
S/Ldr D.A.P. McMullen
Sgt E. McQuaig
F/O J.J. O'Meara
P/O C.M. Mertens (Belgian)
P/O R.A. Mitchell
Sgt T.E. O'Conner
P/O E.H. Patterson
Sgt W. Pearce
P/O J.G. Pippet
P/O J.D. Plesman (Netherlands)
F/Lt L. Prevot (Belgian)
F/O H.R.G. Poulton
P/O Quill
S/Ldr J. Rankin
Sgt D.F. Reeve
P/O J. Roberts

Sgt C. Robinson
Sgt R. Rogers (Rhodesian)
F/O W.N.C. Salmond
Sgt T.W. Savage
P/O Schuren
Sgt J.W. Slade
P/O Snowball
Sgt J.Stewart
P/O J.K. Stewart (Rhodesian)
F/Lt P.C.F. Stevenson
Sgt Stone
Lt E.S. Stromme (Norwegian)
F/Lt J.S. Taylor
P/O A.R. Tidman
Sgt C. Thomas
F/Lt Thomson
Sgt Thornber
Sgt L.Trunley (Australian)
P/O O. Ullested (Norwegian)
Sgt W. Walker
Sgt H. Warnock (Australian)
F/Sgt V. Worrall
P/O E.O. Watson
F/Lt B.W. Wicks
Sgt G.H. Wickson
Sgt Wise
P/O H.F. Withy
P/O W.D. Wolff (Netherlands)
Sgt J. Yarra

### No. 66 Squadron

F/Lt H. Allen
F/O J. Brunner
P/O R. Burke
F/Lt P. Chappell
F/Sgt R. Casburn
F/Sgt B. Deakes
F/Lt A. Deytrikh
F/Lt G. Elcombe
Sgt R. Emery
S/Ldr W. Foster
F/O D. Francis
Sgt J. French
P/O M. Fulford
F/O A. Furniss-Roe
F/O T. Hamer
Sgt A. Hopkins
Sgt R. Housden

F/Lt A. Jackson
S/Ldr K. Lofts
P/O R. Logan
F/Sgt V. Lonnen
W/O A. McKibben
F/Sgt C. Neal
F/Sgt W. Nixon
F/O L. Parsons
P/O C. Reeder
F/O S. Rodgers
Sgt G. Simon
F/Sgt V. Tidy
F/Sgt G. Thomas
F/O W. Varey
Sgt L. Verbeeck
W/O J. Woodward

## No. 81 Squadron

P/O P.J. Anson
Sgt J.R. Baker
F/Lt L.G. Bedford
S/Ldr R. Berry
Sgt Bubes
Sgt G. Bullion
P/O H.A. Byford
P/O J.R. Chandler
F/Sgt Crewe
F/O R.J. Curtis
P/O P.B.L. Evans
Sgt Davibrooke
Sgt P.A. Dixon
F/Sgt H. Fenwick
P/O M.A. Le Fevre
Sgt J. Friar
Sgt R. Guillermin (French)
Sgt A.W. Hardy
P/O C. Haw
Sgt D. Husband

P/O W.S. Large
Sgt J.M. Lock
Sgt L. Lowrey
F/Lt J. Manak (Czech)
F/Lt K.A. McKay
Sgt S.P. Moston
Sgt V.C. Parker
F/Sgt E. Reilhac (French)
F/Sgt V.J. Reed
F/Sgt J.B. Rigby
W/Cdr Sanhelm
P/O A.E. Shackleton
Sgt A.H. Stodhart
Sgt P.J. Turner
Sgt G. Vaillant (French)
F/Lt Walbor
F/Lt J.E. Walker
W/O K.L. Waud
P/O A.G. Winchester

## No. 122 Squadron

Sgt P.S. Ballantine
Sgt Barrett
F/Lt P.P.C. Barthropp
P/O Bland
P/O H. Booth
Sgt D. Bostock
P/O Butler
P/O Collignon
P/O J.L. Crisp
Sgt G.F. Crowley
Sgt W.E. Dunsmore
P/O J.G. Durkin
P/O Edwards
F/Lt F. Fajtl
F/Sgt G.J. Foreman
P/O Fowler
P/O Giddings
P/O W.G. Goby
F/Lt Griffith
P/O R.E. Hardy
F/Lt H.J.L. Hallowes
F/O C. Haw
P/O B.M.G. de Hemptine (Belgian)
Sgt Hubbard
Sgt G.S. Hulse
Sgt S.D. James
Sgt J. Jacques
F/Sgt S.D. Jones
P/O R.L. King
F/Lt D.E. Kingaby
F/Lt T. Kruml
P/O Le Gal
Sgt Livesey

Sgt McDonald
F/O I.R. MacIntyre
Sgt McIntosh
Sgt A.M. McPherson
Sgt J.J. Matthews
P/O D.G. Mercer
S/Ldr R. Miller
Sgt Morrison
Sgt Mortimer
P/O J.Y.F.F. Muller (Belgian)
P/O Mulliner
P/O Maynard
F/Sgt G.K. Nadam
Sgt Park
Sgt P. Paris
P/O T.L. Parker
Sgt Peet
P/O D.A. Piggott
P/O W.B. Poulton
P/O W.A. Prest
S/Ldr L.O. Prevot (Belgian)
Lt E. Reilnac
Sgt E.E.J. Regis
Sgt R.A.J. Ribout
F/O W.T.E. Rolls
Sgt K.G. Silsand (Norwegian)
Sgt T. Skjeseth (Norwegian)
P/O C.P. Snow
P/O Van de Poel (Dutch)
P/O Wilkin
F/Lt A. Williams

## No. 129 Squadron

Sgt L. Adkins
F/O J.P. Bassett
P/O A. Bradshaw
F/O J. Byrne
F/O N.H. Cain
Sgt J.S. Carmichael
Sgt G. Cliff
F/Lt R.J. Conroy
P/O G.R. Dickson
Sgt E.W. Edwards
W/O A.J. Foster
F/Sgt A.B. Harrop
F/Lt C. Haw
F/Lt A.J. Hancock
F/Sgt T. Hetherington
F/O Hood
S/Ldr H.A. Gonay
F/Lt Gaze
F/Lt A.C. Leigh
Sgt R.O. Long
Sgt L.G. Lunn
F/O J.D. McKay

F/Lt G.A. Mason
F/O F.H. Maywhort
Sgt D.H. Nelson
P/O P.A. Nicholson
F/Lt A.G. Osmond
F/Sgt Payne
Sgt G.F. Pyle
F/Sgt Rigby
Sgt N.Roggenkamp
F/O Rosser
F/O D.F. Ruchwaldy
F/Lt Sanderson
F/Lt Smets
F/Lt Stoop
W/O R.L. Thomas
S/Ldr P.V. Tripe
P/O M. Twomey
F/Lt E.A. Watson
F/Lt N.J. Wheeler
Sgt Wood
F/Sgt C. Woodhall
F/Sgt M.F.S. Young

## No. 132 'City of Bombay' Squadron

S/Lt P. Beraud
P/O D.W. Burgess
Sgt R.A. Carr
F/Sgt T.W. Cooper
P/O E.J. Cowen
F/Lt D. Fopp
Sgt E.F. Greenshields
P/O B.J. Hammond
Sgt W.J. Johnston
P/O J.F. Kelman

Sgt F.C.D. McCulloch
P/O T. Nesbitt
Sgt R.D. Petchey
S/Ldr J.R. Ritchie
P/O A.G. Russell
P/O V.J. Sumpter
F/Lt B.J. Thomas
Sgt T. Wallace
Sgt A. O'B Weekes

## No. 154 Squadron

P/O F.A. Aikman
F/Sgt E.Artus
F/Sgt A.R. Bray
Sgt P.J. Brown
Sgt N. Bruce
F/Sgt J.G. Buiron
S/Ldr D. Carlson
P/O H.W. Chambers
Sgt H.D. Constain
Sgt A.E. Cooper
Sgt M. Davies
Sgt I.M. Dawson
F/Lt A.F. Eckford
Sgt J.F. Farrell
Sgt F.J. Flote
W/Cdr B.E. Finucane

F/Sgt G. Le Gal (French)
P/O I.T. Garrett
Sgt J. Hall
Sgt E. Hansen
F/Lt G.A. Harrison
Sgt G.M. Haase
Sgt R. Hassell
F/Lt G.T. Hugill
W/Cdr P. H. Hugo
P/O C.E. Hurt
F/Sgt D.F. Livingston
Sgt J. Tarbuck
P/O W.L. Thompson
F/O A.S. Turnbull
Sgt J. Warrington
Sgt J.S. Whaley

## No. 222 'Natal' Squadron

F/Lt Barrett
Sgt J.E. Barrie
F/O R.F. Bass
Sgt J.E.R. Beaven
F/O Beedham
F/O Bern
P/O V.G. Le Blanc (Belgian)
P/O G.M. Braidwood
P/O N. Juul-Buchwald
F/O Burge
F/Lt H.P.Lardner-Burke
F/Lt E. Cassidy
F/O J.D. Clements
F/O J.B. Collins
F/Sgt T.W. Cooper
Sgt J. Cordery
Sgt Cosgrove
F/O F.C. Cryderman
F/Sgt P.S.W. Daniel
W/O R.M. Davidson
F/O E.G. Dutton
S/Ldr P.R. Ellis
Sgt J.J.M. Fromoat
Sgt A.R. Fulton
F/O G.C.D. Green
F/Lt J.E. Hall
F/O W. Haider
F/Lt Hancock
Sgt T.B. Hannan
P/O H. Hlado
F/Sgt T.B. Hannan
S/Ldr E.J.F. Harrington
F/Lt R.B. Hesselyn
S/Ldr R.F. Inness

Sgt C.A. Joseph
F/Sgt J. Kjelbeck
F/Lt Lazenby
F/O Leigh
Sgt J.A. Leneham
F/Lt D.F. Lenton
P/O Le Gal
Sub/Lt W. Long
F/O G.A. Mason
F/Sgt A. McKibban
P/O P.A. Morgan
F/Sgt Morris
F/Lt Omissi
Sub/Lt G.P.L. Pardoe
F/Sgt R.H. Reid
P/O O. Smik
F/O J. Stenton
S/Ldr G.F. Stonehill
F/O H.L. Stuart
F/Lt R.A. Sutherland
Sgt G. Tate
F/Lt Tofield
F/O Thiriez
F/Lt W.J. Thompson
F/Sgt J.M.V. Thomson
Sgt A.E. Townsend
F/Lt P.V.K. Tripe
F/Sgt H.E. Turney
F/Sgt S.G. Walton
F/Sgt Webster
F/O E.D. Whalen
F/Sgt T.G. Winslow
Sgt T. Wyllie

## No. 229 Squadron

P/O D. Andrews
F/Lt H.J. Burrett
F/Sgt J. Butterworth
F/Sgt K.E. Clark
P/O F.R.M. Cook
F/Sgt J. Cookson
Lt R. Cumming
F/Sgt F.W. Doidge
F/O A.C.S. Ensell
Maj N.F. Harrison
Sgt A.L. Haupt
F/Sgt R.E. Hayes
W/O H.G. Head
F/Lt W.D. Idema
F/Lt I.W. Jones

F/O N.G. Langford
Sgt T.J. O'Reilly
F/Sgt J.D. McKenzie
P/O J.C.G. McDougall
F/Lt G. Mains
F/Sgt J. Manley
F/Sgt W.H. Norton
F/O G.C.S. Pearson
W/O S.E. Price
P/O J. Shirlore
F/Lt R.H. Small
F/O G.W. Symons
F/O H.A. Terris
P/O G. Walker

## No. 239 Squadron

F/O Bassett
P/O Brooks
F/O Fryer
F/O Goodwin
F/Lt Green
F/O Hallas
P/O La Coombe

P/O Lambros
P/O Lawson
W/Cdr Legge
S/Ldr McClean
F/O McLeod
F/O Martin
P/O Quixley

## No. 274 Squadron

Sgt C.J. Aldred
F/O G.J. Aylott
W/O S.G. Barker
F/O D.G. Bickford-Smith
Sgt R.C. Cole
P/O A.C. Cooper
Sgt J. Douay
S/Ldr J.F. Edwards
F/O W. Foulston
P/O C.R. Furtney
F/Lt J.R.S. Halford
F/O C.S. Hunton
W/O T. McCloy
F/O J.M. Mears

P/O R.E. Mooney
F/Lt J. Olmstead
P/O B. Ott
F/Sgt W. Pretlove
P/O N.J. Purce
W/O A.M. Ross
Sgt W.J. Stark
F/O G.A. Stroud
F/O A. Ustenov
F/Sgt W.B. Weir
W/O J. Westcott
F/Sgt F.A. Wilks
F/Lt L.A. Woods
F/O W. Woolfries

## No. 278 Squadron (Air Sea Rescue)

F/Lt Allanson
P/O Bedford
W/O Beneke
F/O J.O. Blank
F/O P. Bland
F/O Bothwell
W/O Boxall
F/Lt D.L. Boys
F/O Brown
F/Lt L. Buchanan
F/Lt Chappell
W/O Cowling
F/O R.A. Elliot
W/O Emblem
Lt Emmett
F/Sgt Evans
F/O J.V. Fleggs
F/Lt Garden
W/O Goozee
S/Lt Carr-George
W/O Hollitt
F/O Hyde
W/O Johnston
F/Lt D. King
F/Lt E.G. Langdon
F/Lt Macloud
W/O Martin
F/Lt Millar
P/O McLaren
W/O McVeigh
F/O Moore

Sgt S.J. Moore
Sgt Morley
P/O Murland
F/O Murray
W/O Orr
F/O H.J. Owen
W/O Penn
F/Lt K.M. Pendray
F/O E. Pert
F/Sgt Pleasents
F/Lt E.C. Rankin
W/O Reeder
F/Lt W.M. Rowan
W/O Saville
F/O Scott
S/Ldr S. Skinner
F/O Skinner
F/Lt W.B.H. Statham
W/O Stephen
W/O Sumner
W/O Symonds
F/Lt Thompson
F/Sgt Tripp
LAC Westbrook
W/O Williams
W/O R.C. Whitaker
F/O J.W. Whitley
W/O Wilson
F/Sgt Vickery
F/O L.T. Young

## No. 313 Czech Squadron

Sgt Bondsch
Sgt Borkoves
Sgt Bonischy
Sgt P. Brazda
Sgt K. Cap
Sgt Dohnal
F/O Drbahlan
Sgt Ednisch
P/O F. Fajtl
P/O S. Fejfar
P/O V. Foglar
F/Lt J. Himr
Sgt V. Hcrak
Sgt J. Hlouzek
P/O V. Jicha
P/O Kasel
Sgt Kocfelda
Sgt B. Konvalina
Sgt Kotiba
Sgt O. Kresta

Sgt J. Kucera
Sgt O. Kucera
Sgt Lauf
Sgt Mares
P/O V. Michalek
F/Lt K. Mrazek
F/O Muzika
Sgt K. Pavlik
Sgt Prevost
Sgt F. Pokorny
P/O J. Prihoda
Sgt Reznick
Sgt S. Spacek
Sgt V. Truhlar
F/Lt K. Valasek
Sgt J. Valenta
P/O F. Vancl
Sgt Vavriner
Sgt Vykoukal
Sgt M. Zauf

## No. 340 Squadron

S/Lt Albert
Capt Bechoff
S/Lt Boudier
Sgt Bouguen
Lt Bournier
Lt Chauvin
Lt Congnard
Adj R.G. Darbin
Adj Debel
Sgt Dumas
S/Lt Durand
Adj Durbourgel
Cdt B. Duperior
Lt Gilbert
Adj Guignard

Capt de Labouchere
S/Lt Lamcort
S/Lt Kennard
S/Lt Kerlan
S/Lt Massart
S/Ldr Moynet
S/Lt R. Mouchotte
Sgt Reeve
Lt Renaud
Lt Schloesing
S/Lt Simon
Sgt Taconet
Lt de Tedesco
Sgt Thibaud

## No. 349 Squadron

F/O H. Bailly
S/Ldr I.G. de Bergendal
F/Sgt Van de Bosch
F/Lt A. Drossaert
F/O J. Ester
F/O J. Fromont
F/O H. Goldsmith
F/Sgt G. Halleux
F/O A. Lemaire
F/O P. Libert

F/Sgt H. Limet
F/O J. Maskens
F/S J. Van Moikot
F/Lt J. Morai
F/Sgt A. Moureau
F/O M. Sams
F/Lt G. Seydel
F/O M. Straut
F/O H. Taymans

### No. 350 Belgian Squadron

Sgt R.A. Alexandre
P/O P. Arend
Sgt F. Boute
S/Ldr A.L. Boussa
P/O A. Claesen
P/O L. Collignon
F/O W.P. Demerode
F/O S. Fejfar
F/O L.V. Flohimont
S/Ldr D.A. Guillaume
Sgt L. Harmel
P/O R. De Hasse
Sgt L. Heimes
Sgt A. Herreman
Adj F.H.E. de Labouchere
Sgt F.P. Lewis
Sgt H. Limet

P/O H.E. Marcel Bel
P/O W. de Merode
Sgt Michiels
F/Lt I. Du Monceau
P/O de Patoul
F/O P. Piercot
F/O E. Plas
F/O A. Plisner
S/Ldr L. Prevot
Sgt Rosse
Sgt J. Rigole
Lt Rougeteh
P/O G.M. Seydel
F/O H. Smets
Sgt J. Vanlerbergh
P/O R. Vanderpoel
P/O F.A. Venesoen

### No. 403 'Wolf' Squadron RCAF

P/O K. Anthony
P/O Ball
Sgt Belcher
P/O Carrillo
F/Lt Cathels
Sgt Collinson
P/O Colvin
Sgt Crisp
F/Lt Christmas
Sgt Cranham
P/O N.R.D. Dick

P/O Ford
Sgt Gilbertson
S/Ldr B.G. Morris
Sgt MacDonald
F/O McKenna
F/O Price
Sgt Rainville
Sgt Rychman
Sgt Stones
P/O W.Waldon
P/O Wood

### No. 411 'Grizzly Bear' Squadron RCAF

F/Lt W.Ash
F/Lt Boomer
Sgt Booth
P/O Brady
Sgt Brown
P/O J.R. Chamberlain
P/O J.R. Coleman
P/O Connolly
Sgt D.A. Court
Sgt Curtis
F/Lt W.G.G. Duncan-Smith
P/O Eakins
P/O Evans
Sgt Gourdeau
Sgt Grant
Sgt Green
Sgt Gridley
Sgt Hartney
Sgt T.D. Holden
Sgt Lapp
Sgt Long
P/O McFarlane
P/O McLeod

P/O R.W. McNair
Sgt McDougall
Sgt Mara
Sgt Matheson
Sgt Mills
Sgt Mitchell
Sgt Mowbray
P/O Morrison
S/Ldr R.B. Newton
Sgt Nutbrown
Sgt Randall
Sgt Reid
Sgt Ritchie
S/Ldr R.B. Pitcher
W/Cdr Powell
Sgt Semple
Sgt Sharun
Sgt Sills
F/Lt Smith
Sgt Taylor
S/Ldr P.S. Turner
F/Lt Weston

## No. 453 RAAF Squadron

F/Lt K.M. Barclay
P/O J. Barrian
Sgt R.G. Clemesha
Sgt H.I. De Cosier
P/O R.J. Darcey
F/Lt W.A. Douglas
P/O R.S. Ewins
Sgt J. Ferguson
Sgt R.C. Ford
Sgt J.R. Furlong
F/O G.G. Galway
F/O E.N.W. Gray
Sgt L.J. Hansell
Sgt Hansen

F/Lt Harrington
Sgt G.R. Leith
P/O R.J. Long
Sgt F.R. McDermot
Sgt A.R. Menzies
Sgt B.T. Nossiter
S/Ldr J.R. Ratten
P/O D.J. Reid
Sgt Stansfield
Sgt F. Swift
P/O F.T. Thornley
Sgt W.W. Waldron
Sgt Watehouse
F/Lt J.W. Yarra

## No. 485 RNZAF Squadron

W/O E.G. Atkins
F/O R.L. Baker
P/O W.F. Bern
F/Lt L.S. Black
P/O A.W. Burge
F/Sgt D.F. Clarke
F/O R.M. Clarke
F/O M.A. Collett
F/O H.G. Copland
P/O J.G. Dasent
F/O R.H. De Tourret
F/O A.J. Downer
F/O H.M. Esdaile
F/O N.E. Frehner
F/Lt P.H. Gaskin
F/Lt B.E. Gibbs
F/Lt L.P. Griffith
F/Lt D. O'Halloran
F/Lt J.A. Houlton
S/Ldr M.R.D. Hume

F/O T.R.D. Kebbell
W/O E.N. Leech
F/Lt K.C. Lee
F/O R.A. Manners
F/Lt M.C. Mayston
S/Ldr J.B. Niven
S/Ldr W.A. Newenham
F/O H.W.B. Patterson
F/Sgt Robbins
F/O D.A. Roberts
P/O J.J. Robinson
F/O A.B. Stead
F/Sgt W.T.H. Strahan
F/O I.D.S. Strachan
F/O G.J. Thompson
F/Lt F. Transom
F/O H.S. Tucker
F/Lt J.F.P. Yeatman
F/Lt L.S.M. White

## No. 504 Squadron

P/O P.D. Bailey
Sgt W.B. Bielby
F/Sgt K.G. Brookes
F/O A.E. Budd
Sgt Flamer-Caldera
Sgt W. Cheesbrough
F/Sgt A.G. Clark
F/Sgt F. Cowling
F/Lt D.G.S.R. Cox
Sgt W.B. Direby
F/O P.J. Doyle
F/Sgt J. Faulkner
F/O W.E. Francis
P/O H.G. Gordon
P/O J. Gough
S/Ldr H.J.L. Hallowes

F/O L. Jaworowski
Sgt E. Jayawardena
F/Lt M. Kellet
Lt K.M. Kopperud
P/O L.E. Laws
F/Lt R.A. Milne
F/Sgt E. Mitchell
P/O J. Seelenmeyer
F/Sgt R.B. Stacey
F/Sgt J. Stewart
F/O G. Strange
P/O M.R. de-Sylva
F/O W.J.J. Warwick
F/Sgt C.S. Wright
W/O White

## No. 567 Squadron
### Anti-Aircraft Co-Operation

F/Sgt Baldwin
S/Ldr R. Joyce-Bond
F/Lt Bartlett
F/O Birtwhistle
F/Sgt Brees
F/Sgt Colquhoun
W/O Dandridge
F/Sgt Daniel
F/Sgt Downing

F/O Follett
Sgt Lawes
F/Lt Milne
F/Sgt Powell
F/O Rhodes
W/O Robinson
Sgt Verran
F/Sgt M.L. Williams

## No. 603 Squadron

Sgt W.J. Allard
Sgt W.J. Archibald
Sgt H. Bennett
P/O H. Blackall
P/O R.J. Burleigh
P/O P.J. Delorme
F/Lt W.A. Douglas
F/Lt W.G.G. Duncan-Smith
P/O J.A.R. Falconer
F/O S.G.H. Fawkes
S/Ldr T.H.T. Foreshaw
F/O G.K. Gilroy
Sgt Hunter
Sgt W.J. Jackman
P/O N.H.C. Keable
Sgt Lamb

F/Lt M.J. Louden
P/O Maclachlan
F/O L. Martel
F/O K.J. McKelvie
F/O J.S. Morton
Sgt Neil
P/O C.A. Newman
F/O H.G. Niven
P/O H.A.R. Prowse
P/O W.A.A. Read
Sgt L.E. Salt
Sgt A.D. Shuckburgh
F/O D. Stewart-Clark
S/Ldr F.M. Smith
Sgt G.W. Tabor
F/O J.A. Walker

## No. 611 Squadron

Sgt Asken
F/Lt R.G.A. Barclay
Sgt Barlow
W/Cdr E.R. Bitmead
Sgt Breeze
F/Lt J.B.H. Bruinier
Sgt A.R. Boyle
Sgt Burnham
Sgt D.A. Bye
P/O C.N.S. Campbell
P/O A. Carey-Hill
Sgt J. Claxton
Sgt W.P. Dales
Sgt Darkin
Sgt A.S. Darling
Sgt J.K. Down
P/O W.G.G. Duncan-Smith
Sgt G.T. Evans
Sgt D.E. Fair
P/O E.F.M. Fayolle
Sgt B.W. Feely
Sgt J.E. Gadd
P/O M.E. Gardiner

P/O D.G. Gibbins
Sgt Gilligan
Sgt W.M. Gilmour
Sgt A.E. Gray
Sgt W.E. Grainger
Sgt C.E. Graysmark
Sgt T. Griffiths
F/Lt J.C.F. Hayter
F/Lt B. Heath
Sgt L.Hemmingway
P/O E.L. Hetherington
Sgt A.P. Holdsworth
P/O R. Van de Honert
Sgt W.R. Irwin
Sgt L.E.H. Jenner
P/O R.A. Johnston
Sgt M.R. Ingram
P/O H.M. Langley
P/O E.J. Lamb
Sgt A.C. Leigh
F/Lt E.S. Lock
Sgt Limpenny
Sgt M.K. McHugh

**No. 611 Squadron (continued)**

Sgt G.A. Mason
F/Lt S.T. Meares
Sgt W.H.L. Milner
Sgt T.M. Ormiston
P/O A.E. Pennings
F/O P.S.C. Pollard
F/Lt Powell
P/O J.F. Reeves
P/O J.W.Y. Roeper-Bosch
F/Lt B.W. Sanderson
S/Ldr F.S. Stapleton
P/O H.E. Sadler
F/O W.N.C. Salmond

P/O N.J. Smith
P/O D.A. Stanley
Sgt Summers
P/O J.R.G. Sutton
Sgt N.G. Townsend
F/Lt E.H. Thomas
Sgt Thomas
Sgt R.A. Turlington
F/Lt D.A Watkins
F/O Watkinson
F/O T.D. Williams
Sgt K.S. Wright

# APPENDIX H

## Spitfire aircraft flown from RAF Hornchurch 1941-1944

Serial numbers of known aircraft, their arrival date at the squadron or final fate and that of the pilot who flew them, if known.

### No. 41 Squadron

| Serial No. | | Date of arrival or final fate | | Pilot |
|---|---|---|---|---|
| P7281 | Spitfire MKIIs | 24.10.40 | | Sgt Darling |
| P7283 | | 24.10.40 | | Sgt Gilders |
| P7284 | | 24.10.40 | Sent to No.54 Squadron on 22.2.41 | P/O Wells |
| P7299 | | 25.10.40 | | Sgt Angus |
| P7300 | | 24.10.40 | Sent to No.54 Squadron on 22.2.41 | F/Lt Lovell |
| P7302 | | 05.11.40 | Shot down on 20.2.41 | Sgt McAdam killed |
| P7322 | | 24.10.40 | Shot down on 20.2.41 | Sgt Angus missing |
| P7354 | | 24.10.40 | | F/O Brown |
| P7371 | | 24.10.40 | Sent to No.54 Squadron on 22.2.41 | Sgt Beardsley |
| P7443 | | 24.10.40 | Sent to No.54 Squadron on 22.2.41 | Sgt Baker |
| P7448 | | 24.10.40 | | F/O Cory |
| P7508 | | 27.10.40 | Sent to No.54 Squadron on 22.2.41 | F/Lt Ryder |
| P7548 | | 01.11.40 | Damaged during Ops on 1.1.41 | P/O Mackenzie |
| P7558 | | 10.11.40 | Sent to Civilian Repair Unit 4.4.41 | F/Lt Ryder |
| P7590 | | 16.11.40 | | Sgt Beardsley |
| P7610 | | 19.11.40 | Sent to No.54 Squadron on 22.2.41 | P/O Briggs |
| P7612 | | 03.01.40 | Sent to No.54 Squadron on 22.2.41 | F/Lt Lovell |
| P7618 | | 01.12.40 | | |
| P7619 | | 01.12.40 | | |
| P7666 | 'Royal Observer Corps' | 21.11.40 | Shot down 20.4.41 – See No.54 Sqdn | S/Ldr D.O. Finlay |
| P7689 | | 09.02.41 | | |
| P7738 | 'City of Nottingham' | 12.12.40 | | F/Lt Lovell |
| P7739 | | 24.12.40 | | |
| P7816 | | 06.02.41 | Crashed at Charing, Kent on 21.2.41 | Sgt Gilders killed |

### No. 54 Squadron

| Serial No. | | Date of arrival or final fate | | Pilot |
|---|---|---|---|---|
| P7281 | Spitfire Mk IIs | 22.02.41 | | |
| P7283 | | 12.02.41 | | Sgt Thompson |
| P7284 | | 22.02.41 | | Sgt Panter |
| P7299 | | 22.02.41 | | P/O Lawrence |
| P7300 | | 22.02.41 | Shot down on 3.3.41 | P/O Lockwood killed |
| P7302 | | 20.02.41 | | |

| | | | | |
|---|---|---|---|---|
| P7308 | | 22.05.41 | | |
| P7310 | | 18.06.40 | From No.41 Squadron | |
| P7370 | | 22.02.41 | From No.41 Squadron | |
| P7352 | | 04.08.41 | | P/O Tuckson |
| P7354 | | 22.02.41 | | Sgt Cordell |
| P7371 | | 22.02.41 | | Sgt Cooper |
| P7383 | | 17.03.41 | | Sgt Cordell |
| P7384 | | 22.02.41 | | P/O Colebrook |
| P7443 | | 24.02 41 | Failed to return 26.2.41 | Sgt Squire |
| P7508 | | 22.02.41 | From No.41 Squadron | Sgt Aitkin |
| P7557 | | 03.04.41 | | Sgt Kean |
| P7610 | | 22.02.41 | Crashed into hangar 3.4.41 | Sgt Thompson |
| P7612 | | 22.04.41 | | F/Lt Gribble |
| P7618 | | 22.04.41 | | |
| P7666 | 'Royal Observer Corps' | 22.02.41 | Shot down on 20.4.41 | F/O J. Stokoe safe |
| P7689 | | 22.02.41 | Shot down on 12.3.41 | Sgt Burtenshaw killed |
| P7738 | 'City of Nottingham' | 22.02.41 | From No.41 Squadron, damaged by AA fire 17.4.41 | F/O J.Stokoe |
| P7739 | | 25.02.41 | From No.41 Squadron | |
| P7743 | 'Brentwood' | 04.08.41 | | SGT Plasil |
| P7744 | 'Bow Street Home Guard' | 04.08.41 | | |
| P7746 | 'City of Bradford I' | 04.08.41 | | |
| P7756 | 'Pampero IV' | 13.04.41 | | F/O E.J Charles |
| P7816 | | 22.02.41 | Crashed near Ashford, Kent 24.2 1941 | Sgt Hall |
| P7818 | | 25.02.41 | | P/O Powling |
| P7823 | | | | F/O Grant-Govern |
| P7833 | 'Portadown' | 05.04.41 | Shot down 7.5.41 | Sgt Kean killed |
| P7846 | 'Newfoundland III' | 18.09.41 | Shot down on 3.10.41 | Sgt Ward killed |
| P7911 | 'City of Birmingham' | 04.08.41 | | Sgt Fenton |
| P7916 | | 04.08.41 | | Sgt Beresford |
| P7918 | 'Northampton' | 24.02.41 | | P/O Stokoe |
| P7920 | 'The Red Rose' | 24.02.41 | Force-landed at Grays, Essex 11.3.41 | Sgt Black |
| P7963 | | 28.02.41 | | W/Cdr Farquhar |
| P7976 | | 26.02.41 | | P/O Pont |
| P7979 | | 06.03.41 | | Sgt Beresford |
| P7980 | | 06.03.41 | | |
| P7981 | | 30.03.41 | | P/O Sewell |
| P8023 | | 07.05.41 | | |
| P8090 | | 04.08.41 | | |
| P8198 | | 28.03.41 | | P/O Batchelor |
| P8233 | | 04.08.41 | | Sgt Faulkner |
| P8267 | | 26.04.41 | | |
| P8380 | 'Black Velvet' | 04.08.41 | | |
| P8373 | | 04.08.41 | | F/Sgt Pavlu |
| P8426 | | 08.05.41 | | |
| P8700 | | 10.07.41 | | Sgt Worrall |
| P8744 | 'Wonkers' | 07.07.41 | | F/O Wilcocks |
| P8754 | Spitfire MkVs | 07.07.41 | Shot down 11.7.41 | F/Lt Gardiner PoW |
| P8792 | | 27.07.41 | | F/Sgt Crisp |
| R6722 | | 10.05.41 | Damaged by Me109s 25.6.41 | F/Lt R. Mottram |
| R7222 | | 25.05.41 | Shot down on 5.7.41 | Sgt Knox killed |
| R7225 | | 25.05.41 | | Sgt Tullitt |
| R7256 | | 25.05.41 | | Sgt Schade |
| R7259 | | 25.05.41 | Shot down on 25.6.41 | S/Ldr Kayll PoW |
| R7260 | 'Bristol Air Raid Warden' | 19.06.41 | | S/Ldr Gaunce |
| R7264 | | 25.05.41 | Shot down on 14.7.41 | Sgt Panter PoW |

| | | | | |
|---|---|---|---|---|
| R7266 | | 26.05.41 | | Sgt Ashurst |
| R7267 | 'Bromley & District' | 26.05.41 | Damaged on ops 18.6.41 | F/O Charles |
| R7268 | | 25.05.41 | Shot down on 23.7.41 | F/O Cookson killed |
| R7269 | | 25.05.41 | Shot down on 9.7.41 | P/O Batchelor PoW |
| | | | | |
| R7279 | 'King's Messenger' | 25.05.41 | | F/O Charles |
| R7295 | 'The Pastures' | 26.05.41 | Ditched in sea 16.6.41 | P/O Grant-Govern safe |
| R7303 | | 23.04.41 | Shot down on 22.7.41 | P/O Jones PoW |
| W3109 | | 08.06.41 | Shot down on 17.9.41 | Sgt Overson killed |
| W3169 | 'Pensa Cola' | 07.06.41 | Shot down on 9.7.41 | P/O Baxter killed |
| W3323 | 'The New Forest' | 23.06.41 | Shot down on 25.6.41 | Sgt Beresford PoW |
| W3216 | 'Maidenhead' | 26.06.41 | Shot down on 17.7.41 | Sgt Laing killed |
| W3332 | 'Hendon Griffon' | 24.07.41 | | P/O Keynes |
| W3437 | 'Kaapstad II' | 11.07.41 | | P/O Page wounded |
| W3513 | | 10.10.41 | | P/O Shuckburgh |
| W3573 | | 24.07.41 | | F/Lt Rose |
| W3620 | | 22.08.41 | Shot down on 4.9.41 | P/O Evans killed |
| W3630 | 'Kuwait' | 27.07.41 | | F/Lt Page |
| W3653 | 'E A Doncaster' | 25.07.41 | Shot down on 17.9.41 | Sgt Preece |
| W3712 | | 25.8.41 | Shot down on 31.8.41 | F/Lt Mottram killed |
| W3772 | 'Moray' | 07.09.41 | | S/Ldr Orton killed |
| AB808 | | 29.08.41 | Shot down on 4.9.41 | P/O Harris killed |
| AB813 | | 25.08.41 | Shot down on 17.9.41 | Sgt Draper killed |
| AB814 | | 25.08.41 | | |
| AB 819 | | 29.08.41 | | P/O Tuckson |
| AB845 | | 25.08.41 | | |

### No. 64 Squadron

| Serial No. | | Date of arrival or final fate | | Pilot |
|---|---|---|---|---|
| K9862 | Spitfire MkI | 19.07.40 | | P/O Gray |
| K9950 | | 29.09.40 | Fire in flight, pilot baled out 28.11.41 | P/O Salmond |
| N3059 | | 12.12.40 | | Sgt Savage |
| N3108 | | 24.10.40 | | Sgt Stone |
| N3122 | | 17.12.40 | | P/O Watson |
| R6684 | | 14.08.41 | | P/O Chadwick |
| R6700 | | 08.06.40 | | Sgt Matthews |
| R6763 | | 06.12.40 | | P/O Jones |
| R6972 | | 23.08.40 | | Sgt Choron |
| R6975 | | 24.07.40 | | P/O Pippet |
| R6977 | | 06.12.40 | | P/O Donahue |
| P6769 | Spitfire MkIIs | 11.12.40 | | Sgt Cooper |
| P7384 | | 16.11.40 | | |
| P7389 | | 10.06.41 | | P/O Divoy |
| P7555 | | 14.01.41 | | |
| P7562 | | 16.01.41 | | |
| P7605 | | 16.01.41 | | |
| P7626 | | 16.01.41 | | P/O Beake |
| P7678 | | 16.01.41 | | P/O Rowden |
| P7690 | | 16.01.41 | | |
| P7695 | | 16.01.41 | | |
| P7747 | | 16.01.41 | | |
| P7751 | 'City of Bradford VI' | 16.01.41 | | |
| P7770 | | 06.02.41 | | P/O Campbell |
| P7778 | | 14.01.41 | Failed to return after sweep 23.2.1941 | |

| | | | | |
|---|---|---|---|---|
| P7781 | | 14.01.41 | | P/O Roberts |
| P7784 | | 23.03.41 | Shot down on 9.4.41 | P/O Rowden killed |
| P7818 | | 24.02.41 | | |
| P7994 | | 15.03.41 | | Sgt Anderson |
| P7840 | 'Mountains O Mourne' | 14.02.41 | | Sgt Thornber |
| P7881 | | 15.02.41 | | P/O Roberts |
| P8031 | | 15.03.41 | | S/Ldr Heath |
| P8035 | | 28.07.41 | | Sgt Doherty |
| P8084 | 'Garfield Western VI' | 11.04.41 | | Sgt Campbell |
| P8135 | | 22.03.41 | | S/Ldr Kain |
| P8277 | | 26.04.41 | | Sgt Thomas |
| P8345 | | 27.08.41 | | Sgt Thomas |
| P8365 | 'Rotterdam' | 15.06.41 | | P/O Conrad |
| P8428 | | 14.06.41 | | Sgt Inkster |
| P8468 | | 02.07.41 | | P/O Campbell |
| P8513 | | 05.07.41 | | F/Lt Prevot |
| P8704 | | 14.08.41 | | P/O Taylor |
| P9450 | | 02.06.41 | Shot down 5.12.41 | Sgt Hopgood killed |
| P9555 | | 16.08.40 | | S/Ldr MacDonell |
| P9556 | | 16.08.40 | Force-landed in Rotherfield, Sussex 21.12.41 | |
| X4321 | | 14.12.40 | | P/O Watson |
| X4481 | | 24.11.40 | | P/O Hawkins |
| X4611 | | 27.11.40 | | P/O Tidman |
| X4647 | | 20.11.40 | | P/O Lawson-Brown |
| X4770 | | 27.11.40 | | P/O Donahue |
| W3563 | Spitfire MkVBs | 14.11.41 | | P/O Slade |
| W3802 | | 14.11.41 | Shot down 28.3.42 | Sgt Robinson PoW |
| W3815 | 'Sierre Leone II' | 14.11.41 | | P/O Savage |
| W3839 | 'Kettering District' | 14.11.41 | | P/O Mertens |
| W3947 | | 14.11.41 | | Sgt Robinson |
| AA372 | | | | |
| AA937 | | 05.12.41 | | P/O Slade |
| AB490 | | 11.04.42 | | Sgt Rodgers |
| AB786 | | 14.11.41 | | P/O Conrad |
| AB921 | | 14.11.41 | | P/O Taylor |
| AD182 | | 21.11.41 | | S/Ldr Kain |
| AD252 | | 14.11.41 | | Sgt Pearce |
| AD271 | | 14.11.41 | | Sgt O'Conner |
| AD320 | 'Palembang Oeloe' | 14.11.41 | | Sgt Bennett |
| AD474 | | 18.11.41 | | P/O Colvin |
| BL232 | | 09.01.42 | | P/O Taylor |
| BL382 | | 09.01.42 | | Sgt Walker |
| BL571 | | 13.04.42 | | P/O Baraw |
| BL717 | | 04.06.42 | | Sgt Dickerson |
| BL724 | | 02.04.42 | Failed to return on 8.4.42 | P/O Conrad missing |
| BL725 | | 16.02.42 | | F/Lt Prevot |
| BM120 | | 25.04.41 | | P/O Donnet |
| BM129 | | 20.05.42 | | Sgt McQuaig |
| BM132 | | 15.06.42 | | F/Sgt Goode |
| BM154 | | 12.04.42 | Damaged on Ops 8.6.42 | Sgt Rodgers |
| BM191 | | 27.03.42 | Failed to return on 4.4.42 | P/O Divoy PoW |
| BM194 | | 27.03.42 | | F/Lt Ullsted |
| BM254 | | 25.04.42 | Shot down 29.6.42 | F/Sgt Goode killed |
| BM268 | | 21.05.42 | Shot down 8.6.42 | Sgt Warnock killed |
| BM289 | | 15.04.42 | | P/O Withy |

| | | | | |
|---|---|---|---|---|
| BM320 | | 16.04.42 | Shot down 17.5.42 | Sgt Bennett PoW |
| BM322 | | 17.06.42 | | F/Sgt Batchelor |
| BM347 | | 13.04.42 | | F/Lt Eckford |
| BM348 | | 12.04.42 | | Lt Stromme |
| BM362 | | 12.04.42 | | F/Sgt O' Conner |
| BM356 | 'Champion' | 12.04.42 | | F/Lt Kingaby |
| BM373 | | 13.04.42 | | Sgt Walker |
| BM409 | | 15.04.42 | | P/O Thomas |
| BM415 | | 24.05.42 | | Sgt Rodgers |
| BM464 | | 31.03,43 | From No.222 Sqdn | |
| BM465 | | 19.05.42 | | Sgt Johnston |
| BM475 | | 25.04.42 | Shot down 17.5.42 | P/O Barrow killed |
| BM476 | | 25.04.42 | | F/Lt Kingaby |
| BM486 | | 04.06.42 | | |
| BM488 | | 04.06.42 | | Sgt Wickson |
| BM490 | | 04.06.42 | | Lt Austeen |
| BR140 | | 24.06.42 | | Lt Ullsted |
| BR142 | | 31.08.42 | Damaged on Ops on 31.8.42 | Lt Johnson |
| BR370 | | 09.07.42 | | Sgt Roberts |
| BR581 | | 22.06.42 | Shot down 19.8.42 | S/Ldr Duncan-Smith safe |
| BR592 | | 08.07.42 | Failed to return on 11.10.42 | P/O Dowler PoW |
| BR594 | | 19.07.42 | | Lt Austeen |
| BR596 | | 22.05.42 | Shot down 11.10.42 | Lt Stromme killed |
| BR600 | | 10.07.42 | | P/O Kingaby |
| BR601 | | 10.07.42 | | P/O Withy |
| BR602 | | 11.07.42 | Shot down 7.9 42 | Sgt Dickenson killed |
| BR603 | | 09.07.42 | Crash-landed 26.9.42 | Sgt Calder injured |
| BR604 | Spitfire MkIXs | 09.07.42 | Shot down 19.8.42 | Sgt McQuaig killed |
| BR605 | | 09.07.42 | Ditched in sea 1.8.42 | Sgt Dickenson safe |
| BR624 | | 05.07.42 | | P/O Donnet |
| BR625 | | 19.07.42 | | F/Lt Thomas |
| BR977 | | 15.07.42 | Shot down 19.8.42 | P/O Stewart killed |
| – – – – | | – – – | Shot down 11.9.42 | P/O Dowler PoW |
| BR980 | | 04.08.42 | Shot down 5.9.42 | Sgt Mason safe |
| BS105 | | 25.07.42 | Damaged on Ops on 3.8.42 | F/Lt MacPhail |
| BS126 | | 14.09.42 | | P/O Patterson |
| BS150 | | 30.08.42 | Shot down 5.9.42 | F/Lt Thomas killed |
| BS227 | | 30.08.42 | | S/Ldr Gaze |
| BS278 | | 04.09.42 | Failed to return on 27.1.43 | Sgt McKoy killed |
| BS280 | | 23.08.42 | | Sgt Wise |
| BS282 | | 25.08.42 | Damaged on 18.1.43 | P/O Dowler |
| BS315 | | 13.09.42 | | Sgt Loftus |
| BS400 | | 18.08.42 | | F/O Patterson |
| BS439 | | 08.09.42 | | S/Ldr Gaze |
| BS441 | | 10.09.42 | | F/Lt Kingaby |
| BS444 | | 12.09.42 | | F/Sgt Batchelor |
| BS539 | | 15.11.42 | | Sgt Ledington |
| BS544 | | 21.10.42 | | Lt Austeen |
| EN132 | | 17.11.42 | Crash-landed at Hornchurch 24.3.43 | Sgt Marshall |
| EN180 | | 22.11.42 | Damaged on Ops on 6.12.42 | Sgt Bern |
| EN522 | | 16.02.43 | | F/Lt Donnet |
| EN525 | | 13.02.43 | | P/O Kelly |

## No. 66 Squadron

| Serial No. | | Date of arrival or final fate | | Pilot |
|---|---|---|---|---|
| EN554 | Spitfire MkVs | 07.03.43 | | Sgt French |
| EN557 | | 07.03.43 | | Sgt Hopkins |
| EN563 | | 07.03.43 | | F/Sgt Neal |
| EN565 | | 02.12.43 | | F/O Parsons |
| EN568 | | 30.12.43 | | P/O Burke |
| EN575 | | 30.12.43 | Failed to return on 25.1.44 | |
| EN635 | | | | F/O Francis |
| MH350 | Spitfire MkIXs | | | F/Lt Elcombe |
| MH422 | | 26.11.43 | | F/O Varey |
| MH455 | | 26.11.43 | | F/O Hamer |
| MH489 | | 26.11.43 | | F/Sgt Casburn |
| MH501 | | 20.08.43 | | P/O Reeder |
| MH715 | | 08.06.43 | | W/O Woodward |
| MH723 | | 17.02.44 | | F/Sgt Hopkins |
| MH872 | | 01.10.43 | | F/Lt Jackson |
| MJ143 | | 09.02.44 | | P/O Logan |
| MJ150 | | 24.01.44 | | F/O Varey |
| MJ154 | | 25.01.44 | | F/Lt Deytrikh |
| MJ175 | | 25.01.44 | | F/Sgt Thomas |
| MJ176 | | 25.01.44 | | Sgt Emery |
| MJ178 | | | | F/Lt Deytrikh |
| MJ180 | | 09.02.44 | | F/Lt Jackson |
| MJ182 | | 26.11.43 | | S/Ldr Lofts |
| MJ794 | | | | F/Sgt Lonnen |
| MK287 | | | | F/O Varey |
| MK297 | | 17.02.44 | | P/O Chappell |
| MK619 | | 20.02.44 | | F/Sgt Hopkins |

## No. 81 Squadron

| Serial No. | | Date of arrival or final fate | | Pilot |
|---|---|---|---|---|
| AR389 | Spitfire MkVbs | 07.06.42 | | F/Sgt Crewe |
| AR395 | | 07.06.42 | | F/Lt Walker |
| AR398 | | 03.06.42 | Crash-landed on 3.8.42 | Sgt Mosten safe |
| BL640 | | 05.04.42 | Failed to return on 5.5.42 | |
| BL809 | | 30.04.42 | Sent to No.64 Sqdn on 3.5.43 | P/O Large |
| BL811 | | 30.04.42 | Air collision with BM463 on 2.6.42 | F/Sgt Reed killed |
| BM137 | | 29.07.42 | | W/O Ward |
| BM141 | | 22.07.42 | Shot down on 29.7.42 | P/O Shackleton killed |
| BM158 | | 17.05.42 | | P/O Evans |
| BM181 | | 30.07.42 | | F/Lt Bedford |
| BM227 | | 08.06.42 | Shot down on 29.7.42 | P/O Evans |
| BM228 | | 08.06.42 | | P/O Anson |
| BM299 | | 06.06.42 | | P/O Anson |
| BM315 | | 01.05.42 | | P/O Haw |
| BM351 | | 01.05.42 | | F/Lt Walker |
| BM363 | | 04.06.42 | | F/Sgt Chandler |
| BM364 | | 30.04.42 | | Sgt Friar |
| BM369 | | 30.04.42 | | F/Lt Bedford |
| BM376 | | 31.07.42 | Damaged during ops on 26.8.42 | P/O Large safe |
| BM378 | | 29.04.42 | | P/O Anson |
| BM382 | | 03.06.42 | | Sgt Husband |

| BM410 | | 29.04.42 | Struck by BM468 on 2.6.42, damaged | F/Sgt Reed |
|---|---|---|---|---|
| BM423 | | 29.04.42 | | F/Sgt Crewe |
| BM455 | | 29.04.42 | | P/O Haw |
| BM460 | | 13.05.42 | | F/Lt Walker |
| BM461 | | 13.05.42 | Force-landed on 15.7.42 | F/Lt Walker |
| BM463 | | 13.05.42 | Air collision with BL811 on 2.6.42 | Sgt Guillermin killed |
| BM468 | | 30.04.42 | Overshot landing at Hornchurch on 2.6.42 | Sgt Moston |
| BM471 | | 30.04.42 | | W/O Waud |
| BM473 | | 14.03.42 | Crash-landed on 14.7.42 | P/O Shackleton |
| BM640 | | 30.04.42 | | Sgt Lock |
| BM645 | | 07.06.42 | | Sgt Turner |

## No. 122 'Bombay' Squadron

| Serial No. | | Date of arrival or final fate | | Pilot |
|---|---|---|---|---|
| AB368 | Spitfire VBs | 17.03.42 | | Sgt Skjeseth |
| AB 859 | | 29.08.42 | Shot down on 16.9.42 | Sgt Nadan killed |
| AD381 | 'The Plessey Spitfire' | 17.07.43 | | F/O MacIntyre |
| AR399 | | 23.06.42 | Force-landed | P/O Snow safe |
| AR400 | | 06.05.42 | Shot down on 17.5.42 | F/Lt Barthropp PoW |
| AR402 | | 09.06.42 | Shot down on 27.8.42 | Sgt Silsand killed |
| AR420 | | 09.06.42 | Failed to return on 27.8.42 | Sgt Shaw killed |
| BL812 | 'Lichfield' | 01.09.42 | | |
| BL813 | | 18.04.42 | Shot down on 24.4.42 | S/Ldr Miller killed |
| BL814 | | 18.04.42 | Ditched in sea on 7.6.42 | |
| BL348 | | 18.04.42 | Shot down on 17.5.42 | P/O Muller PoW |
| BL462 | | 01.03.42 | Shot down on 24.4.42 | P/O Hardy PoW |
| BL812 | 'Lichfield' | 01.09.42 | | Sgt Paris |
| BM127 | | 25.06.42 | | F/Lt Griffiths |
| BM135 | | 11.08.42 | Shot down on 27.8.42 | P/O Shaw killed |
| BM198 | | 11.08.42 | | F/Lt Griffiths |
| BM203 | | 14.06.42 | | P/O Mulliner |
| BM210 | | 26.04.42 | Shot down on 5.5.42 | S/Ldr Fajtl safe |
| BM241 | | 14.04.42 | Shot down on 1.5.42 | P/O Poulton PoW |
| BM242 | | 20.06.42 | Shot down on 30.7.42 | Sgt McPherson killed |
| BM244 | 'Spen Valley Spitfire' | 16.05.42 | Shot down on 30.5.42 | Sgt Skjeseth killed |
| BM252 | 'Bombay City' | 06.05.42 | | Sgt Williams |
| BM266 | | 26.04.42 | Shot down on 30.7.42 | S/Ldr Prevot safe |
| BM269 | | 10.04.42 | Shot down on 5.5.42 | Sgt Ribout killed |
| BM309 | | 10.07.42 | | P/O Collignon |
| BM311 | | 06.05.42 | Damaged on Ops 17.5.42 | Sgt McPherson |
| BM318 | | 09.07.42 | | Sgt Matthews |
| BM321 | | 18.04.42 | Shot down on 5.5.42 | F/Lt de Hemptine killed |
| BM329 | | 10.04.42 | Shot down 15.7.42 | Sgt James killed |
| BM349 | | 14.04.42 | Shot down on 9.8.42 | Sgt Matthews killed |
| BM352 | | 10.04.42 | Shot down on 30.7.42 | P/O Durkin killed |
| BM373 | | 06.06.42 | | Sgt McIntosh |
| BM404 | | 14.04.42 | Shot down on 17.5.42 | F/Sgt Jones killed |
| BM483 | | 25.06.42 | | Sgt Silsand |
| BM520 | | 19.05.42 | | P/O Van de Poel |
| BM552 | | | | P/O Durkin |
| BM643 | | 14.05.42 | | P/O Prest |
| BM644 | | 08.06.42 | | F/Lt Williams |

| | | | | |
|---|---|---|---|---|
| BR632 | | 12.02.43 | | F/Lt Kruml |
| BR636 | | 12.02.43 | | P/O Le Gal |
| BS109 | | 19.09.42 | | P/O Prest |
| BS272 | | 11.08.42 | | |
| BS281 | | 25.09.42 | | Sgt McIntosh |
| BS283 | | 19.09.42 | | Sgt McIntosh |
| BS285 | | 25.09.42 | Shot down on 15.10.42 | Sgt Regis killed |
| BS286 | | 19.09.42 | | P/O Le Gal |
| BS290 | | 25.09.42 | | Sgt Hulse |
| BS336 | | 22.09.42 | | P/O Mercer |
| BS345 | | 25.09.42 | | Sgt Lawson |
| BS346 | | 25.09.42 | Shot down on 6.12.42 | P/O Parker killed |
| BS347 | | 21.09.42 | | Sgt Peet |
| BS348 | | 01.10.42 | | P/O Piggott |
| BS349 | | 30.09.42 | Shot down on 8.11.42 | F/Sgt Foreman killed |
| BS350 | | 30.09.42 | Shot down on 2.12.42 | P/O King killed |
| BS351 | | 01.10.42 | | Sgt Peet |
| BS387 | | 01.10.42 | | P/O Mercer |
| BS386 | | 12.01.43 | | Sgt Booth |
| BS430 | | 22.09.42 | | Sgt Ballantine |
| BS439 | | 12.01.43 | | P/O Goby |
| BS461 | Spitfire Mk IXs | 26.09.42 | | F/Lt Haw |
| BS464 | | 26.09.42 | | S/Ldr Kilian |
| BS545 | 'Brazil No.1' | 27.10.42 | | |
| BS546 | 'O Guaran' | 27.10.42 | Shot down on 26.2.43 | Sgt Crowley killed |
| EN472 | | 13.02.43 | Shot down on 26.2.43 | P/O Mercer killed |
| EN473 | | 13.02.43 | | S/Ldr Kingaby |
| EP107 | | | Shot down on 13.2.43 | F/Lt Stevenson killed |
| EP385 | | 11.08.42 | | Sgt Mercer |

## No. 129 'Mysore' Squadron

| Serial No. | | Date of arrival or final fate | | Pilot |
|---|---|---|---|---|
| MA596 | Spitfire MkIXs | 25.06.43 | Shot down on 14.7.43 | P/O Dickson safe |
| MH377 | | 14.08.43 | | |
| MH384 | | 18.08.43 | | P/O Young |
| MH385 | | 14.08.43 | Force-landed at South Foreland, Kent | Sgt Roggenkamp injured |
| MH386 | | 22.08.43 | | F/O Ruchwaldy |
| MH414 | | 11.08.43 | | F/Lt Watson |
| MH415 | | 11.08.43 | Used in The Longest Day film | S/Ldr Gonay |
| MH418 | | 14.08.43 | | F/Sgt Payne |
| MH422 | | 09.08.43 | Shot down on 6.9.43 | |
| MH425 | | 12.08.43 | Shot down on 22.12.43 | P/O Bradshaw PoW |
| MH433 | | 12.08.43 | | F/Sgt Long |
| MH436 | | 14.08.43 | | F/O Twomey |
| MH438 | | 14.08.43 | | |
| MH440 | | 14.08.43 | Shot down on 27.9.43 | F/O Rosser killed |
| MH441 | | 14.08.43 | Shot down on 22.12.43 | F/O Cain killed |
| MH442 | | 14.08.43 | Shot down on 6.9.43 | F/O McKay killed |
| MH445 | | 14.08.43 | | F/Lt Mason |
| MH446 | | 13.08.43 | Ditched into sea 4.9.43 | F/O Maywhort safe |
| MH447 | | 12.08.43 | | P/O Wood |
| MH449 | | 14.08.43 | | |
| MH454 | | 14.08.43 | | F/Sgt Byrne |

| Serial No. | | Date of arrival or final fate | | Pilot |
|---|---|---|---|---|
| MH471 | | 26.08.43 | Shot down on 5.9.43 | Sgt Carmichael killed |
| MH472 | | 14.08.43 | Shot down on 24.9.43 | F/Lt Mason PoW |

## No.132 'City of Bombay' Squadron

| Serial No. | | Date of arrival or final fate | Pilot |
|---|---|---|---|
| AA725 | Spitfire MkVs | 12.07.42 | F/Lt Thomas |
| AA836 | | 01.09.42 | P/O Burgess |
| AB369 | | | Sgt Chiddenton |
| AD393 | 'Goenteor' | 10.03.42 | P/O Coleman |
| BL671 | | 19.08.42 | P/O Nesbitt |
| BL713 | | 06.10.42 | F/Sgt Cooper |
| BL688 | | 13.03.42 | Sgt O'B Weekes |
| BL716 | | 01.04.42 | P/O Sumpter |
| BL718 | 'Rindsjani' | 10.03.42 | Sgt Johnston |
| BL719 | | 23.03.42 | Sgt Carr |
| BL731 | | 15.03.42 | Sgt McCulloch |
| BL775 | | 13.03.42 | S/Ldr Ritchie |
| BL781 | | 15.03.42 | Sgt Wallace |
| BL847 | | 01.09.43 | P/O Russell |
| BL930 | | 04.04.42 | Sgt Greenshields |
| BM411 | | 28.04.42 | P/O Hammond |

## No. 154 'Motor Industries Gift' Squadron

| Serial No. | | Date of arrival or final fate | | Pilot |
|---|---|---|---|---|
| X4342 | Spitfire Mk1 | 13.06.42 | | F/Sgt Le Gal |
| P8757 | Spitfire MkVBs | 13.06.42 | Collided with BM453 on 29.6.42 | Sgt Davies injured |
| W3373 | | 26.06.42 | | F/Sgt Bray |
| W3899 | | 01.07.42 | | P/O Aikman |
| AB490 | | 19.07.42 | | F/Lt Harrison |
| AD467 | | 13.06.42 | | Sgt Artus |
| AR393 | | 22.06.42 | | Sgt Artus |
| AR431 | | 14.06.42 | | F/Sgt Buiron |
| BL238 | 'Scott of Mafeteng' | 13.06.42 | | F/Sgt Livingstone |
| BL338 | | 14.03.42 | | P/O Turnbull |
| BL518 | | 24.06.42 | | Sgt Bruce |
| BL717 | | 12.07.42 | | P/O Aikman |
| BL776 | | 13.06.42 | | Sgt Farrell |
| BM120 | | 13.07.42 | | P/O Garrett |
| BM127 | | 08.06.42 | | F/Sgt Buiron |
| BM129 | | 15.07.42 | | W/O Buiron |
| BM132 | | 08.06.42 | | Sgt Artus |
| BM194 | | 15.07.42 | Shot down on 30.7.42 | P/O Hurt killed |
| BM207 | 'Dominant Factor' | 08.06.42 | | P/O Aikman |
| BM248 | | 08.06.42 | Crash-landed on 27.8.42 | F/O Turnbull wounded |
| BM289 | | 19.07.42 | | Sgt Hassell |
| BM308 | | 02.06.42 | Shot down on 15.7.42 | W/Cdr Finucane killed |
| BM318 | | 09.07.42 | From No.122 Sqdn | P/O Aikman |
| BM322 | | 12.07.42 | | P/O Chambers |
| BM323 | | 03.06.42 | Failed to return on 21.6.42 | F/Lt Hugill missing |
| BM347 | | 12.07.42 | | Sgt Hansen |
| BM348 | | 12.07.42 | | Sgt Warrington |
| BM356 | 'Champion' | 12.07.42 | | F/Sgt Bray |

| BM362 | | 12.07.42 | | Sgt Haase |
|-------|--|----------|--|-----------|
| BM374 | | 08.06.42 | Failed to return on 30.7.42 | Sgt Dawson missing |
| BM415 | | 12.07.42 | Shot down on 28.8.42 | Sgt Hall wounded |
| BM428 | | | | P/O Turnbull |
| BM453 | | 15.06.42 | Collided on landing with P8757 on 29.6.42 | S/Ldr Carlson injured |
| BM465 | | 12.07.42 | From No.64 Sqdn | F/Lt Eckford |
| BM476 | | 14.07.42 | From No.64 Sqdn | |
| BM480 | | 12.06.42 | | |
| BM483 | | 08.06.42 | From No.313 Sqdn | |
| BM486 | | 13.07.42 | Shot down on 14.7.42 | F/Sgt Bray killed |
| BM488 | | 15.07.42 | From No.64 Sqdn | F/Lt Eckford |
| BM510 | | 08.06.42 | Sent to No.611 Sqdn on 17.6.42 | |
| BM571 | | 06.06.42 | | W/O Livingstone |
| BM580 | | 12.06.42 | | Sgt Cooper |
| BM582 | | 12.06.42 | | Sgt Dawson |
| BM588 | | 13.06.42 | | P/O Thompson |
| BM593 | | 13.06.42 | | P/O Chambers |
| BM624 | | 15.06.42 | | F/Sgt Le Gal |
| EN798 | | 12.06.42 | | Sgt Brown |
| EN900 | | 12.06.42 | | Sgt Brown |
| EN915 | | 12.06.42 | | P/O Hurt |
| EP288 | 'Canadian Pacific' | 25.06.42 | | P/O Garrett |

## No. 222 'Natal' Squadron

| Serial No. | | Date of arrival or final fate | | Pilot |
|------------|--|-------------------------------|--|-------|
| W3127 | Spitfire MkVs | 31.03.43 | | F/O Whalen |
| W3250 | 'Central Province IV' | 03.04.43 | | F/O Le Blanc |
| W3848 | 'Travancore II' | 19.05.43 | | Sgt Hannan |
| AA920 | | 04.04.43 | | F/Lt Burke |
| AA936 | | 31.03.43 | | P/O Stuart |
| AB814 | | 31.03.43 | | P/O Braidwood |
| AR340 | | 31.03.43 | | F/S Cooper |
| AR362 | | 31.03.43 | | Sgt Barrie |
| AR373 | | 31.03.43 | | F/Sgt Turney |
| AD383 | | 31.03.43 | | F/Lt Tripe |
| AD474 | | 31.03.43 | | F/O Cryderman |
| AD475 | | 31.03.43 | | S/Lt Long |
| BL233 | | 31.03.43 | | F/Sgt Daniel |
| BL302 | | 31.03.43 | | Sgt Cordery |
| BL516 | | 31.03.43 | | F/O Clements |
| BL638 | | 31.03.43 | | F/O Stenton |
| BM152 | | 31.03.43 | | Sgt Joseph |
| BM464 | | 15.01.43 | | F/O Thiriez |
| BR141 | | 19.05.43 | | P/O Stonehill |
| BR636 | Spitfire MkIXs | 19.05.43 | Shot down on 27.5.43 | P/O Le Blanc killed |
| BS281 | | 19.05.43 | | F/O Mason |
| BS286 | | 19.05.43 | | P/O Hlado |
| BS345 | | 19.05.43 | | S/Ldr Ellis |
| BS347 | | 19.05.43 | | S/Ldr Compton |
| BS348 | | 19.05.43 | | P/O Le Gal |
| BS374 | | 19.05.43 | | P/O Hesselyn |
| BS386 | | 19.05.43 | | F/Lt Lenton |

| BS405 | | 19.05.43 | Shot down on 13.6.43 | F/Lt Hall PoW |
|---|---|---|---|---|
| BS461 | | 19.05.43 | | F/Lt Sutherland |
| BS512 | | 19.05.43 | | P/O Smik |
| LZ924 | | 19.05.43 | | P/O Morgan |
| MA244 | | 16.07.43 | | W/O Davidson |
| MA735 | | 16.07.43 | | S/Ldr Kingaby |
| MH353 | | 13.08.43 | | S/Ldr Heppell |
| MH371 | | 13.08.43 | | F/Sgt Webster |
| MH389 | | 29.08.43 | Shot down on 8.9.43 | Sgt Townsend PoW |
| MH390 | | 21.08.43 | Shot down on 27.9.43 | F/Sgt Hannan evaded capture |
| MH415 | | | | F/Sgt Kjelbeck |
| MH424 | | 14.08.43 | | F/Sgt Winslow |
| MH429 | | 11.08.43 | Shot down on 31.8.43 | F/Sgt Thomson PoW |
| MH430 | | 15.08.43 | | Sgt Leneham |
| MH434 | | 13.08.43 | | F/Lt Lardner-Burke |
| MH435 | | 12.08.43 | Struck by MH451 on 1.9.43 | |
| MH439 | | 13.08.43 | | F/Lt Lazenby |
| MH451 | | 15.08.43 | Struck MH435 while taxying 1.9.43 | |
| MH491 | | 06.09.43 | | F/O Green |
| MH494 | | 06.09.43 | | F/Sgt Reed |
| MH496 | | 26.08.43 | | F/O Collins |
| MH506 | | 12.09.43 | Crash-landed at Broadstairs, Kent, 2.10.43 | F/O Stuart safe |
| MH753 | | 12.09.43 | | Sgt Cosgrove |
| MH783 | | 24.09.43 | Shot down on 3.10.43 | F/Lt Hesselyn PoW |
| MH987 | | 13.09.43 | Crashed in Channel on 23.9.43 | F/O Thiriez killed |
| MJ201 | | 06.11.43 | | F/Lt Omissi |
| MJ232 | | 28.10.43 | | F/Lt Broad |
| MJ253 | | 06.11.43 | | F/Lt Lenton |

## No. 229 Squadron

| Serial No. | | Date of arrival or final fate | Pilot |
|---|---|---|---|
| BS340 | Spitfire MkIXs | 29.04.44 | P/O Andrews |
| BS393 | | 29.04.44 | P/O Andrews |
| MA220 | | | F/O Terris |
| MA817 | | 29.04.44 | P/O Shirlore |
| MH372 | | 29.04.44 | Lt Cummings |
| MH835 | | 29.04.44 | F/Sgt Manley |
| MH855 | | 29.04.44 | W/O Price |
| MH909 | | | F/O Symons |
| MJ220 | | 11.05.44 | P/O Cook |
| MJ310 | | 29.04.44 | F/O Ensell |

## No. 274 Squadron

| Serial No. | | Date of arrival or final fate | Pilot |
|---|---|---|---|
| BS284 | Spitfire MkVs | 09.05.44 | F/O Hunton |
| JK118 | | 20.04.44 | W/O Westcott |
| JK195 | | 31.04.44 | W/O Ross |
| JK710 | | 30.04.44 | P/O Mooney |
| JK764 | | 25.04.44 | F/O Hunton |
| JL249 | | | F/O Bickford-Smith |
| JL328 | | | W/O McCloy |

| BS128 | SpitfireMkIXs | 15.05.44 | F/Lt Olmstead |
|-------|---------------|----------|---------------|
| BS474 | | 13.05.44 | F/Lt Wood |
| MA579 | | 15.05.44 | F/Lt Halford |
| MA585 | | 22.04.44 | F/O Stroud |
| MH362 | | 16.04.44 | P/O Mooney |
| MH438 | | 11.05.44 | F/O Woolfries |
| MH853 | | 13.05.44 | F/Sgt Wilks |
| MH939 | | 22.04.44 | S/Ldr J.F. Edwards |
| MJ129 | | 19.05.44 | P/O Purce |
| MK256 | | 16.04.44 | F/Sgt Weir |

## No. 278 Air Sea Rescue Squadron

| Serial No. | Aircraft | Pilot/Crew |
|------------|----------|------------|
| BV475 | Vickers-Armstrong Warwick | F/Lt Statham |
| | | F/O Elliot |
| | | F/O Blank |
| | | F/O Bland |
| | | W/O Wilson |
| | | W/O Emblem |
| BV478 | Vickers-Armstrong Warwick | F/Lt Chappell |
| | | W/O McVeigh |
| | | W/O Sumner |
| | | W/O Boxall |
| | | W/O Hollitt |
| | | Sgt Morley |
| BV485 | Vickers-Armstrong Warwick | S/Ldr Skinner |
| | | F/O Moore |
| | | F/O Brown |
| | | F/O Scott |
| | | F/Sgt Tripp |
| | | F/Sgt Pleasents |
| BV528 | Vickers-Armstrong Warwick | F/Lt Garden |
| | | W/O Beneke |
| | | W/O Saville |
| | | W/O Johnston |
| | | F/Sgt Evans |
| BV529 | Vickers-Armstrong Warwick | P/O MacLaren |
| | | W/O Goozee |
| | | W/O Martin |
| | | W/O Penn |
| | | P/O Murland |
| HF968 | Vickers-Armstrong Warwick | F/O Bothwell |
| | | F/O Pert |
| | | W/O Orr |
| | | W/O Symonds |
| | | W/O Stephen |
| L2254 | Saunders Roe-Walrus | W/O Reeder |
| | | F/O Murray |
| L2284 | Saunders Roe-Walrus | Lt Emmett |
| | | P/O Cummings |
| L2292 | Saunders Roe-Walrus | P/O Bedford |
| | | LAC Westbrook |
| W2735 | Saunders Roe-Walrus | Lt Langdon |
| | | Sgt Morley |

## Supermarine Spitfire MkVs

| | | |
|---|---|---|
| W3234 | 13.10.44 | F/Lt Thompson |
| W3368 | 13.10.44 | F/Lt Allanson |
| W3718 | 27.09.44 | F/Lt Thompson |
| AA931 | 27.09.44 | F/Lt Millar |
| AD562 | 24.04.44 | F/Lt Thompson |
| EN948 | 13.10.44 | F/Lt Carr-George |

## No. 313 Czech Squadron

| Serial No. | | Date of arrival or final fate | | Pilot |
|---|---|---|---|---|
| W3177 | Spitfire MkVs | 21.10.41 | | P/O Jicha |
| W3969 | | 26.10.41 | | F/O Muzika |
| AA757 | | 21.10.41 | | |
| AA765 | 'Hyderabad' | 24.10.41 | | F/Lt Fejfar |
| AA865 | | 26.10.41 | Shot down on 10.4.42 | Sgt Truhlar PoW |
| AA869 | | 24.10.41 | Shot down on 18.3.42 | Sgt Zauf killed |
| AA909 | | 23.03.42 | | Sgt Cap |
| AA918 | | 29.01.42 | | F/O Vancl |
| AB358 | | | | P/O Jicha |
| AB916 | | 26.10.41 | | Sgt Spacek |
| AD196 | | | | P/O Michalek |
| AD197 | | 25.02.42 | Shot down on 27.3.42 | P/O Michalek killed |
| AD250 | | | | P/O Jicha |
| AD276 | | 13.01.42 | | F/O Muzika |
| AD290 | | 08.01.42 | | P/O Jicha |
| AD299 | | | | Sgt Pokorny |
| AD353 | | 22.10.41 | | F/O Vancl |
| AD361 | | 21.10.41 | | Sgt Ednisch |
| AD380 | | 24.10.41 | | F/Sgt Foglar |
| AD384 | | 21.10.41 | Damaged during Ops on 12.4.42 | Sgt Kresta PoW |
| AD390 | | 24.10.41 | | Sgt Spacek |
| AD394 | | 25.01.42 | | F/Lt Fajtl |
| AD424 | | | Damaged during Ops on 11.1.42 | Sgt Hcrak |
| AD465 | | 21.10.41 | | F/O Kasel |
| AD494 | | | | Sgt Valenta |
| AD509 | | | | Sgt Borkoves |
| AD572 | | 07.12.41 | | F/O Muzika |
| AD782 | | | | Sgt Kocfelda |
| BL480 | | 15.01.42 | Shot down on 10.4.42 | Sgt Pokorny killed |
| BL513 | | | | P/O Vykoukal |
| BL578 | | 29.01.42 | | P/O Kasal |
| BL581 | | 17.01.42 | | P/O Vykoukal |
| BL970 | | 30.01.42 | | F/O Drbahlan |
| BL973 | | 30.03.42 | | St Horak |
| BM117 | | 30.03.42 | | Sgt Jicha |
| BM127 | | 30.03.42 | | F/O Vancl |
| BM132 | | 18.05.42 | | P/O Prihoda |
| BM137 | | 18.04.42 | | W/O Foglar |
| BM203 | | 18.04.42 | | |
| BM207 | | 06.05.42 | | F/Lt Vancl |
| BM209 | | 17.04.42 | Force-landed at Benenden, Kent on 5.5.42 | P/O Kucera |
| BM227 | | 18.04.42 | | |

| | | | |
|---|---|---|---|
| BM242 | 24.04.42 | | Sgt Prerost |
| BM248 | 17.04.42 | | F/Lt Vancl |
| BM261 | 14.04.42 | Failed to return on 5.5.42 | Sgt Pavlik missing |
| BM263 | 12.04.42 | | P/O Kucera |
| BM301 | 14.04.42 | Failed to return on 17.5.42 | F/Lt Fejfar missing |
| BM314 | 22.05.42 | | Sgt Borkoves |
| BM317 | 11.04.42 | | Sgt Reznick |
| BM322 | 08.05.42 | | |
| BM323 | 11.04.42 | | Sgt Borkoves |
| BM328 | 11.04.42 | | Sgt Horak |
| BM357 | 11.04.42 | Shot down on 24.4.42 | Sgt Brazda killed |
| BM374 | 11.04.42 | | Sgt Kotiba |
| BM483 | 06.05.42 | | F/Sgt Mares |
| BM510 | 14.05.42 | | Sgt Dohnal |
| BM517 | 06.05.42 | | |

## No. 340 'Ile de France' Squadron

| Serial No. | | Date of arrival or final fate | | Pilot |
|---|---|---|---|---|
| W3127 | Spitfire MkVs | 09.03.42 | | Sgt Dumas |
| W3457 | 'Cynon Valley' | 09.03.42 | Shot down into sea on 9.8.42 | Lt Kerlan safe |
| W3705 | | 01.08.42 | Shot down on 5.9.42 | Adj Dubourgel |
| W3947 | | 18.04.42 | Shot down on 4.5.43 | |
| AA743 | | 01.03.42 | | Adj Dubourgel |
| AB814 | | 20.08.42 | | Lt Gilbert |
| AB849 | | 04.05.42 | Sent to No.41 Sqdn on 20.11.42 | Adj Guignard |
| AD118 | | 20.08.42 | | S/Lt Kennard |
| AD513 | | 31.07.42 | Sent to No.131 Sqdn on 27.10.42 | Lt Chauvin |
| AR363 | | 27.03.42 | | S/Lt Kennard |
| BM312 | | 12.04.42 | | Lt Renaud |
| BM324 | | 12.04.42 | | Cdt Duperier |
| BM343 | | 29.04.42 | | Capt Bechoff |
| BM400 | | 19.08.42 | Shot down on 5.9.42 | Sgt Taconet |
| BM584 | | 01.06.42 | | Adj Debel |
| BM596 | | 08.05.42 | | Sgt Bouguen |
| BL262 | | 12.08.42 | Shot down into sea off Dieppe 19.8.42 | Adj Darbin killed |
| BL329 | | 17.03.42 | | S/Lt Durand |
| BL469 | | 04.05.42 | | Lt Gilbert |
| BL556 | | 09.09.42 | | Sgt Reeve |
| BL596 | | 17.03.42 | | |
| BL603 | | 17.03.42 | Shot down on 5.9.42 | Capt de Labouchere |
| BL765 | | 02.03.42 | | S/Lt Kerlan |
| BL780 | | | | Adj Guignard |
| BL788 | | 07.04.42 | | Sgt Taconet |
| BL803 | | 17.03.42 | | Capt Mouchotte |
| BL854 | | 20.08.42 | Shot down on 5.9.42 | Sgt Thibaud |
| BL859 | | 01.03.42 | | Capt Bechoff |
| BL862 | | 01.03.42 | Sent to No.334 Sqdn on 2.11.43 | Sgt Reeve |
| BL905 | | 20.07.42 | | Sgt Bouguen |
| BL908 | | 17.03.42 | Failed to return from ops on 23.8.42 | |
| EN889 | | 05.06.42 | | Sgt Kennard |
| EN908 | | 05.06.42 | Sent to No.411 Sqdn on 3.11.42 | Capt de Labouchere |

## No. 349 (Belgian) Squadron

| Serial No. | Date of arrival or final fate | | Pilot |
|---|---|---|---|
| MH610 | 01.03.44 | Failed to return on 28.4.44 | F/O Maskens |
| MJ230 | 16.02.44 | | F/O Bailly |
| MJ353 | 16.02.44 | | F/O Libert |
| MJ369 | 16.02.44 | | F/S Moureau |
| MJ879 | 16.02.44 | | F/Lt Drossaert |
| MJ889 | 16.02.44 | | F/O Straut |
| MJ962 | 16.02.44 | | F/O Fromont |
| MK136 | 17.02.44 | | F/Lt Seydel |
| MK153 | 01.03.44 | | F/S Limet |
| MK175 | 28.01.44 | | F/S Halleux |
| MK253 | 25.02.44 | | F/O Sams |
| MK354 | 16.02.44 | | F/S Van de Bosch |
| MK368 | 16.02.44 | | F/O Ester |

## No. 350 (Belgian) Squadron

| Serial No. | | Date of arrival or final fate | | Pilot |
|---|---|---|---|---|
| P8549 | Spitfire MkII | 02.06.42 | | Sgt Harmel |
| W3236 | Spitfire MkVs | 12.09.42 | | P/O de Patoul |
| W3262 | | 12.09.42 | | P/O de Merode |
| W3370 | | 12.09.42 | | P/O Seydel |
| AB967 | | 06.07.42 | | Sgt Herreman |
| AD113 | | 12.09.42 | | F/Lt Boussa |
| AD228 | 'Cheshire County II' | 24.05.42 | | Sgt Flohimont |
| AD231 | 'West Borneo II' | 12.09.42 | | S/Ldr Guillaume |
| AD475 | Spitfire MkVs | 11.02.42 | Damaged in ops on 19.8.42 | P/O Venesoen unhurt |
| AD550 | | 10.02.42 | Shot down on 12.12.42 | F/O Demerode evaded capture |
| AR373 | | 17.06.42 | Damaged in ops on 19.8.42 | Sgt Alexandre unhurt |
| AR380 | | 20.07.42 | Shot down on 19.8.42 | P/O Marcel Bel unhurt |
| AR452 | | 04.12.42 | | G/Capt Lott |
| AR515 | | 30.11.42 | Crash-landed on 12.12.42 | F/O Plisner safe |
| AR592 | | 02.12.42 | Shot down on 22.1.43 | Sgt Flohimont killed |
| BL540 | | 11.12.42 | | Sgt Limet |
| BL696 | | 01.07.42 | | P/O Arend |
| BM196 | 'Brentford & Chelsea' | | | Sgt Boute |
| BM258 | | 16.08.42 | | Sgt Rigole |
| BM381 | | 17.04.42 | | F/O Smets |
| BM564 | | 30.04.42 | | P/O de Merode |
| EE723 | | 13.12.42 | | P/O Siroux |
| EE738 | | 09.12.42 | | Sgt De Jaegher |
| EE743 | | 09.12.42 | | Sgt Dancot |
| EE745 | | 13.12.42 | | Sgt Wustefield |
| EE766 | | 13.12.42 | | Sgt Groensteen |
| EN769 | | 31.07.42 | Hit overhead cables, force-landed on 13.8.42 | F/Lt Boussa unhurt |
| EP288 | 'Canadian Pacific II' | 29.11.42 | | P/O Le Large |
| EP640 | | 26.11.42 | Failed to return on 28.3.43 | |
| EP699 | | 30.11.42 | | P/O Gallatay |

## No. 403 'Wolf' Squadron RCAF

| Serial No. | | Date of arrival or final fate | | Pilot |
|---|---|---|---|---|
| P7280 | Spitfire MkVbs | 17.07.41 | | P/O Ball |
| P7622 | | 19.07.41 | | Sgt Rychman |
| P7886 | | | | P/O Gilbertson |
| P8233 | | 19.07.41 | | Sgt Stones |
| P8373 | | 24.07.41 | | P/O Dick |
| P8726 | | 16.07.41 | | S/Ldr Morris |
| P8740 | | 04.08.41 | Shot down on 21.8.41 | S/Ldr Morris PoW |
| P8744 | 'Wonkers' | 04.08.41 | Crash-landed at Orsett, Essex on 19.8.41 | Sgt MacDonald |
| R7260 | | 19.06.41 | Crashed in sea on Ops on 19.8.41 | P/O Dick safe |
| R7266 | | 04.08.41 | Shot down on 9.8.41 | P/O Walden killed |
| R7279 | | 04.08.41 | Shot down on 21.8.41 | Sgt MacDonald PoW |
| R7256 | | 04.08.41 | | Sgt Crisp |
| R7279 | 'King's Messenger' | 04.08.41 | | P/O Carrillo |
| R7301 | | 04.08.41 | | P/O Walden |
| R7342 | | 04.08.41 | Shot down on 19.8.41 | P/O Anthony PoW |
| R7343 | 'Hexham & District' | 11.08.41 | | Sgt MacDonald |
| R7352 | | | | P/O Ford |
| R7422 | | | | F/O Price |
| W3114 | | 04.08.41 | Crash-landed at Manston 16.8.41 | S/Ldr Morris unhurt |
| W3436 | 'Midland Banker' | 04.08.41 | | F/Lt Christmas |
| W3438 | | 04.08.41 | Failed to return 21.8.41 | F/O McKenna missing |
| W3446 | 'Jennifer' | 04.08.41 | | Sgt Belcher |
| W3453 | 'County of Reading' | 04.08.41 | | F/O Price |
| W3502 | 'Wolds & Buckrose' | 04.08.41 | | P/O Wood |
| W3573 | | 04.08.41 | Failed to return 19.8.41 | P/O Walden killed |
| W3630 | 'Kuwait' | 04.08.41 | | P/O Ball |

## No. 411 'Grizzly Bear' Squadron RCAF

| Serial No. | | Date of arrival or final fate | | Pilot |
|---|---|---|---|---|
| X4257 | Spitfire Mk1 | 08.11.41 | | Sgt Mowbray |
| W3215 | 'Marksman' | 02.10.41 | Failed to return 24.3.42 | |
| W3570 | | 16.10.41 | | Sgt Randall |
| W3639 | Spitfire MkVs | 02.10.41 | Shot down on 16.12.41 | P/O Chamberlain killed |
| W3853 | | 01.11.41 | | Sgt Hartney |
| W3951 | | 02.10.41 | | Sgt Taylor |
| AA833 | | 06.10.41 | Struck hangar on landing on 8.1.42 | Sgt Mara |
| AA836 | | 11.10.41 | | P/O McNair |
| AA839 | | 03.10.41 | | Sgt Nutbrown |
| AA840 | | 02.10.41 | Shot down on 8.12.41 | Sgt Court killed |
| AA844 | | 02.10.41 | Air collision with AB265 on 28.2.42 | Sgt Long |
| AA939 | | | | P/O Evans |
| AB181 | 'One from Avro' | 10.12.41 | | F/Lt Boomer |
| AB183 | | 11.12.41 | | P/O Brady |
| AB268 | | 09.01.41 | Failed to return on 24.3.42 | W/O Gridley missing |
| AB281 | | 08.01.42 | Shot down on 23.3.42 | P/O Ash PoW |
| AB284 | | 29.12.41 | | Sgt Matheson |
| AB804 | | 24.12.41 | | Sgt Sharun |
| AD117 | | 03.10.41 | Failed to return on 16.12.41 | Sgt Holden missing |
| AD132 | 'Bihar III' | 02.10.41 | | Sgt Holden |

| AD259 | | 11.10.41 | | Sgt Holden |
|---|---|---|---|---|
| AD261 | | 10.10.41 | | S/Ldr Pitcher |
| AD263 | 'Miss ABC II' | 10.10.42 | | F/Lt Weston |
| AD264 | 'Paisley' | 02.10.41 | Shot down on 8.12.41 | P/O Coleman killed |
| AD299 | | 11.10.41 | | Sgt Green |
| AD356 | 'Black Eagle' | 16.10.41 | | Sgt Green |
| BL464 | | 27.03.42 | | Sgt Ritchie |
| BL638 | | 01.03.42 | | P/O McLeod |
| BL980 | | 03.03.42 | | P/O Eakins |

### No. 453 RAAF Squadron

| Serial No. | | Date of arrival or final fate | | Pilot |
|---|---|---|---|---|
| W3574 | Spitfire MkVs | 11.10.42 | | Sgt Stansfield |
| AA936 | | 12.10.42 | | Sgt Leith |
| AB792 | | 13.09.42 | Shot down on 11.10.42 | Sgt Nossiter killed |
| AD298 | | 10.09.42 | Shot down on 11.10.42 | Sgt Menzies killed |
| AD386 | | 01.09.42 | | Sgt Ferguson |
| AR296 | | 12.10.42 | | Sgt Waldron |
| AR340 | | 23.11.42 | | Sgt Barrian |
| AR362 | | 23.11.42 | | F/Lt Yarra |
| BL516 | | 19.09.42 | | S/Ldr Ratten |
| BL593 | | 11.07.42 | | Sgt Ford |
| BL631 | | 15.11.42 | | F/Lt Harrington |
| BL899 | | 11.07.42 | | P/O Long |
| BL923 | | 11.10.42 | Shot down on 31.10.42 | Sgt Furlong killed |
| BL983 | | 11.10.42 | | Sgt Ford |
| BM152 | | 25.07.42 | | Sgt Swift |
| BM255 | | 11.07.42 | | P/O Blumer |
| BM523 | | 11.07.42 | | Sgt Clemesha |
| BM631 | | 11.07.42 | | Sgt De Cosier |
| EN786 | | | Shot down on 31.10.42 | Sgt Galway safe |
| EN824 | | 23.06.42 | | Sgt Watehouse |
| EN914 | | 11.07.42 | | Sgt McDermott |
| BS400 | Spitfire MkIX | 02.04.43 | Shot down on 22.6.43 | F/O Gray PoW |

### No. 485 RNZAF Squadron

| Serial No. | | Date of arrival or final fate | | Pilot |
|---|---|---|---|---|
| BL369 | Spitfire MkVs | 11.11.43 | | F/Sgt Collett |
| BL634 | | 11.11.43 | Damaged on hitting sea on 21.12.43 | F/Lt Gibbs |
| BL729 | | 11.11.43 | | F/O Kebbell |
| JK762 | | 04.07.43 | Shot down on 20.10.43 | F/O Baker killed |
| JK979 | | 31.07.43 | | F/Lt Black |
| EN557 | | 04.07.43 | | F/O Roberts |
| EN559 | | 04.07.43 | Shot down on 20.10.43 | F/O Thompson killed |
| EN560 | | 10.03.43 | | F/O Thompson |
| EN563 | | 04.07.43 | | F/Sgt Frehner |
| EN565 | | 04.07.43 | | F/Lt Strachan |
| EN568 | | 23.09.43 | | S/Ldr Hume |
| MH350 | Spitfire MkIXs | 06.08.43 | | F/O Copland |
| MH364 | | 06.08.43 | Shot down on 20.10.43 | F/Sgt Transom safe |
| MH422 | | 09.08.43 | | F/O Dasent |
| MH455 | | 25.10.43 | | F/Sgt Clarke |

| | | | |
|---|---|---|---|
| MH501 | | 24.08.43 | F/O Tucker |
| MH819 | 'Red Rose III' | 08.10.43 | F/O Baker |
| MH872 | | 08.10.43 | F/Lt Griffith |
| MH879 | | 08.10.43 | F/O Stead |
| MJ964 | | 07.02.44 | F/Sgt Downer |
| MK198 | | 11.02.44 | F/Lt de Vere |
| MK202 | | 23.02.44 | F/Sgt Esdaile |
| MK252 | | 13.02.44 | F/O De Tourret |
| MK280 | | 09.12.43 | W/O Kearins |
| MK302 | | 13.02.44 | F/Sgt Eyre |
| MK347 | | 11.02.44 | F/O O'Halloran |

### No. 504 Squadron

| Serial No. | | Date of arrival or final fate | Pilot |
|---|---|---|---|
| P8585 | Spitfire MkVs | 15.10.43 | F/O Budd |
| P8785 | | 10.10.43 | F/Sgt Stacey |
| AB981 | | 15.12.43 | F/Sgt Stewart |
| AD185 | | 10.10.43 | P/O Laws |
| BL725 | | 10.10.43 | F/Sgt Brookes |
| BL390 | | 10.10.43 | F/Sgt Stewart |
| BL564 | | 12.01.44 | F/Sgt Brookes |
| BM493 | | 10.10.43 | Sgt Jayawardena |
| BM529 | | 10.10.43 | F/O Doyle |
| BM642 | | 10.10.43 | F/O Budd |
| BR179 | | 10.10.43 | F/Sgt Faulkner |
| BS472 | | 10.10.43 | F/Sgt Wright |
| EN951 | | 10.10.43 | Sgt Flamer |

### No. 567 Squadron Anti-Aircraft Co-Operation

| Serial No. | Aircraft | Pilot |
|---|---|---|
| LF577 | Hawker Hurricane | F/Sgt Daniel |
| LF584 | | F/Sgt Williams |
| JN546 | Miles Martinet | F/Sgt Brees |
| | | Sgt Lawes |

### No. 603 'City of Edinburgh' Squadron

| Serial No. | | Date of arrival or final fate | | Pilot |
|---|---|---|---|---|
| | Spitfire MkVs | | | |
| P8603 | 'Nabha I' | 11.11.41 | Shot down on 8.12.41 | F/O Fawkes killed |
| P8720 | | 27.07.41 | | P/O Fawkes |
| P8784 | | 12.09.41 | | F/Lt Smith |
| P8786 | | 17.11.41 | Shot down on 8.12.41 | P/O Falconer PoW |
| P8796 | | 22.08.41 | Crashed into sea on 19.12.41 | S/Ldr Foreshaw injured |
| R7221 | | 25.05.41 | Shot down on 27.9.41 | Sgt Allard PoW |
| R7223 | | 16.05.41 | | Sgt Hunter |
| R7226 | | 16.05.41 | | F/O Prowse |
| R7227 | | 16.05.41 | Shot down on 23.7.41 | Sgt Jackman PoW |
| R7229 | 'Stafford I' | 16.05.41 | | P/O Newman |
| R7230 | | 16.05.41 | | F/Lt Hamilton |

| R7272 | | 16.05.41 | Failed to return on 26.6.41 | P/O Newman missing |
|---|---|---|---|---|
| R7299 | 'Aitch-Aitch' | 16.05.41 | | F/O Douglas |
| R7300 | | 16.02.41 | Shot down on 21.8.41 | P/O Falconer wounded |
| R7305 | | 09.06.41 | | P/O Douglas |
| R7333 | 'The Kirby I' | 19.06.41 | Shot down on 8.12.41 | Sgt Bennett |
| R7335 | | 19.06.41 | | Sgt Neil |
| R7339 | | 16.05.41 | Shot down on 4.7.41 | F/O Prowse PoW |
| R7341 | | 17.07.41 | Shot down on 23.7.41 | P/O Blackall killed |
| R7345 | | 16.05.41 | Crash-landed due to enemy action on 21.6.41 | F/O Stewart-Clarke wounded |
| W3110 | | 16.05.41 | Force-landed on 23.6.41 | F/O W.A Douglas wounded |
| W3111 | | 16.05.41 | Failed to return on 7.6.41 | P/O Burleigh missing |
| W3112 | | 27.06.41 | | Sgt Cook |
| W3113 | | 27.06.41 | | F/O Griffiths |
| W3121 | | 22.06.41 | Shot down on 24.6.41 | F/O McKelvie killed |
| W3128 | | 22.06.41 | | P/O Griffiths |
| W3138 | 'Cawnpore' | 27.06.41 | Damaged by enemy fighter on 30.6.41 | S/Ldr Louden |
| W3233 | | 07.08.41 | Shot down on 27.9.41 | Sgt Archibald killed |
| W3242 | 'Crispin of Leicester' | 22.06.41 | Damaged by enemy AA fire on 30.6.41 | Sgt Ruchwaldy |
| W3266 | | 11.08.41 | | F/Lt Sutherland |
| W3364 | | 22.06.41 | Force-landed on 24.6.41 | Sgt Lamb wounded |
| W3369 | | 26.06.41 | Failed to return on 22.7.41 | P/O Delorme missing |
| W3502 | 'Wolds & Buckrose' | 26.09.41 | | Sgt Bennett |
| W3379 | | 17.09.41 | | P/O Thomas |
| W3569 | | 25.07.41 | | F/Lt Walker |
| W3632 | 'Bahrein' | 24.07.41 | | F/Lt Scott-Malden |
| W3698 | | 22.08.41 | | Sgt Hurst |
| X4389 | | 29.09.41 | Shot down on 13.10.41 | Sgt Shuckburgh killed |
| AD502 | | 22.10.41 | | F/Lt Smith |

### No. 611 'West Lancashire' Squadron

| Serial No. | | Date of arrival or final fate | | Pilot |
|---|---|---|---|---|
| N3280 | Spitfire Mk1 | 24.10.40 | | Sgt Townsend |
| P9335 | | 24.10.40 | Damaged in Ops on 12.12.40 | F/O Pollard |
| R6765 | | 24.11.40 | | Sgt Leigh |
| R6759 | | 08.11.40 | | F/Lt Heath |
| R6887 | | | | Sgt Down |
| R6986 | | 24.11.40 | | Sgt Leigh |
| R7025 | | 16.02.41 | | P/O Stanley |
| X4017 | | 24.10.40 | | G/Capt Broadhurst |
| X4060 | | 30.12.40 | | P/O Johnston |
| X4253 | | 24.10.40 | | Sgt Gilligan |
| X4258 | | 15.11.40 | | P/O Smith |
| X4317 | | 24.10.40 | | Sgt Breeze |
| X4547 | | 24.10.40 | Shot down on 5.2.41 | P/O Sadler killed |
| X4589 | | 24.10.40 | | P/O Williams |
| X4592 | 'St George' | 25.10.40 | Shot down on 25.2.41 | P/O Stanley killed |
| X4620 | 'Falkland Island VII' | 05.11.40 | Crash-landed on 22.4.41 | Sgt Limpenny |
| X4662 | | 08.11.40 | | F/O Pollard |
| X4667 | | | | Sgt Burnham |
| X4817 | Spitfire MkII | 27.12.40 | | S/Ldr Bitmead |
| P7314 | | 28.02.41 | | F/O Pollard |

| | | | | |
|---|---|---|---|---|
| P7355 | | 21.02.41 | Damaged by enemy fighter on 15.4.41 | Sgt Limpenny |
| P7368 | | 28.02.41 | Hit fence on landing at Hornchurch 13.3.41 | Sgt Darling safe |
| P7494 | | 21.02.41 | | |
| P7558 | | 04.01.41 | | P/O Sutton |
| P7606 | | 21.01.41 | | Sgt Townsend |
| P7607 | | 21.02.41 | Force-landed in Channel on 13.5.41 | P/O Askew |
| P7609 | | 25.02.41 | Damaged by enemy fighter on 15.4.41 | Sgt Burnham |
| P7628 | | 28.02.41 | | Sgt Smith |
| P7629 | | 02.03.41 | | P/O Lamb |
| P7698 | 'Zanzibar II' | 28.02.41 | | |
| P7774 | | 21.12.40 | Shot down on 28.4.41 | P/O Pennings killed |
| P7776 | | 21.02.41 | Damaged on landing on 16.5.41 | Sgt Breeze |
| P7817 | | 24.02.41 | Shot down on 7.5.41 | Sgt Claxton killed |
| P7883 | 'Grahams Heath' | 14.03.41 | | P/O Reeves |
| P8539 | Spitfire MkVs | 08.07.41 | | Sgt Hemmingway |
| P8561 | 'Kalahari' | 25.06.41 | | |
| P8603 | 'Nabha I' | 29.06.41 | | |
| P8743 | | 17.07.41 | | |
| P8756 | | 14.07.41 | Shot down on 7.8.41 | Sgt Holdsworth PoW |
| P8780 | | 11.07.41 | | P/O Van de Honert |
| P8581 | | 08.07.41 | Failed to return on 14.7.41 | P/O Dexter killed |
| R7208 | 'City of Liverpool III' | 13.05.41 | | Sgt Summers |
| R7209 | 'City of Liverpool I' | 13.05.41 | Failed to return on 22.6.41 | P/O Pollard missing |
| R7213 | | 06.06.41 | | |
| R7217 | | 13.05.41 | Collision on landing with R7255 on 6.6.41 | |
| R7218 | 'Retford & District' | 18.05.41 | | |
| R7230 | 'Brenda' | 15.05.41 | | Sgt Smith |
| R7231 | 'Grimsby II' | 13.05.41 | Collided with R7306 while taxying on 26.6.41 | Sgt Gilman |
| R7253 | | 13.05.41 | Damaged by enemy fighter on 23.6.41 | P/O Pollard |
| R7254 | | 13.05.41 | Damaged by enemy fighter on 4.6.41 | F/Lt Reeves |
| R7255 | | 15.05.41 | Struck R7217 while landing on 6.6.41 | Sgt Townsend |
| R7263 | 'Stafford II' | 16.05.41 | | S/Ldr Stapleton |
| R7268 | 'The Swan' | 25.05.41 | | F/O Williams |
| R7271 | 'Beverley & District' | 15.05.41 | | Sgt Summers |
| R7274 | 'West Riding' | 13.04.41 | | Sgt Burnham |
| R7277 | 'Foremost' | 15.05.41 | Failed to return  on 8.7.41 | Sgt Feely missing |
| R7291 | 'Trustworthy' | 15.05.41 | | Sgt Gilman |
| R7293 | 'Sans Touche' | 03.07.41 | Failed to return on 3.7.41 | Sgt McHugh missing |
| R7296 | 'Newbury II' | 02.11.41 | | Sgt McHugh |
| R7304 | | 15.05.41 | Damaged by enemy fighter on 4.6.41 | |
| R7306 | | 10.06.41 | | Sgt Thomas |
| R7309 | | 15.9.41 | | |
| R7349 | | 13.05.41 | Failed to return on 24.6.41 | F/Lt Bye missing |
| W3226 | | 29.06.41 | | |
| W3230 | | 28.06.41 | | |
| W3242 | 'Crispin of Leicester' | 22.06.41 | Damaged by AA fire 30.6.41 | F/Lt Lock |
| W3243 | 'The Falkirk of Bairn' | 22.06.41 | | |
| W3244 | 'Devon Squadron' | 20.05.41 | | |
| W3246 | 'Devon Squadron' | 22.06.41 | Shot down on 23.7.41 | F/O Sutton PoW |
| W3247 | 'City of Hull III' | 22.06.41 | Shot down on 26.8.41 | Sgt Gray missing |
| W3248 | 'Letchworth' | 22.06.41 | | |
| W3257 | | 08.07.41 | Failed to return after strafing enemy on 3.8.41 | F/Lt Lock missing |

| | | | | |
|---|---|---|---|---|
| W3260 | | 30.06.41 | | |
| W3261 | | 29.06.41 | | Sgt Ingram |
| W3309 | 'The Wiltshire' | 25.06.41 | | F/Lt Lock |
| W3311 | | 25.06.41 | Shot down on 6.7.41 | Sgt Smith PoW |
| W3318 | Jewellery Watch Trades | 29.06.41 | Damaged on Ops on 16.8.41 | Sgt Milner |
| W3325 | 'Newcastle on Tyne' | 25.06.41 | Shot down on 9.7.41 | P/O Johnstone missing |
| W3327 | 'Horsham & District' | 25.06.41 | Shot down on 21.10.41 | P/O Reeves killed |
| W3328 | 'The Flying Fox' | 25.06.41 | | F/Lt Hayter |
| W3329 | 'Spirit of Uruguay' | 25.06.41 | Failed to return on 21.7.41 | Sgt Grainger missing |
| W3442 | 'Progress II' | 14.07.41 | Shot down on 27.9.41 | Sgt Evans PoW |
| W3443 | 'Cape Town I' | 03.07.41 | | P/O Johnstone |
| W3445 | 'Cape Town II' | 10.07.41 | | Sgt Boyle |
| W3515 | | 15.07.41 | Shot down on 20.9.41 | P/O Smith killed |
| W3761 | 'Blue Nose' | 15.08.41 | | |
| W3802 | | 10.09.41 | | Sgt Milner |
| W3804 | | 10.09.41 | | Sgt Dales |
| W3815 | 'Sierre Leone II' | 29.08.41 | | |
| W3816 | 'The Shopmate' | 29.08.41 | Shot down on 20.9.41 | F/Lt Barclay safe |
| W3818 | | 29.08.41 | | |
| W3838 | 'Valparaiso' | 15.09.41 | Shot down on 27.10.41 | P/O Carey-Hill killed |
| AB786 | | 06.08.41 | | Sgt Boyle |
| AB855 | | 06.08.41 | | |
| AB921 | | 07.09.41 | | Sgt Milner |
| AB984 | 'West Borneo III' | 02.10.41 | Crashed on 5.11.41 | Sgt Dales killed |
| AD252 | | 25.09.41 | | F/Lt Powell |
| AD271 | | 30.09.41 | | Sgt Dales |
| AD312 | 'Cambridge' | 01.10.41 | | Sgt Barlow |
| AD359 | | 22.10.41 | | Sgt Darkin |
| AD425 | 'Ardu Spitfire' | 22.10.41 | | F/O Watkinson |

# APPENDIX I

## List of Roads named after RAF Hornchurch Pilots, RAF Commanders and Airfields

**Pilots' names**
Adnams Walk
Bader Way
Beaumont Crescent
Bennions Close
Berry Close
Bouchier Walk
Boulter Gardens
Broadhurst Way
Carbury Close
Crawford-Compton Close
Dawson Drive
Deere Avenue
Denholm Close
Dewey Path
Dowding Way
Edridge Close
Esmonde Close
Finucane Gardens
Franklin Road
Freeborn Gardens
Gillam Way
Gilroy Close
Gray Gardens
Hayes Drive
Hesselyn Drive
Hillary Close
Hugo Gardens
Kilmartin Way
Kingaby Gardens
Leathart Close
Lock Close
Lovell Walk
Malan Square
Mermagen Drive
Mungo-Park Road
Park Mews
Pease Close
Robinson Close
Ryder Gardens
Sarre Avenue

**Pilots' names**
Scotney Walk
Simpson Road
Sowrey Avenue
Stephen Avenue
Tempest Way
Tuck Road
Wells Gardens

**RAF Airfields**
Aldergrove Walk
Bradwell Close
Coltishall Road
Debden Walk
Detling Close
Digby Walk
Duxford Close
Fairlop Close
Gosport Drive
Hawkinge Way
Kirton Close
Leconfield Walk
Manston Way
Martlesham Close
Penrith Cresent
Northolt Way
Pembrey Way
Roborough Walk
Rochford Close
Stansted Close
Tangmere Cresent
West Malling
Wittering Way

**RAF Related**
Airfield Way
Astra Close
Blenheim Court
Squadrons Approach

# APPENDIX J

Author's Note – Corrections and additions to
*Hornchurch Scramble Volume 1.*

The following has been included since further research of the first volume found that certain facts were printed incorrectly.

Chapter 1 – Page 1 should read Northolt, not North Weald.

Page 4 William Leefe Robinson's aircraft serial no was 2693, not 2092.

Page 7 again as above.

Page 9 Robinson was shot down on the 5th April 1917, not the 8th.

Page 15 Captain James McCudden paid the airfield a visit on the 8th August to visit members of No.46 Squadron. He did not receive the notification of his Victoria Cross until he was at Sutton's Farm in March 1918.

# APPENDIX K

## Map of RAF Hornchurch 1942

This shows the layout of the three hangars with the original No. 1 Flightway, which ran north to south until a second flightway was opened up across from east to west in 1942, shutting the South End Road which ran alongside the station. The Officers' Mess was situated across the road from the main entrance.

# APPENDIX L

## OPERATIONS ROOM - MASONIC HALL, ROMFORD

SENTRIES \GATES/ SENTRIES (Password changed every day)

ENTRANCE DOORS STAIRS TO
OPS. DIAS

OBS. CORPS/ARMY   RAISED DAIS   CONTROLLER OPS 'B'   INTELLIGENCE
PRINTER A

Stairs ___                                                    Stairs
____        PLOTTER
____                    OPERATIONAL MAP ON                    ___
                        TABLE – COVERING THE                  ___
                        SOUTH EAST AND
Tannoy                  CHANNEL PLUS 12
System      PLOTTER     GROUP

        PLOTTER                                PLOTTER
                    PLOTTER    PLOTTER                      The
                                                        Only Safety
                                                          Doors

PANELS SHOWING STATE OF SQUADRONS INC.

SATELLITE STATIONS ETC., UNDER OUR

COMMAND

| | R.T.O. CABINS | DOOR TO OPS. |
| | STAGE | |
| SIGNALS OFFICERS | 2 TELEPRINTERS – DIRECT LINES TO UXBRIDGE & STANMORE | TRAFFIC OFFICE WITH 2 TELEPRINTERS & RAF WIRELESS OPS |

| CORRIDOR | | | |
| STAIRS TO OVERHEAD WORKSHOP | BATTERY ROOM | TOILETS & STOVE FOR HEATING | TELEPHONE EXCHANGE |

# APPENDIX M

**RAF Hornchurch 'At Home' Programme**

# APPENDIX O

## THE HORNCHURCH WING

The air that we breathe was theirs to defend
And they did so with no hesitation
Their skill and their love to the bitter end
Was their gift to us and the nation.

So how can we forget them
Kin and strangers who gave their all
Ours is the freedom that once was theirs
And our streets, now their only roll-call.

Let us pay tribute to Hornchurch
And the parts that were played in each war
So the likes of the Sowreys, Malans and Bouchiers
Are remembered forever more.

Yet, making a gift for the future
A future where sense is the key
Where our children can learn that peace is the way
The only way nations should see.

Our planet could be such a wonderful place
To live in, to love in, to be,
If lessons we've learned could be put to good use
For the future of humanity.

M. Patricia Churchill

# BIBLIOGRAPHY

The books listed below are recommended by the author as essential background reading for those interested in Sutton's Farm and RAF Hornchurch.

*Aces High*, Christopher Shores and Clive Williams, Grub Street 1994

*Battle of Britain Then and Now MkV*, Winston Ramsey, After the Battle 1980

*Fighter Squadrons in the Battle of Britain*, Anthony Robinson, Arms & Armour 1987

*Fighter Squadrons of the RAF and their Aircraft*, John Rawlings, MacDonald & Co 1969

*First Things First*, Eric Smith, Ian Henry Publications Ltd 1992

*Fly for your Life*, Larry Forrester, Frederick Muller Ltd 1956

*Hornchurch Scramble, The Definitive History Vol 1*, Richard C. Smith, Grub Street 2000

*Men of the Battle of Britain*, Kenneth G. Wynn, Gliddon Books 1989

*Paddy Finucane Fighter Ace*, Doug Stokes, Kimber 1983

*Nine Lives*, A/Cdr Alan Deere, Wingham Press Ltd 1992

*Raiders Approach*, S/Ldr H.T. Sutton, Gale & Polden 1956

*Richard Hillary, The Definitive Biography*, David Ross, Grub Street 2000

*Park*, Vincent Orange, Grub Street 2001

*Smoke Trails in the Sky*, Tony Bartley, Kimber 1984

*Spitfire into Battle*, W. Duncan-Smith, John Murray Ltd 1981

*Spitfire The History*, Morgan and Shacklady, Key Publishing Ltd 1987

*Sutton's Farm and RAF Hornchurch 1915-41*, S/Ldr H.T Sutton, Crown Copyright 1953

*Tally-Ho: Yankee in a Spitfire*, A.G. Donahue, Macmillan & Co Ltd 1943

*Tigers*, The Story of No.74 Squadron, Bob Cossey, Arms & Armour 1992

*The Air Battle of Dunkirk*, Norman Franks, Grub Street 2000

*The Last Enemy*, Richard Hillary, Macmillan & Co Ltd 1942

*The Narrow Margin*, Derek Wood and Derek Dempster, Tri-Service Press Ltd 1990

*The Zeppelin Fighters*, Arch Whitehouse, Robert Hale Ltd 1968

Documents, Station and Squadron Operation Books etc, consulted at the Public Record Office, Kew, London.

| | | |
|---|---|---|
| No.19 Squadron | Operations Book | Air/27/252 |
| | Combat Reports | Air/50/10 |
| No.39 Squadron | Operations Book | Air/27/406 |
| No.41 Squadron | Operations Book | Air/27/424 |
| | Combat Reports | Air/50/18 |
| No.54 Squadron | Operations Book | Air/27/511 |
| | Combat Reports | Air/27/21 |
| No.64 Squadron | Operations Book | Air/27/590 |
| | Combat Reports | Air/50/24 |
| No.65 Squadron | Operations Book | Air/27/593 |
| No.66 Squadron | Operations Book | Air/27/597 |
| No.74 Squadron | Operations Book | Air/27/640 |
| | Combat Reports | Air/50/32 |
| No.92 Squadron | Operations Book | Air/27/743 |
| No.122 Squadron | Operations Book | Air/27/915 |
| No.129 Squadron | Operations Book | Air/27/934 |
| | Combat Reports | Air/50/46 |
| No.222 Squadron | Operations Book | Air/27/1371/1372 |
| | Combat Reports | Air/50/85 |
| No.226 Squadron | Operations Book | Air/27/1558 |
| No.229 Squadron | Operations Book | Air/27/1477 |
| No.239 Squadron | Operations Book | Air/27/1455 |
| No.264 Squadron | Operations Book | Air/27/1553 |
| No.274 Squadron | Operations Book | Air/27/1587 |
| No.278 Squadron | Operations Book | Air/27/1604 |
| No.313 Squadron | Operations Book | Air/27/1697/1698 |
| No.340 Squadron | Operations Book | Air/27/1738 |
| No.349 Squadron | Operations Book | Air/27/1744 |
| No.350 Squadron | Operations Book | Air/27/1744 |
| No.403 Squadron | Operations Book | Air/27/1780 |
| No.411 Squadron | Operations Book | Air/27/1803 |
| No.453 Squadron | Operations Book | Air/27/1892 |
| No.485 Squadron | Operations Book | Air/27/1933 |
| No.567 Squadron | Operations Book | Air/27/2039 |
| No.600 Squadron | Operations Book | Air/27/2059 |
| No.603 Squadron | Operations Book | Air/27/2079 |
| | Combat Reports | Air/50/167 |
| No.611 Squadron | Operations Book | Air/27/2110 |
| RAF Hornchurch 1915-1941 | Operations Book | Air/28/384 |
| RAF Hornchurch 1942-1945 | Operations Book | Air/28/385 |

| RAF Hornchurch 1946-1950 | Operations Book | Air/28/1050 |
| RAF Hornchurch 1951-1955 | Operations Book | Air/28/1214 |
| RAF Hornchurch 1956-1960 | Operations Book | Air/28/1369 |

IF YOU HAVE ENJOYED THIS BOOK, AND THE FIRST VOLUME,
*HORNCHURCH SCRAMBLE*, VISIT THE LARGEST COLLECTION
OF SUTTON'S FARM & RAF HORNCHURCH MEMORABILIA
& ARTEFACTS ON DISPLAY AT

HOUSED WITHIN THE PURFLEET HERITAGE & MILITARY
CENTRE, CENTURION WAY, PURFLEET, ESSEX

OPEN EVERY SUNDAY FROM APRIL TO NOVEMBER
AVAILABLE FOR SCHOOL AND GROUP BOOKINGS
DURING WEEKDAYS

TELEPHONE 01708-523409/866764

WEBSITE WWW.BIGWIG.NET/HOGMAN/PURFLEET.HTM

MEMBERSHIP OF THE PURFLEET HERITAGE/HORNCHURCH
WING IS AVAILABLE

# INDEX

**GENERAL – PLACE NAMES**